C000175881

PAUL &
THE UNSEARCHABLE
RICHES OF CHRIST

SOTIRIOS CHRISTOU

Other books published by Sotirios Christou

The Priest & The People Of God – 2003
Evangelism & Collaborative Ministry – 2004
Anglican & Beyond Repair? – 2005

Published by Phoenix Books, Cambridge
Telepone 01223 514593

To the glory of God and Christ – in whom are hid all the treasures of wisdom and knowledge – Colossians 2: 12.

Christ is the image of the invisible God, the first-born of all Creation: for in him all things were created, in heaven and on earth, visible and invisible, whether thrones or dominions or principalities or authorities – all things were created through him and for him. He is before all things and in him all things hold together. He is the head of the body, the church: he is the beginning, the first-born from the dead that in everything he might be pre-eminent. For in him all the fullness of God was pleased to dwell and through him to reconcile to himself all things, whether on earth or in heaven, making peace by the blood of his cross. Colossians 1: 15-20.

CONTENTS

CHAPTER ONE

A FUTURE FULL OF PROMISE

CHAPTER TWO

THE CONVERSION OF ST. PAUL
THE TAMING OF THE BEAST

CHAPTER THREE

PAUL'S PRAYERS

CHAPTER FOUR

PAUL'S EXPERIENCE OF CHRIST

CHAPTER FIVE

WHO WANTS A THORN?!

CHAPTER SIX

PAUL'S PHILOSOPHY OF MINISTRY

CHAPTER SEVEN

PASTOR AND THEOLOGIAN
PAUL THE PASTOR

PAUL THE THEOLOGIAN
JUSTIFICATION BY FAITH

APPENDIX

PREFACE

My adolescent phase at being an author was surprisingly rekindled on my twins' birthday on 18th November 2005. In God's providence, as no door of opportunity to return to ministry had materialised, I was at a loss about what to do next. Then quite out of the blue, the idea came to me to write a book about Paul and Christ. A couple of days later, I had an outline of some of the chapter headings, and so I began to write.

There are innumerable books on Paul and I myself have a reasonably modest selection, as is evident from my bibliography. So what exactly is distinctive about mine, apart from the title? I have approached Paul from the perspective, that he is a paradigm for us in a number of ways. His prayers reveal a rich vein of spirituality and immense depth, that are timeless models that can enrich our own intercessions. He went from being a stranger to Christ, to knowing him intimately – a paradigm of what Christ longs for his church. His experience of Christ and his 'philosophy of ministry,' are also challenging paradigms for ministry in the 21st century. Equally, his thorn in the flesh, is a paradigm that shows how the Lord works through our weaknesses, as we serve him.

Paul is a figure you invariably come across in lectionary readings and sermons on his letters, without necessarily having a coherent picture of him as a person. This is not really possible unless you have an overall view of his cultural, historical and spiritual background – and a good idea of why he wrote his letters. Being reasonably well resourced has enabled me to provide such a coherent framework.

The Paul that we are familiar with through our church connections, can lead us to having an image of him that is a lop-sided caricature. He can easily come across as a rather intense man, 'mouthing off doctrine' in his letters, to correct the churches and sort out controversies. There is some truth in this, because he was passionate about his theology. But, on closer examination of the Biblical material, I have been surprised by what I found out about Paul – and I have been a Christian for 40 years. I have discovered new facets of his personality, that I had not previously been aware of. He has come alive to me as never before.

Paul's letters generally portray him as a very joyful and an extremely loving man, a gregarious apostle who excelled at making loyal friends. He also comes across as a profoundly spiritual man, deeply committed to prayer, whose all consuming passion is to live for Christ, and share Christ with others – regardless of the cost. His letters also reveal an accomplished literary ability, that is quite outstanding. Unless you understand the style used by the speakers of his day, you will not fully appreciate the genius of his rhetorical skill.

As we learn about Paul, we also learn more about Christ through his letters – and through the apostle, Christ shows what he can do through a life, surrendered to his Lordship. Paul is also the example par excellence, of growing in the grace and knowledge of Christ. In the 21st century, discovering afresh the unsearchable riches of Christ, and proclaiming them to the nation, may well be a catalyst in the renewal of the Church.

Sotirios Christou
Cambridge February 14th 2006

ACKNOWLEDGMENTS

For the faithfulness of their prayers during the past few years, I owe an incalculable debt of gratitude to Jan Hudson, Ken and Judy Duke, and Eva and Mandy Hanlon – members of St. Andrew's in West Sussex, where I served them as a minister until the summer of 1998. I would also like to thank Guy Brandon, for looking through my manuscript and for the suggestions he made. Equally, I would like to thank Margaret Pollard, for her very artistic and creative front cover design. I am glad she ignored my suggestion, and came up with her own much better idea. I have known Margaret since 1984, when I was a student at St. John's College in Nottingham, where here late husband Noel Pollard was my tutor.

I am also grateful to the Lord as I believe he gave me the idea for this book – although of course, I take responsibility for what I have written. I trust that it is not too presumptuous to say, I also believe the Lord guided me to write my first book, and never remotely considered that he would inspire three of the four books I have written. In my book I have included the chapter on 'Who Wants A Thorn?' which was unpublished material, along with a revision of, 'The Conversion Of St. Paul' and 'Paul The Pastor,' from my 2nd and 1st books respectively.

As I devoted myself to the discipline of writing, my manuscript has flowed almost seamlessly, as I have immersed myself in my studies. My familiarity with Paul's letters during the past 40 years as a Christian, has obviously contributed to this. Also my exposition of his letters, has allowed me to capitalise on my primarily calling to preach and teach, and to utilise the commentaries in my resource library, along with my books on Paul. When I was a theological student 20 years ago, I only owned four books, so I consider myself fortunate to have accumulated a modest resource library, of almost 400 commentaries and 800 other books on various aspects of ministry.

As it evolved I found my chapter on 'Paul's Philosophy Of Ministry' fascinating, and consider it to be relevant for the formation of ministers today. This chapter has been a catalyst that has enabled me to come to terms with, and make sense of, what I have been through these past few years. I have enjoyed learning from others about Paul, and greatly valued what I have learned from my own Biblical studies. Also I love the fresh encounter with familiar truths about Christ – and the Colossian prayer, that 'Christ can fulfil all our aspirations' – is one of my favourite. This is not only relevant for Christians, but has an evangelistic impact too.

Last, but not least, I would like to thank the team at Vision, in Cambridge, for producing such an attractive book.

INTRODUCTION

As you read the New Testament it is an inescapable fact, that Paul is a central figure as he wrote a large percentage of it (although there is mixed opinion amongst scholars about which letters he wrote). Nevertheless, he cannot be ignored and is very much 'in your face.' You cannot escape his influence or circumnavigate him. You may love him or be infuriated by him. And you may find aspects of his theology controversial or awe-inspiring, unpalatable or stimulating. This is not surprising, as C. K. Barrett has pointed out:

> Diverse attitudes to Paul have persisted throughout the ages. He has been hated and loved, understood and misunderstood.[1]

Whatever we think or feel about Paul he is an integral part of Christian tradition, and his teaching about Christ is almost unrivalled in its panoramic scope. Clearly, he has had an incalculable influence throughout the centuries, and is firmly established in our ecclesiastical heritage.

K. Haacker reiterates the fact that, 'Opinions about Paul have always been divided. He had been a man of conflict before his sudden conversion on the road to Damascus, bitterly opposed to the Jesus movement. He remained a subject of controversy after that event, not only among his conservative Jewish countrymen but also within the early church... Positive or negative judgements on Paul are usually based upon some well-known doctrinal statements of his, isolated from the argument of their context and quoted without regard to the circumstances of his life and times. Instead of such more or less arbitrary opinions, to do justice to the person and work of the apostle demands a careful consideration of the character of our sources and an interpretation of his teaching, as conditioned by his social and religious background and as part of his ministry of founding and fostering young churches in the Mediterranean world outside Judea.'[2]

We know that Paul's Jewish name was Saul, and as he was from the Tribe of Benjamin, it is almost certain that he was named after the first King of Israel. Also as a Roman citizen he would have been known as Paulos, a common Graeco-Roman name, as having two names was fairly common for Jews in his day. Tradition has it that Paul was short, had bow legs (probably because of the 39 lashes he received five times), a Roman nose, thick eyebrows and may have been stocky, because of the physical nature of being a tentmaker. He was obviously no Adonis, yet arguably his personality compensated for his appearance.

The Greek for Paul means 'little,' and Onesiphoros in the 2nd century described him as a rather small man. 'Yet the power of the man was unmistakable. "Strongly-built" the account ran on, 'he is full of grace, for at times he looked like a man, at times like an angel.'[3] This sounds like poetic license, bearing in mind the unpleasant ailment of his eyes, which he refers to in Galatians 4: 14-15. But who is to say that on occasions, the glory of the Lord wasn't reflected in his countenance, as 2 Cor. 3: 18 testifies, 'And we all with unveiled face, beholding the glory of the Lord are being changed from one degree of glory into another.'

One of things that stands out in Paul's letters, is his passion for the truth. He had the courage to preach the gospel of Christ crucified, and refused to tone down his message, to please people and endear himself to them. He also showed courage in taking on his critics and opponents the Judaizers, who systematically went around the churches he founded advocating the necessity of circumcision, and questioning Paul's authority and credentials as an apostle. O'Connor comments on the seriousness of this issue, that threatened his entire ministry when in effect he says, 'the deliberate opposition by the Judaizers carried the real possibility, that it would be systematically extended to the other churches he founded. His credibility and his gospel were at stake. His whole future was endangered.'[4] The future of the church was also precarious, because without the tireless work of the apostle, Christianity as we know it, may have remained a sect within Judaism, that was eventually swallowed up by the Jewish faith.

We glimpse Paul's passion for truth in the letter to the Galatians, where he confronts these opponents, who insisted his Gentile converts also had to be circumcised. D. Wenham calls Galatians 'A red hot letter, written with great passion and force.'[5] As he writes he is so angry, that he even omits his customary note of thanksgiving to God for them. An extraordinary omission, that reflects how gravely concerned he was about this. His language is forceful and pugnacious: 'I am astonished you are so quickly deserting him, who called you in the grace of Christ, and turning to a different gospel' – 1: 6 and, 'O foolish Galatians who has bewitched you?'– 5:1. He is excruciatingly sarcastic when he says about the intruders, 'I wish they would mutilate themselves' – 5: 12. Equally, he uses strong language in 1: 9, 'If anyone is preaching to you a gospel, contrary to the one you received, let him be accursed.' 'Paul was a formidable opponent who 'responds not with cold argument but with heated emotion.'[6] Or, should we rather say, with heated emotion and the compelling logic of the truth? Either way, we owe an incalculable debt of gratitude to Paul's courage, in defending the truth of the gospel, that he safeguarded and handed down to us as Gentiles.

At the other extreme Paul could be fairly relaxed, and this is seen by his tolerant response to the Christians at Corinth with the 'weaker' consciences, concerning meat offered to idols, in 1 Corinthians 8 & 10. F. F. Bruce also recognises this trait when he says, 'Paul's personal strength of will was not accompanied, as it is by so many, by impatience with lesser mortals. While he himself had a robust and emancipated conscience, he had warm sympathy with those whose conscience was immature and unenlightened: and he would go to almost any length of self-denial in consideration for his weaker brethren. He deplored the inability or unwillingness, of other strong-minded Christians to show them such consideration.'[7]

But this was not always the case, and we must assume this tolerant side of the apostle reflects the mature Paul. We know from Acts 15: 38, that he refused to allow John Mark to accompany him and Barnabas on their trip, as he had withdrawn from a previous mission in Pamphylia – Acts 2: 13. In Acts 15: 39, we learn that a sharp contention – a fierce argument – arose between Barnabas and Paul about this, so they separated with Mark accompanying Barnabas. Paul expected the high standards from others that he set for himself, and at this particular time he could not extend the hand of fellowship, to someone who failed to meet his expectations.

Clearly, as Paul matured, he had to learn to accommodate the failures of others. When they were written his letters reflect his maturity as an extremely loving person, who was very warm and good at establishing relationships. From the evidence it is hard to imagine him being anything other than a thorough extrovert, something E. Stourton echoes when he says, 'To me Paul's letters read like the work of a bachelor with a talent for friendship – a thoroughly gregarious fellow.'[8] F. F. Bruce also affirms Paul's capacity for friendship and being an outgoing person when he says, 'He was eminently 'clubbable,' social, gregarious. He delighted in the company of his fellows, both men and women. The most incredible feature in the Paul of popular mythology is his alleged misogyny. He treated women as persons: we recall his commendation of Phoebe, the deacon at Cenchreae, who had shown herself a helper to him as to many others, or his appreciation of Euodia and Syntyche of Philippi who worked side by side with him in the gospel.

The range of his friendship and the warmth of his affections, are qualities which no attentive reader of his letters can miss. There are scores of people mentioned in the New Testament, who are known to us by name at least, simply because they were friends of Paul. And in his friends he was able to call forth a devotion which knew no limits. Priscilla and Aquila risked their lives for him in a dangerous situation. Epaphroditus of Philippi overtaxed his strength and suffered an almost fatal illness, in his anxiety to be of service to the imprisoned apostle. Timothy readily surrendered whatever personal ambitions he might have cherished, in order to play the part of a son to Paul and help him in his missionary activities, showing a selfless concern for others that matched the apostle's own eagerness, to spend and be spent for them.'[9]

J. D. G. Dunn has this to say about him. 'Paul was the first and greatest Christian theologian. From the perspective of subsequent generations, he is undoubtedly the first Christian theologian. Moreover, he was "first" in the other sense of being pre-eminent among Christian theologians. He belonged to that generation which was more creative and more definitive, for Christianity's formation and theology than any other since. And within that generation, it was he more than any other single person, who ensured that the new movement stemming from Jesus, would become a truly international and intellectually coherent religion. Paul has indeed been called the "second founder of Christianity" who has, compared with the first, exercised beyond all doubts the stronger influence. Even if that should be regarded as an overblown assessment of his significance, the fact remains that his influence and writings have shaped Christianity, as the writing/theology of no other single individual have.

Hence also the claim that he is the greatest theologian of all time. In effect, this is simply to restate the traditional Christian affirmation, of the canonical status of Paul's letters. They were evidently valued by the churches to which they were addressed, cherished as of continuing value for instruction in Christian faith, worship and daily living and circulated to other churches in an ever widening circle of authority, until their canonical status was acknowledged in the 2nd century. One of the principal fascinations of these letters, indeed, is their self-revelatory character – Paul, as a persuader of great forcefulness (judging by the fact his letters have been preserved) great effectiveness, Paul as an irascible protagonist.'[10]

While Paul is unquestionably one of the most influential leaders and theologians in the church, he does not appeal to everyone. As D. Horrell points out, 'For some he was largely responsible for taking the message of Jesus and corrupting it, turning it into a Greek ("Hellenistic") type of religion which Jesus would hardly have recognised, let alone approved. For some, Paul is a social and political radical, who announced a message of liberation and equality for women and slaves, a feminist before his time. For others he is responsible for keeping women and slaves in their place, and for fostering attitudes of misogyny and anti-semitism... Contemporary theologians come to Paul, with questions arising from the contexts they have to address, just as Paul's theology arose because of the particular questions he faced. But different theologians interpret Paul quite differently, and there are major disagreements between various traditions of theology, in terms of their understanding of Paul's gospel... The great diversity of attitudes, should also alert us to the fact, that he is not an easy person to understand.'[11] This is something the apostle Peter echoed when he said: 'There are some things in them (his letters) that are hard to understand...' Although his approach is not so complimentary – 'which the ignorant and unstable twist to their own destruction, as they do other Scriptures' – 2 Peter 3: 16. This sounds like a comment, that Paul himself would have enjoyed making.

Paul's attitude to women can also be interpreted differently, depending on the perspective of the protagonist. D. Horrell in effect says, 'that scholars are by no means unanimously agreed, as to how to assess him on the issue of feminism. For some he is a voice for equality and liberation, for others a voice of domination and women's oppression. He points out that Fiorenza stresses, that any assessment of Paul on this issue, must accept the ambivalent legacy which his letters represent: otherwise he may be somewhat one-sidedly claimed, either as a "chauvinist" or as a "feminist" and "liberationist."

> Paul's impact on women's leadership in the Christian missionary movement is double-edged. On the one hand he affirms Christian equality and freedom. He opens up a new independent lifestyle for women, by encouraging them to maintain free of the bondage of marriage. On the other hand, he subordinates women's behaviour in marriage and in the worship assembly to the interests of Christian mission, and restricts their rights not only as 'pneumatics,' but also as women.

In effect, Fiorenza insists, that all history-writing is reconstruction, reflecting the values and commitments of the historian, and that those who claim objectivity for their work, merely conceal their own position of commitment.'[12]

As we know, Paul has had a significant impact on leaders throughout the history of the church. 'It was under the influence of Paul that Irenaeus and Tertullian were able to steady the boat of

Christianity, rocked as it was in the second half of the second century by 'heresy' and competing religious systems.'[13] 'Augustine the Bishop of Hippo in North Africa (354-430), was deeply influenced by Paul's Epistles. He identified in Romans 7 with a self-portrait of the apostle, whose mind was torn in two directions similar to his own. In Paul he sensed a kindred spirit, who identified with his own spiritual state. As a result Augustine exerted a powerful influence, on how he was interpreted for centuries afterwards. Martin Luther (1483-1546) was also famously influenced by Paul's gospel of justification by faith, that brought him liberation from sin and guilt, and liberation from the teaching of the church, that quantified grace as something to be earned or purchased. Luther's theology, central to the Protestant Reformation, is unimaginable without Paul.

In turn John Wesley (1703-1791) the founder of Methodism, with his brother Charles, was touched while listening to a reading of Luther's preface to the Romans, and as is famously known, felt his heart 'strangely warmed.' He wrote, 'I felt I did trust in Christ, Christ alone for salvation: and an assurance was given me that he had taken away my sins, even mine, and saved me from the law of sin and death.'[14]

In contrast to the powerful influence Paul exerted on these men, it is a humbling fact, that the churches he founded were relatively small house-churches. Small Christian communities meeting in homes that belonged to rich Christians, where probably around 20-30 people met together. In reality they numbered among the minority groups in their cities and towns. In a way the house-churches were a subversive sect of the Jewish faith, and probably an irritant to Orthodox Jews. In this respect, we can easily over-estimate, how influential a figure Paul was in these urban settings. M. Hooker echoes this when she says, 'To the outside world, he was totally insignificant – except on those occasions when he was a nuisance to the authorities. And though he undoubtedly planted the Christian gospel, in various strategic cities in the Roman world, the communities he formed were small, and largely ignored or abused by those around them.'[15]

Paul knew he could never repay the debt he owed to Christ's love, that was so generously lavished upon him. This was something which he was acutely aware of since his call to be an apostle, and his letters give the impression that he was a driven man, who had something to prove. This is implied in 1 Cor. 15: 10 when he says, 'I worked harder than all the other apostles.' Equally, this is seen by the fact he refused to receive financial support or patronage when he founded churches, presumably because he did not want anyone to claim his conversion and change of heart, was based on ulterior motives. He willingly worked hard to support himself as a tent maker, and was equally industrious in preaching the gospel, and pastoring his converts.

Paul had a driven temperament and loved to be on the go all the time. When he was not tent making during the day he would have been teaching the Christians, or debating the gospel with those who were willing to listen. When he was guided by the Holy Spirit he was off on his missionary travels, arduous journeys by land and sea, taking in a punishing schedule of evangelism from place to place. He also channelled all his drive into being disciplined, and this is reflected in his letter to Timothy when he says, 'No soldier on civilian service gets entangled in civilian pursuits, since his aim is to satisfy the one who enlisted him. An athlete is not crowned unless he competes according to the rules' – 2 Tim. 2: 4-5. Timothy knew that this reflected Paul's own disciplined commitment to Christ. Similarly in 1 Timothy 4: 7-8 he says, 'Train yourself in godliness...' Again this reflected Paul's discipline as an apostle, in channelling all his drive and energy into serving Christ. Even though he lived under the banner of Christ's grace, he set himself high standards and pushed himself to the limit.

We can perceive this same driveness when he persecuted the church so ferociously and so relentlessly, which indicates he was a passionate man with strong religious convictions. His righteous indignation directed at purging this new sect of Jesus' followers, at times may have made him a somewhat volatile character. One the Christians probably felt had lost control of himself.

In his wildest dreams Paul had no inkling whatsoever, that his letters would reverberate throughout history as Holy Scripture. As I have learned about the historical and sociological backgrounds of these letters – many of which were written to address 'local difficulties' – I have been forcibly struck that in God's providence they became Holy Scripture. In essence, they still read, as the correspondence he wrote to the churches almost 2000 years ago. In retrospect, they may arguably be considered to be his most enduring legacy, eclipsing anything he achieved while he was alive.

Paul was an apostle, whose suffering authenticated his devotion to Christ, and reflected his passionate love for him. Arguably, the way to make sense of Paul, is to grasp that the heart of Christ that pursued and won him over, became the pulse and inspiration of his own. Clearly, and unambiguously, the 'lens' for understanding Paul, is through the person of Christ. It seems extraordinary that as he didn't know Christ when he was alive, he should not only have such a rich experience of him – but also acquire a remarkable understanding of who Christ was, and what he accomplished. This is even more surprising, bearing in mind he was not mentored by any of the apostles who had known Christ. Before his conversion Paul was a stranger to Christ, but when Christ revealed himself to him, he was captivated by Him. Christ was now his all-consuming passion. And as his pilgrimage unfolds, we perceive that Christ was now the 'lens' through which he viewed and interpreted The Law, his own life, Israel, the church and the world. This is a pivotal observation, in understanding Paul and his theology.

Paul is indeed a fascinating Christian leader, teacher and theologian, who had a thorough grasp of the Law and became an outstanding Christian thinker. Luke, in the Acts of the Apostles, presents him as the hero of early mission. Unquestionably, he was a pivotal figure in the early church, and took the gospel to the Gentiles as an evangelist and pioneer church planter. I imagine that if Paul had been alive today, he would undoubtedly have been an influential religious leader. Perhaps he would have been the Archbishops' Adviser on Evangelism. Or perhaps he would have established himself as a national, or international evangelist of great repute. Then again being so well educated, and having a brilliant theological mind, and being a pastor who wore his heart on his sleeve, perhaps he would have been a Bishop, or even an Archbishop. Tom Wright, the Bishop of Durham has this to say about Paul:

> He is one of the most powerful and seminal minds of the first and any century...I persist in regarding him as the intellectual equal of Plato, Aristotle or Seneca.[16]

CHAPTER ONE

A FUTURE FULL OF PROMISE

CULTURAL INFLUENCES

Anyone researching the life of St. Paul, will soon discover that he was exposed to, and influenced by three ancient cultures. He was the product of these temperamentally colourful and creatively rich cultural sources. The amalgamation of this diverse heritage beckoned a future full of promise – and in the background we may discern the hand of the Lord shaping him through his exposure to these formative influences. There was the Jewish culture he was born into, along with the Roman and Greek-Hellenistic cultures which pervaded the ancient world. Donald Coggan, former Archbishop of Canterbury succinctly captures the confluence of these streams of thought.

> Young Saul of Tarsus stood at the point where two rivers met. The first was the river of Judaism – narrow, deep, powerful. The second was the river of the outer world, the broad, open stream of Greek culture (all that is included in the word 'Hellenism') and Roman power. The two rivers met in the important city of Tarsus where Saul was born. He found himself through no choice of his own to be heir to two traditions. He was a citizen of two worlds.[1]

'We tend to associate Paul with Tarsus, and although his letters do not directly confirm his birth from there, they do speak of him spending a lot of time in that general area after his conversion.'[2] Jerome thinks his parents might have lived in Gischala, a village in the mountains of Upper Galilee. Around 4 BC, when he was about two years old, there had been an uprising in the area which was quelled by the Roman authorities, whose custom was to capture some of the residents and sell them as slaves. This may have happened to Paul's parents who would then have been taken to Tarsus their new home, which was the capital of the Roman province, Cilicia Pedias. In Acts 21: 39, we learn that Paul identified himself with Tarsus, 'I am a Jew from Tarsus in Cilicia, a citizen of no mean city. Yet it is still possible he was born in Gischala and moved to Tarsus when he was still very young. So he naturally saw himself as coming from Tarsus, as he lived there from a very young age. Either way, it is the city with which he closely associated himself.

'Tarsus had a history stretching back 4000 years and lay on one side of the great trade routes of the ancient world, linking Syria with Asia Minor and the Aegean. Since the native inhabitants did not exploit the full economic potential of Tarsus, Greek and Jewish colonists were brought in by the Seleucids of Syria in the 2nd century BC.'³ 'Although today it is a town of no great distinction, in Paul's era it was a thriving city, and its university compared favourably with that of Athens. It was also a distinguished centre of Greek culture, including Greek games, the gymnasium and a training place for athletes. Traders fetched their merchandise to it and also brought news of what was happening in the world. Philosophers debated in the streets and Stoicism flourished there.'⁴

'Tarsus was absorbed into the Roman system when Pompey reorganised Asia Minor in 64 BC. Mark Anthony rewarded its loyalty to the memory of Julius Caesar, after his assassination in 44 BC, by granting it freedom and immunity from imperial taxes. Roman interest in Tarsus implies that citizenship was conferred at least on the leading personalities, and as these families grew so the number of Roman citizens increased. This offers us the simplest explanation of how Paul became a Roman citizen, as his parents would automatically have acquired their citizenship, when they were set free by the Roman who bought them.'⁵

F. F. Bruce informs us, 'Alexander the Great saved Tarsus from the retreating Persians in 333 BC. When Julius Caesar visited the city in 47 BC, it adopted the name Iuliopolis in his honour, and after his death it enjoyed the favour of Mark Anthony. It was in Tarsus that the celebrated meeting between Anthony and Cleopatra took place, when she was rowed up the Cydnus in the guise of Aphrodite. The people of Tarsus applied themselves to the study of philosophy, the liberal arts and the whole round of learning in general...so much so that the city in this respect at least surpassed even Athens and Alexandria, whose schools were frequented more by visitors than by their own citizens. Tarsus was what we might call in short a university city, and the students were those who lived there.'[6]

JEWISH BACKGROUND

We have a concise summary of Paul's Jewish roots in his letter to the Philippians in 3: 5-7, 'circumcised on the eighth day, of the people of Israel, of the tribe of Benjamin, a Hebrew of Hebrews, as to righteousness under the Law blameless, a Pharisee.' In Acts 22: 3, he informs us, 'that he was educated at the feet of Gamaliel, according to the strict manner of the Law of our fathers, being zealous for God.' Acts 23: 6, also records Paul saying, 'I am a Pharisee a son of Pharisees.' His Jewish ancestry and religious credentials are impressive indeed, linking him back to the tribe of Benjamin and the Hebrews in the Old Testament. A proud association with the tribe, which could boast the first Hebrew King of Israel, Saul.

It is interesting to hear what the relevance of being a Hebrew was in Paul's day. O'Connor points out, 'Hebrew' carried not only religious or ethnic overtones, but also a linguistic connotation. For example, the high priest "sought out such Hebrews as he had of the highest reputation, who had received an education in Greek as well as their native tongue." The implication of this passage, whose emphasis is not knowledge of the Law but on linguistic ability, is that while few Jews, if any, in the Diaspora knew Hebrew, only some of the Jews in Palestine could write Greek... "Hebrew," because of its linguistic connotation, implied a relationship to Palestine in a way which "Hellenist" did not. Even though these latter may have been Greek-speaking Jews of Jerusalem, use of the ancestral language created a deeper bond with the land. (Although it should be noted that in the 1st century, Hebrew seems to have mainly been a sacred language).

These considerations create a presumption, that when Paul uses "Hebrew," he intends to imply a positive relationship to Palestine through the use of a Semitic language, it is not a mere synonym for Israelite. This is confirmed by J. B. Lightfoot's perceptive insight, that Paul's privileges in Philippians 3: 5, are arranged on a descending scale. A child circumcised on the eighth day, could still be descended from proselytes. But Paul is of the race of Israel. Some Israelites were unable to provide proof of their genealogy. But Paul knew he was of the tribe of Benjamin. The land of Benjamin, however, included Jerusalem where the influence of Hellenism was particularly manifest in the many Jews who spoke Greek. But Paul came from a family which, despite its location in the Diaspora, retained the ancient tongue of the Jews.'[7]

Having been brought up in Tarsus as a young lad, his parents as strict Orthodox Jews would have brought Paul up in a godly home, where he learned the history and the traditions of the Jewish people. At the local Synagogue with his parents, he would have regularly heard the Law read and expounded. So he was familiar with the history of the Jewish people, and acquainted with the Jewish Scriptures – the Pentateuch, the Psalms and the Prophets. As a young lad he also would have accompanied his parents on a pilgrimage to Jerusalem, a journey of around 500 miles, to see the Temple and experience the worship there.

EDUCATION

At some stage as a young man, Paul would have gone to live in Jerusalem and train as a Pharisee. His time there coincided with that of the famous wise teacher Gamaliel, who represented the more liberal and tolerant tradition of interpreting the Law – the grandson of Hillel who had lived until he was 100 years old. If we are not careful, we can unjustly gain a negative view of the Pharisees as religious leaders in Jesus' day, because of the controversial encounters, he had with some of them in the Gospels. It is illuminating to note what D. Coggan says about the Pharisees. 'The movement had begun as a great protest against religious laxity, a century and a half before Christ. The Jewish Law was being broken, its teachings disobeyed, its practices unheeded under pressure from pagan influence and opposition. The Pharisees were those who originally 'separated' themselves from such defilement. They held tenaciously to the tradition of their fathers, and often at the cost of their very lives, bore their witness to their prophets and wise men. As time went on, there were many of them who spoilt the nobility of their movement, by reducing it to a legalistic insistence on observing a complicated code.'[8]

Galatians 1:14, gives us an insight from Paul himself about how dedicated he was as a Pharisee, 'I was advancing in Judaism beyond many Jews of my own age, so extremely zealous was I for the tradition of my fathers.' This affords us a glimpse into his intensely competitive nature, as he undoubtedly excelled in his studies. Living and studying in Jerusalem at the feet of Gamaliel, a famous religious teacher, must have been an intoxicating experience for him. He probably and rightly felt that he was part of an elite group, with honourable intentions of maintaining their religious traditions. And being in Jerusalem, the city where the temple was, where he could worship at the spiritual home of the Jewish people, was equally a privileged opportunity to make the most of.

An integral part of Paul's study, was involved in discussion with fellow students, concerning the interpretation of the Law. O'Connor says, 'Consensus regarding what should be done was hammered out in common study and discussion, so we can infer that he spent considerable time with his fellow disciples. The tendency for Pharisees to concentrate in groups, was reinforced by the commonsense recognition, that life was simplified if one ate with people, who respected the same exigent standards of ritual purity. They could be fully themselves only with like-minded people. Table fellowship was the high point of their life as a group, and because of the purification laws, they could not easily mix so readily with other Jews, and had a tendency to be aloof from them.'[9]

In the Gospels, because of the controversies some of the Pharisees raised with Jesus, we do not get a comprehensive picture of them. Having already referred to Gamaliel, who represented the more liberal Hillel school of Pharisees, there also existed the

Shammaite school, named after its founder Shammai, which advocated a stricter interpretation of the Law. Tom Wright, the Bishop of Durham, informs us:

> Paul himself was from this school of thought, a hard-line Pharisee – what we would call today a militant right-winger. The key issue at stake between 'lenient' and 'strict' interpretations of the Law was not just a matter of religion. Nor was it just about private or personal piety. The key issue was as much 'political' as it was 'theological.' It was about aims and agendas for Israel: for the people, the land and the Temple.[10]

'In the political climate of the Roman Empire, the distinction between the two schools of thought, was that the Hillelites pursued a relaxed policy of 'live and let live.' Their outlook was to let them rule Israel politically, so long as the Jews were allowed to study and practice the Torah – the Jewish Law – in peace. But the Shammaites interpreted the Torah, as saying that Israel should be free from Roman rule, calling no one master and free to serve God. This line of thought led to these Jews being much more radically zealous, not just in outlook but in practice, using violence to achieve their ends. At times the Pharisees from the Shammaite school were also involved in such revolutionary activities.'[11]

Knowing this background makes it easier to understand why some of the Pharisees challenged Jesus, but since Paul sat at the feet of Gamaliel, at first sight it appears problematic to reconcile his hatred towards Christ and the church. However, we may simply deduce that while he may have been enrolled at Gamaliel's school, as a young man by his parents, as he grew older he increasingly identified with the more zealous Pharisees of his day. Bearing in mind that the Jewish people had prophetic expectations of a conquering Messiah, who would overcome the Romans, when once again Yahweh would establish territorial rule for Israel by physical force as in David's day – the radical and zealous outlook of those in the Shammaite school, with their nationalistic fervour, made perfect sense.

HELLENISTIC INFLUENCE

Paul was an influential religious leader and a stranger to Christ, who after his conversion evolved into a literary genius, of almost unparalleled understanding about him. His letters give us an important clue into his educational training, in the Greek rhetorical style of speaking and writing. And as we shall see this is foundational to the composition of his correspondence. C. K. Barrett has this to say about them:

> Paul's letters are the first great theological product of the Christian faith: that is their essential greatness, but they are also a very notable literary phenomenon, marked by an individual, sometimes rough but always powerful, eloquence. They are anything but negligible simply as a piece of Greek literature. This was recognised by those who received and preserved them, and not least by Paul's adversaries.[12]

'Gilbert Murray, Regius Professor of Greek for thirty golden years at Oxford, called him "one of the great figures in Greek literature." We have no direct evidence whatsoever, that Paul was educated at one of the "schools of rhetoric" in his native city, but the way he writes suggests that the distinction "MA, Tarsus" would sit comfortably after his name. It is one of those qualities that make him a uniquely compelling figure, to those who have seen western civilisation as a legacy, which mixes Jewish Religion, Greek thought and Roman energy and order – like the 19th century poet and essayist Matthew Arnold, who wrote extensively about St. . Paul.'[13]

Contradicting Professor Murray's claim, that there is no direct evidence of Paul being educated at one of the schools of rhetoric in Tarsus, is the excellent rhetorical skills he employs in his correspondence, especially in 1 and 2 Corinthians. That this was fortuitous is extremely unlikely. O'Connor concurs with this when he says, 'Tarsus had, "all kinds of schools of rhetoric." From this perspective Tarsus is the perfect illustration that, "For the great majority of students, higher studies meant attending the lectures of an orator and learning with him the art of eloquence." Oratorical skills were the keys to advancement in an essentially verbal culture.

The acquisition of such skills fell into three parts. The base was the theory of discourse which included letter writing. Techniques, rules, formulae, etc, were discussed ad infinitum. The second stage was a little more practical, in so far as it involved the study of the speeches of the great masters of rhetoric. What techniques were used, how did they produce their effects, could they have been bettered? The final stage was the writing of practice speeches.'[14]

Although Paul agrees with the claims of his opponents at Corinth, that he was not an impressive speaker – 2 Cor. 11: 6, this was a matter of personal choice that he alludes to in 1 Cor. 2: 2-5, 'for I decided to know nothing among you, except Jesus Christ and him crucified...and my speech and my message were not in plausible words of wisdom, but in demonstration of the Spirit and of power, that your faith might not rest in the wisdom of men, but the power of God.' Clearly he knew he was capable of an impressive presentation of the gospel, but he deliberately chose not to make use of his rhetorical skill. O'Connor observes, 'Paul's vigorous style of writing, was reinforced by the careful presentation expected of a well trained writer. He quotes G. A. Kennedy's assertion, that Paul was "thoroughly at home in the Greek idiom of his time, and in the conventions of the Greek Epistles." This is borne out by the evidence of rhetorical arrangement, not only in the organisation of whole letters, but also in the parts of 1 Corinthians when he is dealing with different subjects. Manifestly he was so well trained, that his skill was no longer conscious but instinctive.'[15]

In the 'Fools Discourse' in 2 Cor. 11: 1–12: 13, these deeply engrained qualities surface. C. Forbes, after a detailed analysis, rightly concludes, 'What we have seen of Paul's rhetoric, suggests a mastery and an assurance unlikely to have been gained without long practice, and possibly long study as well.' It was in the context of the school of rhetoric, that Paul was exposed to the various strands of Greek philosophy, which formed part of the intellectual equipment of every educated person. In order to balance this stress on his Hellenistic education, it is important to remember that throughout this whole formative period of his life (15-20), he would also have attended the synagogue of Tarsus. There he was exposed to the tradition of Hellenised Judaism, whose towering figure was his contemporary Philo of Alexandria. Owen Chadwick observes, 'how deeply this tradition impregnated his thoughts, is clear from the extensive parallels in his letters to the writings of the Jewish philosopher, despite their very different personalities.'[16]

E. Stourton echoes the impact of Paul's letters, when he says, 'If there is one thing that comes across in Paul's letters it is a sense of intellectual enthusiasm: they are very much the words of a man who grew up in a place, where ideas mattered....Paul's particular literary genius, is down to that "extraordinary Hebrew capacity to put things down as images, to put forward ideas as images." For example, 'O death where is thy sting? O death where is thy victory?' – 1 Cor. 15: 55. 'For now we see through a glass darkly' – 1 Cor. 13: 12.'[17] Equally, we have no difficulty in thinking of other metaphors Paul used, such as 'the Body of Christ' or 'the temple of the Holy Spirit' – to make abstract concepts concrete, and to earth in a tangible way, profound theological truths. Hugh Montefiore, also captures Paul's brilliant mind when he says, 'Paul had insight and a leaping, darting mind. His intellect was pugnacious and it functioned intuitively. It provides us with brilliant epigrams, memorable aphorisms, incisive battle thrusts.'[18]

In this way, Paul shows great originality, as a thinker and innovative theologian. This was something that was to some extent fortuitous, due to the conflict and controversies, he had to resolve in the churches. C. K. Barrett alludes to this when he says, 'Conflict was what made Paul creative.'[19] One of the outstanding aspects of Paul's literary style, is his use of antithesis to make a point. For example old covenant and new covenant: law and grace: flesh and spirit: light and darkness. W. Trilling informs us, 'In the secular rhetoric of the ancient world, in oratory and teaching, antithesis plays a prominent part, as it does in later Christian theology and preaching down the centuries...Paul had a gift for antithesis. A recent work on the subject gives a detailed account, of the contrasts in Paul and draws this conclusion. 'This tells us a good deal about the actual breadth, of the vocabulary of contrasts in Paul. It shows that no thought of any importance whatsoever, in Pauline theology, is formulated other than in contrasts – or should one say, can be formulated that way?'[20] Possibly another influential factor in using this contrasting rhetorical style, is because his conversion marks a demarcation line in Paul's life. Subsequently, he was constantly comparing life under the Law, and his life in Christ. We do not have to be a scholar, to realise the crucible for the formation of his theology, was forged through his own experience of the Law and Christ.

AN ANCIENT PERSONALITY

Having worked with Jewish people many years ago and being from a Mediterranean culture, I found it very interesting to come across B. Witherington's analysis, of how to understand Paul. He points out that ancient persons tended to be very different from modern ones, in the way in which they derived their sense of identity. A fundamental shift has occurred in the approach to ancient persons, and this has largely come from scholars of social history, cultural anthropology and social-scientific theory. This has been a major window, on the apostle to the Gentiles, in the last two decades.

To understand Paul, it is necessary to know what shaped him and his value judgments, and to know how he made sense of his world. He reminds us that the basis of the ancient Greco-Roman world, was that its cultures and subcultures were highly patriarchal. 'His world was, to a greater extent than our Western culture, a male-dominated world. And families in antiquity like other social groups, were based on ancient kinship principles and operated within a group mentality. Individual persons essentially derived their sense of identity, not from what distinguished them from the crowd, but rather from what crowd they were a part of, where they lived, their gender and what values were upheld by their group.'[21] Being from a Mediterranean culture, I can testify that this mentality is still true for Greeks today. This also explains why people from ancient ethnic cultures, in a foreign country such as Britain, congregate together to perpetuate their cultural identity and customs, as their sense of belonging and identity are derived from these.

Another aspect of ancient personality and identity, was how the individual was recognised. They were not addressed by their surnames, but according to whose son or daughter they were. For example, this is seen in the New Testament when the crowd identified Jesus by saying, 'Is not this Jesus the son of Joseph, whose mother and father we know? – John 6: 42. In Jesus' and Paul's day, what identified persons was not how they were different from their parents, but whose child they were. This collective family mentality was all-pervasive in the first century and affected Jewish, Greek and Roman understandings of persons and the world. Similarly, I can remember many years ago when I met other Greek people, I was not introduced as 'Sotirios Christou' – but as Sotirios, the Son of Panayiotis and Andriani – and the villages where my parents came from in Cyprus might also be mentioned. This ancient cultural sense of belonging and identity, still exists in Greek culture today.

Through this background information, Witherington helps us to see, how Paul understood his sense of belonging and identity in Philippians 3: 5-6, where he lists his impressive Jewish heritage and credentials. In effect, he was thinking like an ancient person, for whom the group was the primary source of identity. However, the difference for Paul, was that now he was part of the new family of God in Christ. As we can see in this passage, he re-evaluates the significance he placed on his heritage, as this was now interpreted in the light of his faith in Christ. All the things he mentions about his Jewish roots, are still true, apart from the value he places on them. Only now, his sense of identity, is also complemented by belonging to Christ and the Body of Christ. Understanding this background, gives us a fresh appreciation of the significance Paul placed on Jews, Greeks, Gentiles, male and female all belonging to the Body of Christ. In effect, being in Christ, inaugurated a new corporate humanity for Paul, and introduced a new sense of belonging and identity. One that had great significance and meaning for him.

CHAPTER TWO

THE CONVERSION OF ST. PAUL

THE TAMING OF THE BEAST

The conversion of St. Paul, is like a crime thriller, with a sensational twist at the end. And as this striking conversion unfolds, this persecutor of Christians is dramatically saved. This is indeed a complex drama – not only with an unexpected ending, but because of the intrigue which precedes it. Bearing this in mind, to appreciate the significance of Paul's conversion, '(according to J. B. Lightfoot's dating he was not converted until A.D. 33-34)'we have to take into account his religious background, along with his persecution of the church.[1]

PAUL THE ZEALOT

In Acts 22:3, we learn about Paul from his own lips, 'I am a Jew born at Tarsus in Cilicia, but brought up in Jerusalem at the feet of Gamaliel. Educated according to the strict manner of the law of our fathers, being zealous for God as you are all this day.' Galatians 1: 14, echoes his religious commitment, 'I advanced in Judaism beyond many of my own age among my people, so extremely zealous was I for the tradition of my fathers.' More of his background is also given by him in Philippians 3: 5-6, '...circumcised on the eighth day, of the people of Israel, of the tribe of Benjamin, a Hebrew born of Hebrews: as to the law a Pharisee, as to zeal a persecutor of the church, as to righteousness under the Law blameless.' These verses give an insight into Paul's impeccable, impressive and privileged religious background and heritage. As a result he was full of self-confidence and self-righteousness. He was deeply devout and proud of his rich religious heritage and learning.

To appreciate the intensity of Paul's zealous persecution of the Church, it is helpful to know what motivated him to do this. J. D.

G. Dunn provides us with the illuminating information that enables us to make sense of what motivated him to mount such a sustained attack. In effect he says that 'a surprisingly neglected feature of his testimonies in Galatians about his conversion is his use of the term "zeal." Zeal was evidently a feature of being "in Judaism," of the competitive factionalism which marked Second Temple Judaism after the Macabbees – Gal. 1: 14, of the confidence in Jewish identity which Paul expresses in Phil. 3: 4-6.

In this sense, we may speak of Jewish zeal, as the echo of or response to divine zeal. For deeply rooted in Israel's consciousness of election, was the recognition that their God was himself a "zealot." That Yahweh is "a jealous God" is firmly stated in Israel's foundation documents, typically in the form, "you shall not worship other gods, for I the Lord your God am a jealous God" – Exodus 20: 5…the conclusion was drawn that Israel should maintain exclusiveness of its devotion to Yahweh, and the distinctiveness of its religion in the face of other nations and religions round about. Israel's "zeal" for Yahweh and his Torah – Law – was, a reflection of Yahweh's zeal for Israel.

First, in each case, the zeal was an unconditional commitment to maintain Israel's distinctiveness, to prevent the purity of the covenant set-apartness to God from being adulterated or defiled, and to defend its religious and national boundaries. Second, a readiness to do this by force. In each case, it is the thoroughgoing commitment, expressed precisely in the slaughter of those who threatened Israel's distinctive covenant status, which merited the description "zeal" or "zealots." Thirdly, the fact that this zeal was directed not only against Gentiles, who threatened Israel's boundaries, but against fellows Jews too.

It can hardly be stated that this must be what Paul had in mind, when he speaks of himself as a "zealot" and of his "zeal" manifested in persecution of the church. First, his zeal for the ancestral traditions, was the other side of the coin of his zeal as a persecutor. He would no doubt have understood that as a reflection of God's zeal.'[2] Therefore, we can readily understand Paul's instinctive reaction to persecute the church, because he considered

Jesus was a false prophet who had threatened the Jewish religion and traditions, and had compromised Israel's integrity and purity. As a result, he was ruthless and single-minded, in his zeal to persecute the Christians.

PAUL AND JESUS

As Jesus usually attended Jerusalem mainly for the major religious festivals, it is unlikely that Paul ever met him. There is no record of such a meeting in the Gospels, or from the letters he wrote. As a prominent religious leader based in Jerusalem, he would not have travelled to such places as Capernaum, or Galilee to meet him. However, when Jesus was in Jerusalem, Paul almost certainly would have been aware of this, as news spread throughout the city. Perhaps out of curiosity, he may have joined the crowds as they listened to his teaching, to catch a glimpse of him and hear what he had to say. He may have even been present on one or two occasions, when some of the religious leaders had controversial discussions with Jesus. He may well have been fascinated, as well as infuriated by this unofficial rabbi, who drew large crowds and was popular with the people.

Paul would almost certainly have been familiar with some of Jesus' teaching and claims, even if most of this was reported to him by eye witnesses. He was probably aware of his reputation that he was the Christ and the Messiah, and of his claim of being equal with God – that he would have seen as blasphemous. He was also likely to be aware of the healings and miracles he performed, and aware of his critical attitude to keeping certain aspects of the Law. Moreover, that on occasions he criticised the Pharisees – and probably aware that he spoke of the destruction of the Temple.

We may also perceive that Paul's perspective on Jesus, was influenced by an eschatological outlook. The prophetic expectation in Israel was that the Messiah would be like King David, a conqueror who vanquished their enemies, the Romans, and gave them territorial supremacy once again. 'This embraced the belief that this would also inaugurate and establish the Messianic rule of the Kingdom of God, defeating evil and ushering in the age to come. With Israel as a leading protagonist.'[3]

Bearing in mind Jesus controversial stance about points of the Law, and the Temple, to those like Paul whose nationalistic zeal looked for a conquering Messiah, yielding a sword, he did not fit their messianic description. Instead, they probably thought Jesus was an unorthodox religious leader, and they almost certainly concluded that he was a false Messiah and a false prophet, interpreting his death on the cross as a sign he was cursed by God. Their Messianic expectation was of a liberator in the tradition of Moses and David. Consequently, Paul and others like him, were convinced Jesus was not the Messiah. As a result, he hated the name of Jesus and his followers so much, that he became a blind, deluded and fanatical opponent. From his perspective, we can see that he believed he was defending the Jewish faith from this new sect, which was spreading rapidly and corrupting and undermining Judaism. As he did not believe Jesus was the Messiah, and as he did not believe he rose from the dead, being a dedicated Pharisee, he chose to defend the faith of his fathers. Ultimately, he believed he was a loyal Jew, who was being faithful to God.

The book of Acts portrays Paul as a formidable, and feared opponent of the early church. In Acts 8: 1-3 we gain a glimpse of his violent persecution: 'And Saul was consenting to Stephen's death. And on that day a great persecution arose against the church in Jerusalem...But Saul was ravaging the church, and entering house after house he dragged off men and women and committed them to prison.' Again in Acts 9: 1-2 we read, 'But Saul, still breathing threats and murder against the disciples of the Lord, went to the high priests and asked for letters to the Synagogues at Damascus, so that if he found any belonging to the Way, men or women, he might bring them bound to Jerusalem.'

Calvin describes Paul before his conversion as:

> A man of savage impulses. Truculent and obstinate. A man of blind passions and perverted zeal. A deadly opponent of Christ.[4]

John Stott similarly describes him as:

> A bitter opponent of Christ and his church. Full of hatred and hostile. More wild animal than human being. Having a mind poisoned by prejudice. A wild and ferocious beast.[5]

Charles Swindoll also says about Paul:

> The first pen portrait of Paul is both brutal and bloody. The man looks more like a terrorist than a devout follower of Judaism.[6]

We gain a glimpse into Paul's fearsome reputation in the eyes of the early church, from passages in Acts. In 9: 13, after the Lord asks Ananias to go to Saul, he replies, 'Lord I have heard from many about this man, how much evil he has done to your saints in Jerusalem and how he has authority from the chief priests to bind all who call upon your name.' In 9: 19-21, after his conversion, Paul was proclaiming Jesus in the synagogue at Damascus. And those who heard him were amazed and said, 'Is not this the man who made havoc in Jerusalem of those who called on his name?' In 9: 21 the Greek verb used is 'portheo' which means 'mauled.' In 9: 26, also after his conversion, we see the extent to which the apostles were frightened of him. 'And when Paul had come to Jerusalem he attempted to join the disciples, and they were all afraid of him, for they did not believe he was now a Christian.'

Paul's reputation was undeniably formidable, and he was certainly the last man any Christian in the early church would wish to meet. He was a religious fanatic who was a deadly opponent. From Acts we have a terrifying picture of him – one which Paul himself confirms after his conversion. He says in Acts 26: 9-10, 'I myself was convinced I ought to do many things in opposing the name of Jesus of Nazareth...And I punished them often in all the synagogues and tried to make them blaspheme: and in a raging fury I persecuted them even to foreign cities.' In Galatians 1: 13 he says, 'I persecuted the church of God violently and tried to destroy it.' He also says in 1 Timothy 1: 13, 'I formerly blasphemed and persecuted and insulted Christ.' In retrospect, Paul was obviously fully aware, of his intense and fanatical persecution.

PAUL'S CONVERSION

Although we tend to think of Paul's conversion as sudden, the Lord had been working in his life for quite some time before this, and we can also perceive that there were a number of contributory factors in this. It may well have taken longer than the Lord anticipated, and the delay was due to Paul's resistance to the overtures of grace in his life, as he persecuted the church.

We know that Paul consented to the death of Stephen, and quite likely he was one of the leaders who instigated the initial attack. As Stephen was stoned he prayed, 'Lord do not hold this sin against them' – Acts 7: 60. His courage and forgiveness towards his killers, probably left an indelible mark on Paul, but one he continued to ignore by pursuing and imprisoning other Christians. We can imagine him being exasperated, by the willingness of these Christians to suffer for Christ, and by the reality of their faith and their love for him.

We can readily imagine the early church desperately and earnestly praying, that the Lord would do something about Saul and stop his persecution. They would certainly have prayed for deliverance from this fanatic, and wondered why the Lord hadn't done anything about resolving the situation. Some may even have been inclined to pray along the lines of the Old Testament Psalms, that called on God to rid himself of his enemies.

However, a small minority, mindful of Jesus' teaching may have been praying a blessing on Saul – which in the circumstances didn't make any sense to them, and seemed no solution whatsoever. Although it is speculative, some Christians may have been prompted by the Holy Spirit, to pray what seemed an outrageous prayer – that Saul would become a Christian. On the other hand, as this request was in line with God's will, these perplexed Christians, may have been praying in obedience for this to happen – unlikely though it seemed.

When Christ spoke to Paul on the Damascus road, he said to him, 'It hurts you to kick against the goads' – Acts 26: 14. Before looking at what these goads may have been, it is helpful to learn what this expression meant in his day. 'To kick against the goads,' was a common expression found in both Greek and Latin literature – a rural image, which arose from the practice of farmers goading their oxen in the fields. Goads were typically made from slender pieces of timber, blunt on one end and pointed on the other. Farmers used the pointed end to urge a stubborn ox into motion. Occasionally the beast would kick at the goad. The more the ox kicked, the more it would stab into the flesh of his leg, causing greater pain.'[7]

Here Calvin reminds us, 'that resisting and struggling against the rule and Lordship of Christ in our lives, is a painful experience.'[8] This usually involves a measure of chastisement and discipline, when we are resisting the Lord. As I have revised this study about Paul, the realisation has dawned on me, that we ourselves are not exempt from struggling against the Lord. Jonah resisted the Lord's will and fled in the opposite direction. He, like Paul, discovered there has to be a turning point – where a final decision has to be made. Either to go with God and submit to his will, or to rebel against him. The same is true for us. Only when we have submitted to the Lordship of Christ, in the areas he has been convicting us about, and which we may have been struggling with, shall we find the painful discipline of his goads come to an end.

While we are not specifically told what Paul's goads were, this is almost certainly referring to his resistance on the occasions Christ spoke to him, through the eloquent witness of the Christians he had persecuted. Undoubtedly, it also includes the witness of Stephen who was killed, as he uttered his approval. Equally, it probably refers to the doubts the Holy Spirit had raised in his mind, that Jesus was in fact alive and the Christ the Scriptures spoke of. These goads of his conscience could not be subdued by him – no matter how much he intensified his reign of terror. And as Saul pursued the followers of Christ – so too Christ pursued him.

After his conversion, Paul was the first to admit he was the least of the apostles, and undeserving of the grace and mercy of Christ. He had resisted and struggled against the call to follow him, and refused to accept that he was alive and the Christ. As he reflected on his conversion, he must have been astonished, for as a persecutor of the church he knew how much havoc he had caused: and he knew quite conclusively that he deserved Christ's judgment. His wonder at his mercy and patience, is echoed by him in 1 Timothy 1: 13-14, 'I formerly blasphemed and persecuted and insulted Christ: but I received mercy because I had acted ignorantly in unbelief: and the grace of our Lord overflowed for me with the faith and love that are in Christ Jesus.'

In 'The Priest & The People Of God' – 2003, I mention that 'Paul had plunged into the abyss of sinful self-righteousness, by persecuting the Christians, and if anyone deserved God's judgment it was him.'[9] He knew only too well that he was totally undeserving of Christ's grace – and he could but wonder at the divine love that pursued him. Thankfully for Paul, the grace of Christ absorbed all the hatred, the persecution and violence that he directed at him and the church. But, not only did Christ absorb it, his love overpowered and conquered it. Christ could see his fiercest opponent giving him his allegiance, and becoming a champion for the Gospel. It comes as no surprise, that Paul could testify to the transforming power of Christ.

What would turn out to be an unforgettable journey for Paul, from Jerusalem to Damascus, of around 150 miles took about a week. Along the way he may well have thought about the followers of Christ he would arrest and bring back to Jerusalem. D. Wenham says, 'he must have thought that the Christian movement was pernicious and needed stamping out, and he must have thought that it was God's will for this to happen.'[10] But he had no inkling of the dramatic encounter with Christ that was imminent. We read in Acts 9: 3-9, 'Now as he journeyed he approached Damascus, and suddenly a light from heaven flashed about him. And he fell to the ground and heard a voice saying to him, 'Saul, Saul why are you persecuting me?' And he said, 'Who are you Lord?' And he said, 'I am Jesus whom you are persecuting. But rise enter the city and you will be told what to do.'

The men who were travelling with him stood speechless, hearing the voice but seeing no one. Saul rose from the ground and although his eyes were open he saw nothing. So they led him by the hand and brought him into Damascus. And for three days he was without sight, and neither ate nor drank.' The Greek in verse 5 for I am – 'Ego Eimi,' is loaded with divine significance. It is a reminder of God's description of himself in Exodus 3: 14, 'I am who I am.' The significance of telling the story of his conversion cannot be under-estimated, and Luke underlines its importance by recording it three times in Acts, in chapters 9, 22 and 26. The personal revelation of Christ to Paul, was to be an authentic sign of his call to be an apostle.

Christ had often attempted to arrest Paul's attention, through the witness of the Christians he persecuted, and by convicting him through his conscience. Now he came to unmistakably reveal himself to him. On the Damascus road Christ took hold of Paul. He seized him: he stopped him in his tracks: he broke his rebellious opposition – and he swept away all doubts about who he was.

The devil knew that Christ had earmarked Paul as a servant. He knew the potential of his religious energy if harnessed for the Gospel, and he almost succeeded, in permanently deceiving him about who Jesus was. We should not under-estimate his deceit which had been so subversive, that over a prolonged period of time Paul remained spiritually blind, and indomitable in his opposition to Christ. But the light of Christ when he revealed himself, shone into Paul's heart and mind, and dispelled the devil's deception. Now he could clearly see Jesus was alive and the Christ. F. B. Meyer captures the essence of what happened on that fateful day, when in effect he says, 'the light that had enveloped Jesus in his glory on the Mount of Transfiguration when his face shone as bright as the sun, was the same light that Paul encountered – the glory of God on the face of Jesus was above the brightness of any previous dispensation...this was the final and the permanent outshining of the love of God. There is no conceivable method of Divine manifestation, that can excel the light which shines from the face of Jesus. He was aglow with the shekinah glory.'[11]

Commenting on this light Calvin also says,

> Not only did the light throw him down, and completely reduce him to bewilderment: but also finished him completely. We now have a tamed Paul as it were. The pride

in him is corrected and the ferocity subdued...He is a man who is stunned and confused.[12]

Paul was comprehensively disarmed by Christ. Paul who had been so confident in persecuting the church, had all his grounds for confidence devastatingly taken away from him. The light, the vision and the voice on the Damascus road, were all an objective and undeniable reality of his encounter with the risen Christ. Although blinded by the light of his revelation, Paul could now clearly see who Jesus was. And as he fell on his knees, he surrendered to the Lordship of Christ.

F. F. Bruce succinctly summarises the magnitude that Paul's conversion was to have on Christendom on succeeding generations.

> No single event apart from the Christ-event itself, has proved so determinant for the course of Christian history, as the conversion and commissioning of St. Paul.[13]

This is no exaggeration, as we are only too aware of the debt from Scripture, that the church down the centuries owes to Paul. Having generously lavished the grace of Christ upon him, God knew the ambitious plans he had for him – although in his lifetime, he had no inkling whatsoever, that his letters would be his abiding legacy, that still minister to us today.

In his commentary on Acts, F. F. Bruce shares Sundar Singh's story of his period of bitter hostility to the Gospel, as being a striking modern parallel to Paul's conversion. 'Praying in his room in the early morning he saw a great light. 'Then as I prayed and looked into the light, I saw the form of the Lord Jesus Christ. It had such an appearance of glory and love...I felt that a vision like this could not come out of my own imagination. I heard a voice in Hindustani. 'How long will you persecute me? I have come to save you: you were praying to know the right way.Why do you not take it? The thought then came to me, 'Jesus Christ is not dead but living and it must be he himself.' So I fell at his feet and got this wonderful peace which I could not get anywhere else'[14]

In Acts 9: 8 we learn that Paul arrived in Damascus, and for three days was without sight and without food and drink. He had three days to contemplate his error of monumental proportions in persecuting the church. Three days to reflect on his misdirected zeal, and be horrified he had been so blind and resistant to Christ. Three days to feel remorse for all he had done and to repent before the Lord. Three days for it to sink in, that his theological framework and religious traditions, had to be reconstructed and reconfigured. 'In his heart Paul experienced Damascus as a participation in the Christ event, which gave him a new identity, and at the same time compelled him to restructure his picture of himself and the world.'[15] E. Bock also captures the dramatic impact on Paul's religious consciousness when he says:

> The "conversion of Paul" was above all a new "enlightenment," an expanding and elevating transformation of his consciousness. The light that opened his inner eyes was never again extinguished. The great glory became for him an inexhaustible source of enlightened insight and inspiration. It is clear that the hour of Damascus not only changed Paul's consciousness, but also his being. He was a different man from then on. Yet, the new nature was the consequence of the new consciousness.[16]

T. Wright goes a stage further in seeing the impact of the risen Christ on Paul, when he revealed himself to him. In effect, he says, 'prior to this he imagined that God would vindicate Israel, after her suffering at the hands of pagans at the end of time, so there is an apocalyptic expectation attached to this. When this occurred it would inaugurate the Kingdom of God, defeating evil and ushering in the new age. Now, post Damascus, he could see that God had vindicated Jesus after his death and suffering, by his resurrection. He now saw him as the true Messiah, the true bearer of Israel's God-sent destiny. Therefore, the Age to come had already begun and had already been inaugurated. The death and resurrection of Jesus were themselves the great eschatological event, revealing God's covenant faithfulness. So, his vision on the Damascus road equipped him with an entirely new perspective, which kept its roots deep within this theology.'[17]

During his three days without sight, Paul was praying, and during this time the Lord spoke to him through a vision. We learn from Acts 9: 12 that he saw a man named Ananias come to lay hands on him, to regain his sight. Simultaneously, the Lord also spoke to Ananais in a vision, instructing him to go to Straight Street (which still exists to this day), to the house of Judas and ask for Saul of Tarsus. Understandably, because of his reputation he is somewhat hesitant and questions it. However, the Lord replies, 'Go for he is a chosen instrument of mine, to carry my name before the Gentiles and kings and the sons of Israel: for I will show him how much he is to suffer for the sake of my name' – Acts 9: 15-16. Ananias, his doubts dispelled, obeys the Lord and lays hands on Saul, who receives his sight and is baptised with the Holy Spirit.

After Ananias baptised Paul and he received the Holy Spirit, we can imagine them having a conversation and sharing how each had had a vision from the Lord: with Ananias sharing what the Lord had said to him about his future ministry. Paul, who had terrorised the church for so long, now became its most famous convert. But to his Jewish colleagues back in Jerusalem he would soon be branded a traitor.

STRANGER TO CONFIDANT

After Paul's conversion, our curiosity is aroused, as to exactly how Christ went from being a stranger to him, to becoming his most intimate confidant – and who by all accounts from his letters became an expert in Christology. The question which begs to be asked is this, 'How did this take place?' Tracing a number of events helps us to answer this.

The obvious place to begin, is none other than the occasion when Paul was baptised by Ananias, and received the Holy Spirit. We may perceive that his experience of Christ would have been identical to that of the disciples, who received the Holy Spirit on the day of Pentecost. In my study on Pentecost, in 'Evangelism & Collaborative Ministry' – 2004, I say, 'Once the excitement of Pentecost, and the reception of the Spirit, and seeing around 3000 people converted had taken place – on reflection later that day, the disciples would have all been aware of something unprecedented. After the crowd of converts had dispersed, what spontaneously dawned on them, was that receiving the Holy Spirit meant Christ was now with them in their hearts – and the Father was also with them.

For the disciples at Pentecost, the greatest joy was not just receiving the Spirit, or seeing the 3000 converts - but the experience that Christ and the Father were now present with them. This new awareness of the intimacy of the indwelling Christ and the Father, and this new experience of fellowship with them through the Spirit, brought the disciples into a personal relationship with them. This is the interpretation of baptism in the Holy Spirit at Pentecost. This is a fulfilment of what Jesus himself promised in John 14: 18-20:

> I will not leave you desolate: I will come to you. In that day you will know that I am in my Father, and you in me, and I in you.[18]

Prior to his conversion Christ had been a stranger to Paul, and while he knew about him he certainly didn't know him personally. After receiving the Spirit, his heart was flooded with the indwelling presence of Christ and the Father. Simultaneously, he was immersed in the love of Christ which must have overwhelmed him. The love of Christ poured into his heart, his mind, his spirit and into his entire being. He was acutely aware of being united to Christ, and of his indwelling presence. His theological training had made no provision for this new relationship with Christ, it was completely outside of his religious framework, and from now on he would see everything in a new light. Christ was to be the lens, through which he would interpret his conversion and being a new creation, the Law, and the Jewish faith with Jesus as its Messiah – that also embraced the Gentiles and his mission as an apostle.

Paul undoubtedly felt unworthy as he remembered his persecution of the church. Yet, he was also aware the forgiveness of Christ was cleansing his guilty conscience, of all he had so violently perpetrated. The joy of being in a relationship with Christ and getting to know him, astonished him because he was so undeserving of his grace and love, something that stands out in his letters and for which he is always thankful.

THE HIDDEN YEARS

In Galatians 1: 11-12, 15-22 and 2: 1-2, Paul writes, 'For I would have you know brethren, that the gospel which was preached by me is not according to man. For I neither received it from man, nor was I taught it, but received it through a revelation of Jesus Christ...But when he who had set me apart, even from my mother's womb, and called me through his grace, was pleased to reveal his Son to me, that I might preach him among the Gentiles, I did not immediately consult with flesh and blood, nor did I go up to Jerusalem to those apostles who were before me, but I went away to Arabia and returned once more to Damascus.

Then after three years I went up to Jerusalem to visit Cephas and remained with him fifteen days. But I saw none of the other apostles except James, the Lord's brother. (In what I am writing to you before God I do not lie!) Then I went into the region of Syria and Cilicia. And I was still unknown in person to the churches of Judea that are in Christ.' 'Then after fourteen years I went up again to Jerusalem with Barnabas taking Titus along with me. I went up because of a revelation and set before them – the gospel that I proclaim among the Gentiles.'

Although Paul was now in a relationship with Christ, he still needed time to get to know his Lord. Through his own record in Galatians and the book of Acts, we can see that it was to be many years, before he began his missionary work amongst the Gentiles. As a disciple of Hillel Paul would have been acquainted with the custom of sitting at the feet of his teacher. Perhaps Christ was now calling him to sit at his feet, to learn about him and get to know him intimately. Just as the Holy Spirit drove Jesus out into the desert to be tested, the Spirit may have convicted him of the necessity of getting to know Christ in this way. 'It has even been suggested, that those three years in Arabia, were a deliberate compensation for the there years of instruction which Jesus gave the other apostles...Now he had Jesus to himself, as it were, for three years of solitude in the wilderness.'[19] 'Equally, it would accord with the much more widely attested practice in the history of religions, of a period of withdrawal into an uninhabited region, following a revelatory or a visionary experience, in preparation for some prophet-like role. And the psychological need for such a "retreat" and reconstruction of his theology can well be imagined.'[20] While this may sound plausible, it is extremely unlikely that Paul entertained any thoughts of a prolonged retreat. He was an action man not a recluse. A city dweller who thrived on the hustle and bustle of urban life.

While Paul was in Arabia it was a period of formation for his future ministry. Charles Swindoll perceives, 'I'm convinced it was there, in that barren place of obscurity that Paul developed his theology…it's where he tossed aside his polished trophies and traded his resume of religious credentials, for a vibrant relationship with the risen Christ… It was there, no doubt, he concluded 'whatever things were gain to me I counted as loss for the sake of knowing Christ.'[21]

To a certain extent we have to imagine what Paul's three years in the desert were like, as we are not given a detailed description. Something that J. B. Lightfoot echoes when he says, 'A veil of thick darkness hangs over St. Paul's visit to Arabia. We know neither where he went nor why he went there…Some people think he went into Arabia as a missionary to preach the gospel. Chrysostom describes, "a barbarous and savage people" who lived there, whom Paul went to evangelise. But it is much more likely he went into Arabia for quiet and solitude.'[22] On the other hand, A. N. Wilson perceptively comments on his time in Arabia, 'It would be a mistake to imagine when Paul tells the Galatians that he went into Arabia, that he was taking himself into the desert as contemplative figures, such as the Essenes might do. Paul is essentially an urban figure, his religion essentially an urban phenomenon.'[23]

M. O'Connor helps us to understand the historical context of Arabia that Paul wandered into. 'In his day it was bounded by the whole extent of the Arabian Gulf (the Red Sea) and the Persian Gulf…Arabia could be seen to the east from the tower of Psephinus in Jerusalem. It lay on the desert side of the three easternmost cities of the Decapolis, Damascus, Raphana and Philadelphia. More specifically, it was adjacent to Herodian territory running along the southern border of the Roman province of Syria. Petra was the royal seat of Arabia. Whence the name "Arabia Petrea," or Arabia belonging to Petra. This mountain-encircled city, however, was the capital and the chief city of the Nabataeans.

Paul must have been doing something to draw attention to himself and arouse the ire of the Nabataeans, because he had to return to Damascus, and even three years later the Nabataean authorities still wanted to arrest him – Gal. 1: 17, 2 Cor. 11: 32-33. The only explanation is that Paul was trying to make converts. This first act subsequent to his conversion, confirms his understanding of his commission to preach the gospel among the pagans. (O'Connor then proceeds to explain the historical background, to the violent reaction of the Nabataeans to Paul, although is not necessary to chronicle this.) When he arrived in Arabia around 33 AD, tension would have been building up for some three years because of the political situation. It was certainly not a propitious moment for a Jew to begin preaching, what to an outsider was but a new variety of Judaism. To those Nabataeans who were the objects of his ministry, it could only appear as an attempt to infiltrate, divide and weaken them. What they saw as an invitation to betrayal, would have prompted an immediate and violent reaction. However Paul escaped. Otherwise, there would have been no point in drawing the authorities into the affair, and painting him in such colours that he was still remembered as dangerous three years later – 2 Cor. 11: 32-33.

If the above assessment of the situation is correct, it is unlikely that Paul penetrated very deeply into Arabia. He may not even have reached Bosra: (there were three Nabataean towns further north, Phillopolis, Kanatha and Suweida). If Aretas contemplated armed resistance to Rome, he would have had troops in that area, and Paul would have been a figure of suspicion once he opened his mouth. This makes it improbable that he stayed long. His silence as to the duration suggests that it was very short, since he lists his two weeks in Jerusalem and his three years in Damascus – Gal. 1: 18. The imprudent gesture is important, only in so far as it indicates that from the beginning, he was convinced that his mission was to Gentiles.'[24]

The personal testimony of his hidden years Paul refers to in Galatians, is tantamount to evidence that he had not associated at any great length with the other apostles. Also that Christ had revealed himself to him and called him as an apostle. His emphasis on revelation to the Galatians is of great importance, as he uses it as evidence to authenticate that the gospel he received was from Christ. He uses this to refute any charges that questioned the gospel he was preaching. Leon Morris similarly says:

> This emphatic disclaimer of any contact with earlier believers and their leaders, makes it clear that Paul did not derive his understanding of the Christian message from any who were Christians before him. Specifically, he did not learn from, nor was he commissioned by, those who had been apostles before him. It could not be said that he had had instruction and had misunderstood, what earlier teachers were trying to convey to him. It is of primary importance for Paul that he had been directly commissioned by Christ.[25]

At the same time, J. D. G. Dunn perceptively points out, 'Paul was conscious of resting his authority on what others may have regarded as a delusion. This is presumably part of the explanation for the somewhat curious dialectic, that is such a feature of Paul's description of his relationships, with the leadership of the Jerusalem church throughout these two chapters – Galatians 1-2. The dialectic between them acknowledging their authority, and maintaining his independence of that authority. It was evidently important to him to acknowledge that authority, for in the event they had exercised that authority in his favour: they had ratified his gospel 2: 1-10, and that ratification was crucial both to his own understanding of Jerusalem as the symbolic focus of the gospel, and to the success of his own mission. But they were not the source of that gospel, and having once ratified it – 2: 1-10, they, or their emissaries could not now deny it. Such was the narrow tightrope on which Paul walked, between maintaining the unity of the Christian churches, and the freedom of the gospel.'[26]

We read in Acts 9: 20 – 31, that after his conversion, Paul remained in Damascus for only a short period of time, as the Jews plotted to kill him, because he had betrayed them and joined the Christians. Having escaped by being lowered in a basket down the city wall he went to Jerusalem, though understandably the disciples did not believe he was a Christian. Perhaps this was a subversive plot to cause more mayhem amongst them. But Barnabas took him and brought him to the apostles, and testified on his behalf how the Lord revealed himself to Paul, and how he boldly preached in the name of Jesus. We get the impression Paul was only there a short time, before the Jews again tried to kill him. He may have defected, but his former associates certainly hadn't lost any of their zeal. So, for his own safety, other disciples brought him down to Caesarea and sent him off to Tarsus, where he was known, and where hopefully he would be safe. It is striking to note that ironically with Paul now out of the way, the church throughout all Judea and Galilee and Samaria, had peace and was built up: and walking in the fear of the Lord and in the comfort of the Holy Spirit it was multiplied – Acts 9: 31.

We do not know how long Paul remained in Tarsus, but we can imagine him sharing the good news about Christ as the Messiah, with the residents of the city. Some time after this, in God's providence, Barnabas comes looking for him in Tarsus, to bring him to Antioch to help nurture the church there. This happened because in Antioch the gospel was effective amongst the Gentiles. We read in Acts 11: 20-27, that men of Cyprus and Cyrene, on coming to Antioch spoke to the Greeks, also preaching the Lord Jesus Christ. When this news reached Jerusalem they sent Barnabas, a Greek from Cyprus, to investigate the situation, and in turn he went and recruited Paul to build up the church. D. Wenham says, 'Acts tells us that he made a hundred-mile journey to Tarsus to get Paul...Exactly what made Barnabas do this is impossible to say. But he had met Paul in Jerusalem not all that long before, and had been convinced of the genuineness of his conversion and call.

He introduced him to the apostles and he evidently believed in the young man and his potential.'[27] For a whole year Barnabas and Paul met with the church and taught the people, and it was at Antioch the disciples were called Christians for the first time. Some time later we learn from Acts 13, that they set out on their first missionary expedition under the guidance of the Holy Spirit. In God's providence Paul's ministry was affirmed and authenticated by Barnabas, a respected leader from the Jerusalem church.

After Paul encountered Christ on the Damascus road, he would have progressively sought to learn as much about him, and his earthly life and ministry as he could. One avenue immediately open to him was through the Old Testament Scriptures. His familiarity with God's Word would have been a distinct advantage to him, as he interpreted the Servant Songs in Isaiah such as chapter 53, as prophetically pointing to Christ and being fulfilled by him. And it is more than likely, he would have identified Jesus as the good shepherd in Ezekiel 34 who sought out his people. He inevitably would have linked many of the Psalms with Jesus as the Son of David, and instinctively identified Psalm 22 as pointing to Jesus, in which he utters his cry of dereliction on the cross.

As we have seen, there was also the opportunity to learn more about Christ, from Barnabas and the fellowship at Antioch. Yet another opportunity to learn more about Christ presented itself later on through Luke, who as the author of Acts is the storyteller of Paul's missionary exploits. 'There is an indication that on occasions he was his companion, as we see from Colossians 4: 14 and from 2 Timothy 4: 11– 'Luke alone is with me.' What we may deduce from this is, that Paul learned a great deal about Jesus from him. As the author of Acts in the "we-sections" – "he unobtrusively draws attention to his presence in each case."...Since for Luke's understanding of the early history people were even more important than places, he will surely also have interviewed many eye-witnesses. Some of them will have known Jesus, including perhaps the now elderly Virgin Mary herself, since Luke's birth and infancy narrative, including the intimacies of the Annunciation, is told from her point of view.'[28]

D. Wenham also draws attention to the fact, 'there are real possible clues that Paul knew stories of Jesus' birth, of his baptism and of his transfiguration. The picture that emerges is that Paul probably knew much of what we know of Jesus from the gospels...What is impressive is how traditions of Jesus seem to be important, on just about every topic that Paul discusses in his letters...it seems likely that his evangelistic preaching will have included substantial explanation of Jesus' life and teaching, not just a few credal statements about his death and resurrection. It also seems quite possible that Paul's evangelistic missions will have included a systematic explanation of the story of Jesus – from his birth to his resurrection...The conclusion is all the more likely if the author of Luke's gospel was a companion of Paul, as we have argued. The evidence is that Paul's missionary team included the gospel writer: if it did, then we may conclude that the story of Jesus, was of interest and important within Paul's team.'[29]

CHAPTER THREE

PAUL'S PRAYERS

INTRODUCTION

Prayer is the conversation of friends. It is not a mere convenience for letting God know what we are thinking or what we want. Prayer is that for which we were made. It is at the heart of God's plan of salvation. To understand the tremendous privilege and import of prayer we need to see it in the context of God's purpose to have a relationship with his people. 'It is not possible for us to say, I will pray, or I will not pray, as if it were a question of pleasing ourselves: to be a Christian and to pray mean the same thing, and not a thing which can be left to our own wayward impulses. It is rather, a necessity, as breathing is necessary to life.' (Karl Barth).[1]

As I have been immersed in Paul's prayers that are paradigms for our intercessions, the Lord has impressed on my heart that they are not just to be used functionally. They are to flow from and be inspired by our experience of his love and in turn become an expression of our love for the Lord and for others. This is a reminder that at the heart of prayer, is the joy of communion and fellowship with the Father and Christ. As we gladly give of our time to be in their presence we can bask in their love. Something of this atmosphere of loving adoration comes through in Paul's prayers.

There are different types of intercessions Paul used in his prayers and it is instructive to be aware of them. Prayer was essential to the apostle's evangelistic work. He asked for prayer to have opportunities to preach the gospel, and for God to open doors and give him boldness and confidence to speak about Christ, as in Ephesians 6: 19-20 and Colossians 4: 3-4. Prayer for perseverance and strength of character, and for the growth and maturity of the churches, was also an integral part of his petitions. He also prayed for his fellow Jews to be responsive to the Gospel, because as he says in Romans 10: 1, 'This is my hearts desire.' 'Prayer for Paul also involved the believer's struggle to discern, affirm and participate in doing God's will, against the pervasive influence of the power of evil. He was also aware of the importance of praying for our political leaders and for political stability, to create a peaceful environment to spread the Gospel – 1 Timothy 2: 2.'[2]

Of all the things Paul was involved in, it is relatively easy to miss how prayer was woven into the very fabric of his life and ministry. Whatever he did, or hoped to do, was immersed in prayer. Prayer was not something added on as an afterthought to invoke God's blessing – it was an integral aspect of his ministry. Even when he was imprisoned he exercised a powerful ministry of intercession, as the Spirit laid on his heart the burden of praying for the churches. At the same time we have to look beyond the man, because Paul's prayers were inspired by the Holy Spirit. And through the Spirit, Christ would have impressed on him the importance of praying to God the Father. So the inspiration and origin of his prayers was essentially Trinitarian.

Twenty years ago when I was a student at St. John's College in Nottingham, I led a study on prayer at our home group, that was attached to St. Nick's city centre church. I introduced this by mentioning that the contents of our prayers, usually focus on peoples' circumstances or church events, locally or wider afield. This model of prayer reflects what Paul speaks about in Philippians 4: 6-7:

> Have no anxiety about anything, but in everything by prayer and supplication with thanksgiving let your requests be made known to God. And the peace of God which passes all understanding, will keep your hearts and minds in Christ Jesus.

Bearing this in mind, it was a revelation to discover, that Paul's prayers in the New Testament are essentially spiritual in content. 'It is worth noting that these prayers, as well as other prison prayers deal with the spiritual condition of the inner man and not the material needs of the body. Certainly it is not wrong to pray for the physical and material needs, but the emphasis in these petitions is on the spiritual.'[3]

A closer look at Paul's prayers reveals a structure that we can adopt. Firstly, he is led to pray corporately for the churches he is concerned about, so the scope of his petition embraces all the Christians in the fellowship. Secondly, he also prays consistently and regularly for them, and his prayer combines thanksgiving for them and affirmation of their progress, along with the worship of God and Christ. Thirdly, the content of his petitions begin by being spiritual not practical. For example, that Christians may receive from God more knowledge, love, power or understanding: or to know God's will, or to have a deeper experience of Christ. Fourthly, that this may have an impact in their hearts, which is also seen in their lives and glorifies God.

What is striking about Paul, is that he usually begins his prayers, thanking God for the Christians he is writing to (apart from the Galatians). This almost seems too simple an observation and we might be tempted to think it is insignificant and polite rhetoric. But, it is important, as it is a reminder to thank God for one another. As one commentator says, 'Paul's prayers spring from unaffected delight at the report of the Thessalonians' faith, love and perseverance.'[4] Whenever we have difficulty in getting on with, or relating to other Christians, the way to approach this is to thank God for them in our prayers – because this is his will. This can facilitate our fellowship with one another, even if there are attitudes or conflict that needs to be resolved.

THE PHILIPPIAN PRAYER
BACKGROUND

In the first century Philippi was a modest size city of around 10,000 people, located in the north eastern part of Macedonia on the Aegean sea, 16 km inland and around 180 km north of Thessalonica. It was initially founded as Krenides by Greek colonists from the island of Thasos around 60 BC. However, it was taken over by the father of Alexander the Great, Philip of Macedon in 356 BC. Philippi remained an insignificant city until the Roman conquest of Macedonia in 168 BC, when it became part of a Roman province.

In 42 BC Philippi was the location where Mark Anthony and Octavian, defeated the roman Republican forces of Brutus and Cassius, the assassins of Julius Caesar. Octavian who later became the Emperor Augustus, established Philippi as a Roman colony giving its inhabitants the privilege of Roman citizenship, with property and legal rights and also exemption from poll and land taxes. When Paul arrived in the city in 49 BC, it was an urban political centre with a Roman and Greek population, with Greek being the main language used in everyday life and commerce.

As we know from Acts 16 Paul founded the church at Philippi and it was the first Gentile and Pauline church. The first convert was Lydia and her household, the slave girl he delivered from a spirit of divination and the Philippian jailer and his household: and in his letter he mentions Clement, Euodia, Syntche and Epaphroditus. A particularly warm relationship evolved with this fellowship, as is evident from his letter written to them while he was in prison.

His imprisonment in Rome probably seemed a considerable setback to them all, as it appeared to jeopardise the spread of the gospel and also threaten his own life – because of the imminent threat of his execution. To encourage the Philippians and counteract this perspective, he shares in 1: 12-14, that in fact being in prison had actually served to advance the gospel, as it became known throughout the whole imperial guard and to everyone else that his imprisonment was for Christ. Also, he mentions his confident hope, that through their prayers and the intervention of Christ and the Spirit he would soon be released – 1: 19. Moreover, the emphasis on 'joy' in his letter is also intended to act as an antidote to any negative response to his imprisonment. M. Bockmhuel captures the spirit of his correspondence when he says:

St. Paul's letter to the Philippians sparkles with joy – the sort of life-giving, heart-refreshing joy that is tangibly transforming in its effect on the mundane realities of everyday existence. Philippians is, at the same time, an Epistle of joy tested and refined, written in Roman captivity while Paul awaits trial on a capital charge and is prevented from carrying out the remainder of his life's work.[5]

P. O'Brien informs us, that 'Philippians fits the genre of the ancient art of letter writing and that out of all his correspondence it resembles a "Letter of Friendship." Writing letters was taken very seriously by the ancient Greeks and Romans, and played a prominent role in societal relationships and in politics and business. The correspondence with the Philippians resembles the model of true friendship, between people whose relationship was based on goodwill and loyalty, including trust. It also embraced "virtue" and affection, in the form of mutual goodwill toward the other for his or her own sake: and especially the basic matter of mutual "giving and receiving benefits." Friendship also included a sense of "obligation and expressions of gratitude" (further goodwill). One can easily see that many of these "ideals" are reflected in Paul's relationship to the Philippian believers. Their friendship is further indicated because Paul does not allude to his apostolic authority when writing to them. Instead he appeals to their mutuality in Christ.'[6]

Paul was obviously familiar with this type of literature, and we glimpse an insight into his style by the endearing terms he uses towards them. In effect he writes with his heart on his sleeve, expressing his attachment to them in terms of intimate affection. This is seen when he says, 'My beloved brothers and sisters, whom I long for, my joy and crown' – 4: 1. And, 'It is right for me to feel like this about you all, because I hold you in my heart' – 1: 7.

PAUL'S PRAYER

Paul's prayer for the Philippian Christians is a good example of his pattern and structure of prayer 1: 2-5 & 7-11:

I thank my God every time I remember you. In all my prayers for all of you, I always pray with joy because of your partnership in the gospel from the first day until now…It is right for me to feel this way about all of you, since I have you in my heart, for whether I am in chains or defending and confirming the gospel, all of you share in God's grace with me. God can testify how I long for you all with the affection of Christ Jesus. And this is my prayer: that your love may abound more and more in knowledge and depth of insight, so that you may be able to discern what is best and may be pure and blameless until the day of Jesus Christ, filled with the fruit of righteousness that comes through Jesus Christ to the glory and praise of God.

MUTUALITY IN PRAYER

We know that a close relationship developed between Paul and the Christians at Philippi, who had a special place in their affection and hearts for one another. 'Paul speaks with a remarkable warmth and affection for these Christians and a depth of relationship not plumbed elsewhere.'[7] So as he prays his heart is full of thanksgiving, praise and joy, because they have supported him in spreading the gospel. Moreover, they appear to have been the only church in partnership with him, supporting him in three distinct ways: financially, prayerfully and practically by sending Epaphroditus to minister to him when he was in prison. Paul was touched that they had resumed contact and had sent a gift of money with him which was a tremendous encouragement. Understandably, he is so attached to these Christians that he regularly remembers them with joy in his prayers, and longs to see them with the affection of Christ. 'Paul is deeply grateful for the long, enduring nature of their fellowship and participation in the spreading the gospel – the passion of his life.'[8]

PRAYER FOR A DEEPENING LOVE

P. O'Brien eloquently describes the language of Paul's prayer as having, 'An element of excess and fullness that overflows the set bounds. In this process of overflowing, the existing standards and rules are transcended and what was comparable becomes incomparable.'[9] This alludes to a request for a love that is abundant, generous, overflowing and rich – and is at the very heart of this prayer. It is an ambitious petition, because the Lord wants the best for them.

While the Philippians have a special place in Paul's heart, when he prays for them we perceive that he has been inspired by the Spirit. Instead of initially praying for them to know the right way to live as Christians, he begins with a spiritual request – namely, that their love for the Lord would be a love that increases as it is immersed in fresh knowledge and insight: so they can perceive what is best, right and excellent in any and every given situation. 'Paul's thought is that there are countless decisions in life where it is not a question of making a straight-forward decision between right and wrong. What you need is the extraordinary discernment that helps you perceive how things differ, and then make the best possible choice'[10] In effect, his petition is that their love for the Lord may continue to increase and affect their practical conduct: and the deepening of this love is initiated by the Lord, through the knowledge and insight that comes from him. A. Motyer informs us that:

> The Greek word translated knowledge "epignosis" always refers to knowledge of the things of God, religious, spiritual, theological knowledge. Often it has the idea of seeing right to the heart of the matter, grasping something as it really is...Paul goes on to speak about love abounding in all discernment. The word "aisthesis" occurs only here in the New Testament...The parent verb "aisthanonai" is well established in the meaning to perceive, to grasp the significance of. Aisthesis is the employment of the faculty that makes a person able to make a moral decision. By using the word in double harness with knowledge, Paul links knowing the truth with applying the truth to life.[11]

On the same theme G. Fee has this to say, 'Paul's request for a deepening love, "aisthesis" denotes moral understanding based on experience, hence something close to moral insight. Very likely therefore this phrase is something of an abbreviated equivalent of the similar phrase, in the (roughly contemporary prayer in

Colossians 1: 9) "that by means of all of the Spirit's wisdom (Sophia) and insight (sunesis) you might be filled with the knowledge of God's will…"'Paul is now praying a second thing, that along with an ever-increasing love they may also experience an ever-increasing knowledge (of God and his will) and moral insight.'[12]

In the Old Testament knowing God and the knowledge of God, was connected to wisdom, as in Proverbs 1: 7, 'The fear of the Lord is the beginning of knowledge.' This is further expounded in 2: 1-6:

> My son, if you receive my words and treasure up my commandments, making your ear attentive to wisdom and inclining your heart to understanding: yes if you call out for insight and raise your voice for understanding, if you seek it like silver and search for it as for hidden treasures, then you will understand the fear of the Lord and find the knowledge of God. For the Lord gives wisdom, from his mouth come knowledge and understanding.

Because of his training as a Pharisee, Paul was undoubtedly acquainted with the wisdom literature of the Old Testament, so he was familiar with the emphasis in Proverbs on the knowledge of the Lord. 'To know God meant to be in a close relationship with him because he had made himself known. The knowledge of God began with a fear of him, was linked with his demands and often was described as knowing his will.'[13] Clearly, it is relevant for us to be aware of this. But as Paul is writing to Gentiles, we do not know whether they made this connection.

PRAYER FOR A DISCERNING LOVE

Nevertheless, for the Philippians to acquire a love that is increasingly more knowledgeable and insightful, is in effect a prayer for them to have a love that is more discriminating. M. Bockmuehl says:

> Love's understanding and practical discernment, leads to the ability to determine what really matters. The verb here has the sense of both testing and approving.[14]

While commentators tend to see a link between a love that is increasingly discerning in the moral realm for the Christian, there is also a more subtle nuance that can be detected. In 1: 16 Paul speaks about those 'who preach Christ from envy and rivalry' and then in 2: 3 he says, 'Do nothing from rivalry or self-conceit' and in verse 4 he continues, 'Let each of you look not only to his own interest but also to the interests of others.' In 3: 2 he also says, 'Look out for the evildoers, look out for those who mutilate the flesh' (referring to an insistence on circumcision). His petition for love will enable them to be more discriminating, as they discern the Lord's will in the fellowship: and enable them to test the ulterior motives of those who introduce different teaching. This emphasis on approving and testing is also evident in his exhortation in 4: 6-8.

'Evidence of a deepening love for the Lord will also be seen through an increasing love for one another, because love for God and Christ finds it practical expression in love for others. Paul also wants to see an overflow of love in their relationships which will anticipate his later words of correction.'[15] It is this love that will empower them to be of the same mind and do nothing from vain conceit, and look not only to their own interests but also to the interest of others, and have a servant attitude like Christ – Philippians 2: 2-5. Christian love that is not informed by an increasing knowledge of God's truth, remains shallow and immature. Equally, a thirst for knowledge and truth that is not tempered by a deepening love for the Lord, can sound like 'a noisy gong or a clanging symbol.'

THE EPHESIAN PRAYERS
BACKGROUND

It has been traditionally acknowledged that Paul's letter was written to the Christians in Ephesus, during his imprisonment in Rome around 61- 63 AD. However, the words 'in Ephesus' are not included in some of the more reliable manuscripts, and equally there is no personal acknowledgment in his greeting to indicate that he knew some of them personally. R. Martin says, 'The absence of personal greetings is remarkable, and the suspicion that the author's relationship with the readers is strangely impersonal and indirect – so unlike that of the Paul who wrote to the Galatians and the Philippians – is all but confirmed to the hilt in 1: 15 and 3: 2.'[16]

It is possible the letter is addressing Christians scattered around Ephesus, which had a population of around two hundred and fifty thousand people. It differs from other letters as it does not appear to be addressing any particular situation or problem, and is not directed to a specific congregation. Perhaps, then, it was intended to be read as a circular letter. However, a connection exists between Ephesians and Colossians as they both contain similar themes, which Ephesians expounds in greater depth, drawing heavily on Colossians which was written earlier. Also there is a link between the two letters, as Paul's personal co-worker Tychicus is mentioned in both.

It is illuminating to hear what commentators have to say about this matter. 'The letter to the Ephesians is one of the most significant documents ever written. Samuel Taylor Coleridge called it "the divinest composition of man." It was also John Calvin's favourite and J. Armitage Robinson later described it as the "crown of St. Paul's writing." F. F. Bruce regarded it as "the quintessence of Paulinism" because 'in large measures it sums up the leading themes of the Pauline letters, and sets forth the cosmic implications of Paul's ministry as an apostle to the Gentiles." Among the Pauline writings Raymond Brown claimed, only Romans could match Ephesians "as a candidate for exercising the most influence on Christian thought and spirituality." Moreover, it has had considerable influence on Christian liturgy and piety down the centuries: liturgical prayers and short readings have frequently been taken from Ephesians.'[17]

THE ATMOSPHERE OF PRAYER

The context of Paul's two prayers for the Ephesian Christians, is arguably one of the peaks of his theological comprehension. Here we can detect an ecstatic atmosphere in the background that sets the tone for these petitions. When we arrive at the first request in 1: 17-18, 'that the God of our Lord Jesus Christ, the Father of glory, may give you a spirit of wisdom and revelation in the knowledge of him, having the eyes of your hearts enlightened…,' we realise the remarkable truths Paul has shared leading up to this petition, probably reflects that he already had received these spiritual qualities. If so, he has already been to the lofty heights of the heavenly places, he so vividly describes in this letter. The benediction in 1: 3-14, leading up to the first prayer is almost a liturgical hymn, framed in adoration and ecstatic in style. As Paul writes he is uplifted and filled with a spirit of worship, because of the sublime truths that have been revealed to him. Bishop Handley Moule captures this atmosphere when he says:

> What shall we say to these things? Perhaps the first and best response is the Amen of holy silence…Let us "sit before the Lord" and be still and passive…Let us hear them, in a hush of the soul, without haste, and without talk.[18]

Concerning this benediction John Stott says, 'In the original Greek these twelve verses 1: 3-14 constitute a single complex sentence. As Paul dictates his speech pours out of his mouth in a continuous cascade. He neither pauses for breath nor punctuates his words with full stops.' He quotes John Mackay's musical simile: "This rhapsodic adoration is comparable to the overture of an opera which contains the successive melodies that are to follow." The whole paragraph is a paean of praise, a doxology, or indeed a "eulogy."[19]

The opening of the benediction, 'Blessed be the God and Father of our Lord Jesus Christ,' is a form taken from Jewish Synagogue worship, and commonly called a "berakhah" the Hebrew word for blessing. 'In Ephesians however, the "berakhah" does not replace the introductory thanksgiving: it precedes it…God is to be praised then, because he has bestowed on his people "in Christ" every spiritual blessing.'[20]

As we think about Paul's prayers it is important to remember they are inspired by the Holy Spirit. In this instance he has been led to incorporate the blessing as the introduction to this prayer, which acts as a liturgical benediction that can easily be memorised. Like any masterly piece of literature, it demands careful study to fully appreciate its beauty and meaning. As a lead into prayer this can be a paradigm that enables us to prepare for our petitions, and the wonderful truths contained in it influence the way we approach God in prayer.

This is something I found very helpful when at the beginning of the 1990s, an eclectic church we belonged to in Cambridge with around 300 members, used to hold a prayer meeting on the first Saturday of each month starting with breakfast at 9am. Around fourteen people regularly attended and we used to take it in turn to lead. When it was my turn I devoted the first twenty minutes to thanksgiving, confession, praise and worship. As we came into God's presence we prepared our hearts to intercede using songs and scripture readings, to focus on the Lord's character and what he had done for us. It helped us to approach God with reverence and with a worshipful attitude. When using this model I always found our intercessions flowed more freely and with greater power.

Mark Stibbe's book on prayer, 'Drawing near To God – The Temple Model Of Prayer' has recently been re-printed. He uses this theme as a model to enable us to come into God's presence and prepare our hearts for our intercessions. Here he mentions, 'the importance of seeking the inspiration of the Holy Spirit to help us in our prayer.' He speaks about the three thresholds in this progressive model. 'The first threshold is the entrance to the court of praise, the second is the entrance to the Holy Place and the third is the entrance to the Holy of Holies.'[21] It is a reminder that prayer is not just coming to God to intercede, but that there is a progressive path in prayer. This demands our attention as we focus on the Lord in thanksgiving, confession, praise and worship, before we make our requests.

THE 1ST EPHESIAN PRAYER

Ephesians 1: 15-23:

> For this reason, because I have heard of your faith in the Lord Jesus and your love toward all the saints, I do not cease to give thanks for you, remembering you in my prayers, that the God of our Lord Jesus Christ, the Father of glory, may

give you a spirit of wisdom and of revelation in the knowledge of him, having the eyes of your hearts enlightened, that you may know what is the hope to which he has called you, what are the riches of his glorious inheritance in the saints, and what is the immeasurable greatness of his power in us who believe, according to the working of his great might which he accomplished in Christ when he raised him from the dead and made him sit at the right hand in the heavenly places, far above all rule and authority and power and dominion, and above every name that is named, not only in this age but also in that which is to come: and he has put all things under his feet and has made him the head over all things for the church, which is his body, the fullness of him who fills all in all.

INSPIRED BY THE TRINITY

Writing about Paul's prayers has required considerable thought, to comprehend the truths and the underlying themes running through them. The Christians who received his letters are likely to have been prompted by the Holy Spirit to pray to understand them too. In Paul's theological framework, he has grasped that not only conversion but growth and maturity as Christians, are intimately linked with the initiative and activity of the Trinity – and in turn he has realised this truth is also inseparably linked to prayer. Something he wanted his readers to grasp and comprehend.

Paul has been impressed by the report he received about the Ephesian Christians, and affirms the progress they have made in their faith and love for one another. This is evidence that they have already experienced the grace of the Lord and his love in their lives. As he writes to them, his underlying purpose is that they will realise and grasp, that there is still so much more of God and Christ for them to experience. So the heart of this prayer is that these Christians would grow in their knowledge of God and know him better. This involves God revealing himself to them and is a common theme that permeates Paul's prayers. But, the emphasis here, is that they may know God as their heavenly Father. In

Ephesians 1, He is described as the God and Father of our Lord Jesus Christ and also in this prayer, as the Father of glory. In chapter 3: 14 his theme is taken up again, 'For this reason I bow my knees before the Father.'

We can readily link Paul's emphasis on God as Father with Jesus' teaching, because this was a central theme for him. Jesus taught us to pray using the intimate term, 'Our Father who art in heaven' – Matthew 6: 9 and in 6: 32 he encourages us to trust God as our heavenly Father. In John 17: 6 Jesus also says, 'I have manifested your name to the people.' The name of God that he took great delight in revealing was that of 'Father.' This passage in Ephesians clearly speaks of the indwelling presence of God and having intimate communion with him as Father. It also speaks of being loved by the Father and experiencing his love in our hearts and lives. It is not just an intellectual exercise or an increase in knowledge about him. It is a relationship with him on a personal level. Something M. L. Jones echoed many years ago:

> Paul is concerned that we should have an immediate knowledge of God, a real fellowship with God. To use the current theological expression, we should have an 'encounter' with God. He means a knowledge of God which is personal and intimate…It is almost impossible to put this truth into words, but it means that God should be real to us, and that we should be conscious of him and conscious of his presence.[22]

SPIRITUAL WISDOM & REVELATION

Paul prays for these Christians that 'God will give them a spirit of wisdom and revelation in the knowledge of him…and to know what is the immeasurable greatness of his power in us who believe.' From personal experience he knew that the irrefutable basis of his theology, was that all the spiritual blessings in the heavenly places in Christ flowed from the inexhaustible riches of God's glory. And for the Ephesians to know God more intimately as Father, involved receiving wisdom and revelation about God and his character, along with his power. But this is not just an intellectual awareness or realisation. This is spiritual insight the Holy Spirit gives them in their hearts, to deepen their faith in God as Father, so they might experience more of his fatherly care and power in their lives.

The same is true when he prays for them – 'to have the eyes of their hearts enlightened.' Who will do this? God of course, by his Holy Spirit. He will give them spiritual insight and understanding in their hearts, so they may grasp that Christ in them is their hope of glory, and also reveal to them the glorious inheritance of the saints in and through Christ – that is all the spiritual blessings in the heavenly places: along with the immeasurable greatness of God's power working in their lives as Christians. These are themes for them to contemplate as the Lord answers Paul's prayer.

THE 2ND EPHESIAN PRAYER

Ephesians 3: 14-19:

> For this reason I bow my knees before the Father, from whom every family in heaven and on earth is named, that according to the riches of his glory he may grant you to be strengthened with might through his Spirit in the inner man, and that Christ may dwell in your hearts through faith: that you being rooted and grounded in love, may have power to comprehend with all the saints what is the breadth and length and height and depth, and to know the love of Christ which surpasses knowledge, that you may be filled with all the fullness of God.

A MINISTRY OF INTERCESSION

This prayer is similar to the one in the first chapter and flows in one long sentence. 'You will never hear anything equal to that for eloquence, for elevation of thought, for profundity of language and of conception. It is undoubtedly one of the great mountain peaks of Scripture.'[23] It is clear that this momentous prayer starts at the beginning of chapter three, but is interrupted by an account of Paul's distinctive ministry of sharing the Gospel with the Gentiles. He explains their place within the mystery of the ages, namely, that they have been included in Christ: and are fellow citizens with the saints and members of the household of God. He resumes at 3: 14 with his prayer, 'For this reason I kneel before the Father.' Paul's intercession is a natural extension of his ministry, because he did not just preach and teach about the gospel. His ministry intrinsically contained a profound commitment to intercession, for the maturity of the Ephesian Christians.

It is important to pause and reflect on the significance of this perception, because this has profound implications, especially for those involved in ministry. This is a reminder that Jesus also exercised a profound ministry of intercession for his disciples and those whom he encountered, and that every day he spent time in prayer in communion with his Father. He knew the effectiveness in his ministry was reliant on prayer, and he also knew that prayer released the power of the Holy Spirit. So we can readily imagine Jesus convicting Paul through the Holy Spirit, of the necessity to engage in a disciplined ministry of intercession. While the public arena of his ministry of preaching the gospel and teaching was left behind once he moved on, his private ministry of intercession could continue.

This reminds us how utterly indispensable prayer is for effectiveness in ministry, and for releasing the power of the Holy Spirit to bear fruit in peoples' lives. On two or three occasions in the past few years I have come across a statistic in the church press, that states clergy only spend on average of four minutes a day in prayer. If this is representative of the average minister then this is astonishing. Although I know there are clergy who devote time to prayer, as I can testify from my personal experience. But, what is disturbing, is the failure of those clergy who do not make time for prayer, to realise they are called to devote themselves to a ministry of intercession. Carson accurately perceives how ministry has evolved when he says:

> Part of the problem we ministers in the West face is that while we know we have been called to the ministry of the Word and prayer, several pressures impose themselves, pressures so persistent they end up shaping our values and

our schedules. The pastor's job has been diversified. We no longer give ourselves to the ministry of the Word and prayer, because we have become professional counsellors, fund-raisers, administrators, committee members etc.[24]

The challenge here is to do what the apostles did when faced with an administrative problem. They had obviously learned the importance of prayer from Jesus, and from Acts 6: 1-7 we see that they delegated this administrative task to others saying, 'We will devote ourselves to prayer and the ministry of the word.' And as a result the word of God increased and the number of disciples greatly multiplied in Jerusalem, and a great many of the priests became obedient to the faith' – Acts 6: 7.

Prayer is not only the priority of ministers, but lay leaders and every Christian too, yet in my experience prayer meetings are the ones most poorly attended. Over the years I have been in churches with 200 and 300 members, where only 12-20 people turn up to the prayer meeting. Yet in the spiritual realm effectiveness and fruitfulness flows from our prayers. Time spent in prayer in communion with God and Christ also expresses our reliance upon them. As our hearts focus on them through Scripture and prayer, we are fulfilling the command to love them and to intercede in the power of the Holy Spirit.

REVERENCE IN PRAYER

The subject of God as Father has already been referred to, but in this prayer Paul has a universal vision of God's fatherhood. He is writing to Gentiles and expounding this truth because now they are also God's people. God is not only Father to the Jews but to them as well – an extraordinary truth for them to grasp. Here, Paul reminds us that our approach to God the Father in prayer is one of reverence. While he is aware of the intimacy of addressing God as 'Abba – Father,' he is not casual or over familiar. Pausing to reflect on our approach to God in prayer, as well as in our worship is healthy. Especially if we worship in a church where the style is informal and the leaders dress casually. The danger is we can slip into a casual intimacy that robs us of the 'otherness' of God: his awe and majesty and his holiness and glory. Even though he is an apostle Paul does not come lightly into God's presence, 'He is not on terms of glib familiarity with God. 'Boldness and access with confidence,' yes! But accompanied by 'reverence and Godly fear.'[25]

Here O'Brien says, 'The solemn introduction of verses 14-15 gives great weight to the prayer. Two elements make this unusual: first, the reference to bowing the knee, and, secondly, the turning to one who is humbly addressed as Father and then identified as the one "from whom every family in heaven and on earth derives its name." The more usual posture in Jewish and early Christian prayer was standing, although kneeling was not uncommon. The latter signifies great reverence and submission, especially marking the humble approach of a worshipper, who felt his need so keenly that he could not stand upright before God…The one to whom he bows in homage is called Father, which in the ancient world was not only a term of intimacy, but also one that had overtones of dignity and authority.'[26] 'Kneeling was unusual. It indicates an exceptional degree of earnestness.'[27]

THE TRINITY'S LOFTIEST IDEAL

One of the themes that runs throughout the letter to the Ephesians, is that of 'power' and this is alluded to in Paul's prayers. In 1:19 one of the things he prays, is for these Christians to know and experience, 'the immeasurable greatness of God's power in us who believe, according to the working of his great might.' He follows this up with the staggering statement that this power in us, is the very same power of God that raised Christ from the dead, seated him in the heavenly places and made him Lord. Now, here in chapter 3, his request for power is that they 'may be strengthened with might through God's Spirit in their innermost being, so that Christ may dwell in their hearts by faith – and that they may have power to comprehend with all the saints, the inexhaustible nature of the love of Christ.'

We can readily see that the shape of this prayer is Trinitarian. Paul prays to God the Father, that they may be strengthened by the Spirit in their inner man, so that Christ may dwell in their hearts by faith. The term inner man refers to our spirit, the core of our character and our heart. 'It may include, or at least it affects, all that the New Testament means when it speaks of heart, mind, will and spirit. It is the deep seat of the personality, where the Spirit seeks to have his dwelling and to transform the whole life of a man.'[28] Later on in Ephesians 6, Paul speaks about 'being strong in the Lord and in the strength of his might,' because in the spiritual dimension Christians are being assaulted in their interior life by the devil.

Similarly O'Brien says, 'The sphere in which the strengthening is to take place is "the inner person" a uniquely Pauline phrase in the New Testament. Some have understood this expression to denote the new creation inwardly begotten by the Spirit in those who are united by faith to Christ. However, it is better to understand the inner person as the "interior of our being...the seat of our personal consciousness...and of our moral being." It is the focal point at the centre of a person's life where the Spirit does his strengthening and renewing work. Indeed, the inner self stands in need of empowering given our struggle against sin.'[29]

From his prison cell Paul is praying for the Ephesian Christians to be strengthened and just before this he says, 'So I ask you not to lose heart over what I am suffering for you, which is your glory' – 3: 13. In the next verse he begins his prayer, 'For this reason...' His concern here is surely obvious. He doesn't want them to be discouraged or disheartened, or to lose their faith because of what is happening to him. He wants their faith to remain strong, rather than fail because he is in prison. So he is praying for them to experience the indwelling presence of Christ in their hearts, something that has happened to him during his imprisonment. He wants them to understand that whatever their circumstances, they can be strengthened inwardly by the power of the Holy Spirit, so that regardless of events in their lives Christ's presence in their hearts will strengthen them. As we consider the pressures in our lives this encourages us to pray for one another to be strengthened by the Holy Spirit to be resilient: and that the love of Christ will sustain us regardless of our difficulties or circumstances.

Bishop Handley Moule has this to say about the indwelling presence of Christ:

Coming to them in a sense, in a respect, so deep and great, as to constitute practically a new arrival...What has Christ not been in residence before?...But his presence in us has degrees and advances, it is less and more, it is outer and inner. To drop a metaphor, a life may be truly Christian and yet far from fully Christian: the man may have come really to Christ, and have really cast anchor on Him, and have really confessed Him, and be really seeking to serve Him, yet be keeping back, perhaps quite unconsciously, whole regions of the life from him...Christ must be inducted into the central chamber (the heart), for it is His proper place. And he must be always there.[30]

Paul's prayer inspired by the Holy Spirit expresses the heart of the Trinity for the Church. It is their supreme desire and loftiest ideal – for Christ to dwell in their hearts and to experience his love in all its fullness. For this to take place they need to be empowered and strengthened by the Holy Spirit, because they cannot accomplish this by their own efforts. This truth complements Paul's emphasis in his first prayer for them in chapter one, that God first has to give them a spirit of wisdom and revelation, having the eyes of their hearts enlightened. So for these Christians to increasingly experience the indwelling presence of Christ, they have to first receive from the riches of God's glory – that is his inexhaustible grace. In this instance this means receiving inner power and strength from the Holy Spirit.

The prayer to be strengthened in the inner man has to take place in order for Christ to dwell in their hearts through faith. This implies there is a connection between inner strengthening and their faith. We know that it is through faith we initially receive the Lord Jesus Christ into our hearts and lives. Equally, Paul knows that despite his encounter with Christ on the Damascus road, he subsequently experienced more of Christ through faith. Is this suggesting that once we have been strengthened by the Holy Spirit, we are ready to receive more of Christ through faith? Or alternatively is the phrase 'through faith' connected to our inner strengthening? To be strengthened by the Holy Spirit in our inner man seems to be a general request, and if we link this to 'through faith' it would now imply – the inner strengthening refers to our faith being strengthened spiritually.

H. Hoehner comes close to making the connection between being strengthened and faith, 'The strengthening in the inner person results in the deep indwelling of Christ by means of faith, and this takes place in the hearts of believers. This demonstrates both the work of God's Spirit in strengthening the believer, and the subjective means by which the believer receives this.'[31]

GOD'S INEXHAUSTIBLE SUPPLY

A. Lincoln picks up on God answering Paul's prayer through his inexhaustible riches – in essence the riches of his glory. 'Now this language is taken up in the request that what is already theirs (from chapter one) might continue to be communicated to God's people by the Spirit. Glory denotes the splendour of the divine presence and power. In fact, in Paul "glory" and "power" can be synonymous in terms of God's saving activity – glory may also be linked with the notion of enlightenment in 1: 18 as the power to illuminate.'[32]

Glory and riches are themes in this letter that reflect the character of God. They express the overwhelming generosity of God the Father as a giver, and Paul's use of such language in Ephesians, is an attempt to describe the indescribable. He makes use of hyperbole, to express the inexhaustible nature of the spiritual blessings in the heavenly places God gives, because of the 'riches of his glory.' God gives in abundance – but there is if you like a super-abundance to his giving.

> The resources available to fulfil Paul's confident request are limitless. It is on a scale commensurate with his glory: he gives as lavishly as only he can. It is not surprising therefore that the apostle frequently speaks of 'fullness, riches and abundance.' The one to whom he directed his request gives richly and generously.[33]

Although these Christians have already been sealed with the Holy Spirit – 1: 13, and have shown love towards other Christians – 1:15, there is room for more spiritual growth. As we read the

letter to the Ephesians there is an emphasis on growing up in Christ
and Christian maturity. The Greek word used for the indwelling
presence of Christ in their hearts is a strong one – 'katoikeo' which
means to settle down somewhere. 'This signifies a permanent
indwelling rather than some temporary abode. If Christ has taken
residence in our hearts, he is at the centre of our lives and exercises
his rule over all that we are or do. The implication of the apostle's
prayer, then, is that the more the Spirit empowers their lives, the
greater will be their transformation into the likeness of Christ.'[34]

KNOWING CHRIST MORE FULLY

As Paul's prayer for the Ephesians develops we come to the
petition, 'that you being rooted and grounded in love, may have
power to comprehend with all the saints what is the breadth and
length and height and depth, and to know the love of Christ that
surpasses knowledge, that you may be filled with the fullness of
God.' As we interpret Scripture it is helpful to ask questions of our
text, as usually there is a progression of thought that unfolds – so
that what has gone before helps us to understand what follows. A
simple observation perhaps, but an important one, because the
implication is we cannot pray the second half of this prayer without
the first part. 'The second request presupposes and builds on the
first.'[35]

The request for them to corporately comprehend the love of
Christ that surpasses knowledge, reminds us of Paul's first prayer
in chapter 1: 15-19. There his request is that the Lord will give
them, 'a spirit of wisdom and revelation in the knowledge of him,
having the eyes of their hearts enlightened.' This too is a prayer for
understanding spiritual truths, and it is not stretching it too far, to
see a connection between these two petitions. Essentially in both
instances, he is praying for the Lord to give them spiritual
understanding, and this is something that takes place in the deep
recess of their hearts and spirits. This is not intellectual
comprehension, although there is a rational aspect of realising the
extent of the love of Christ – but it is more than that. It is spiritual
comprehension that sinks into their very souls and into the very

fibre of their being, and that is why there is an emphasis on having the right foundations for this to happen. It is the deeper level of corporately comprehending and then experiencing the love of Christ.

Just as there are different levels of human friendship and love, here we are similarly confronted with the most profound panorama of the love of Christ that surpasses knowledge, because its scope embraces the very fullness of God. This is divine love on an unimaginable level. On those special occasions when our love, and the love of another has merged and we encounter a dimension of love that previously we had not experienced, there is a union of our love and our souls. There is at the same time a new awareness, a new knowledge, a new comprehension of the dimension of human love. We may feel this is an analogy that reflects to some extent, the deeper experience of the love of God and Christ. While this analogy is inadequate it points us to the truth of this prayer, that the love of Christ has another deeper dimension that God wants us to experience corporately. And when it happens there is also a new awareness, a new knowledge, a new comprehension of the limitless dimension of the love of Christ.

Now the climax of Paul's petition for them, 'is to know the love of Christ that surpasses knowledge, so they may be filled with the fullness of God.' However, the right preparation has to take place in their hearts, before they are ready to receive the full extent of Christ's love. We already know they are reliant on God to strengthen them and their faith through his Spirit so that Christ may dwell in their hearts. Then being rooted and grounded in love is also indispensable to comprehending and experiencing the full measure of the love of Christ – that is synonymous to being filled with the fullness of God. As we know rooted and grounded in love refer to the spiritual foundations in their lives. The first metaphor 'being rooted' has botanical overtones and the second 'grounded' has architectural associations. John Stott expresses this concisely when he says: 'These Christians are to have deep roots and firm foundations. Thus Paul likens them to a well-rooted tree and then to a well-built house. In both cases the unseen cause of their stability will be the same: love. Love is to be the foundation on which their life is built.'[36]

One way of interpreting being rooted and grounded in love is to understand this as having firm foundations in the love of God and Christ: and to view all the spiritual blessings of God's grace and the inclusion of the Gentiles in the Gospel as an expression of this remarkable love. Therefore, this prayer may be understood in terms of their being thoroughly grounded in the love of God and Christ, before their hearts are ready to experience this love in a more profound way.

This interpretation is complemented by another interpretation of being rooted and grounded in love. To experience more of Christ's love on a corporate level, reminds us of two aspects of Jesus foundational teaching on this topic. In John 14: 15 he says, 'If you love me you will keep my commandments.' Then in 14: 21 & 23 he also says, 'Whoever has my commandments and keeps them he it is who loves me. And he who loves me, will be loved by my Father, and I will love him and manifest myself to him. If anyone loves me he will keep my word and my Father will love him, and we will come to him and make our home in his heart.' In this instance to be rooted and grounded in love is the obligation to live according to God's Word. Another aspect of Jesus' teaching about love, also comes in John's Gospel in chapter 13: 34-35, 'A new commandment I give unto you, that you love one another: even as I have loved you, that you also love one another.' Clearly, we cannot corporately experience the love of Christ on a profound level, unless we are loving one another and also showing that love by keeping his word.

Paul's petition moves from having the right foundations of love, to having power to comprehend with all the saints the love of Christ in its infinite dimensions. We can be excused for thinking it is easier to offer up this petition than it is to penetrate its meaning. Once again there is an emphasis on receiving divine power to comprehend the love of Christ that surpasses knowledge – in order to be filled with all the fullness of God. How else can you comprehend the incomprehensible? How else can you experience that which is outside of your experience? 'It is obvious that only God himself can impart this knowledge to Paul's readers: not only is he the one whom the apostle petitions, but also the preface to the request implies that divine enabling is essential. The word used (for power to grasp) "carries the nuance of the ability to obtain an objective" while that of knowing, has been "employed to emphasize the difficulty of comprehending the vastness and magnitude of the intended object.'[37]

What we have to remind ourselves in our Western individualistic society, is that to comprehend and experience the love of Christ in all its fullness, has a corporate dimension to it. Of course to some extent this is also possible on an individual level, but the implication of Paul's prayer inspired by the Holy Spirit, is that we shall only grasp hold of and experience the inexhaustible nature of the love of Christ together – on a corporate dimension.

THE COLOSSIAN PRAYER
BACKGROUND

As you look more closely at Paul's letters, you cannot lightly dismiss what the scholars have to say about their authorship. Colossians falls into the category of divided opinion about whether Paul wrote this. This invariably provokes an interest in the cultural, religious and social backgrounds of the recipients of his letters as they can help us to understand their original context.

Colossians is particularly interesting, because it links the Pauline letters scholars consider he wrote, and those that are generally considered post-Pauline: (there is a consensus in Pauline scholarship that Ephesians is considered to be post-Pauline). On making a comparison between the two Epistles, it is readily apparent how similar many of the themes are, and that some are considerably more developed in Ephesians. Although notably in its Christology and ecclesiology, it is significantly less developed than Ephesians. 'Colossians shows us how Pauline thought developed, whether in the late phase of his ministry, or among his close disciples after his death. There is a degree to which Colossians and Ephesians overlap, sufficiently often with very similar phraseology, structure and content. This feature is best explained by Ephesians being written using Colossians as a kind of template.'[38]

Colosse was in the southern part of the Roman province in Asia Minor that today is modern Turkey. Four or five hundred years before Paul's day it had been a large and wealthy city. Its wealth was generated by its position on the main road from Ephesus and Sardis to the Euphrates and by its wool industry. Close by were the cities of Laodicea and Hieraplois, which later flourished under Roman rule while Colosse declined. All were to be found in the fertile Lycus valley. 'A significant feature of these cities was the presence of a substantial Jewish minority. According to Philo, Jews were very numerous in every city in Asia Minor.'[39] We learn from Colossians 1: 6-7, that the church was founded by Epaphras, and it is likely he also founded the churches at Laodecia and Hierapolis.

THE COLOSSIAN HERESY

There is a well established tradition of the 'Colossian heresy,' about which there has been a great deal of conjecture during the past 100 years. This heresy represents the false teaching that undermined the pre-eminence of Christ, and which prompted Paul to write to counteract this error, which in 2: 8 is described as 'philosophy and empty deceit.' Here Dunn says, 'In the present century the dominant tendency has been to understand the threat to the Colossian Christians more simply (!) in syncretistic terms. Perhaps, then, as M. D. Hooker in particular has argued, the situation in Colosse, with its threat and potential trouble was quite different – not false teaching targeted on and already winning support among the members of the church(es) in Colosse, but simply the temptation to conform to more traditional or pervasive ideas and practices, or the attractiveness of teachings on offer from one or more other groups in Colosse – 2: 4.'[40]

Perhaps the Christians were influenced more by the spirit of their age, as they assimilated beliefs from their syncretistic religious environment. But whatever the false teaching may have been, clearly Paul expounds the supremacy of Christ over any earthly philosophy and human traditions. It is in this context that he presents his theology about the pre-eminence of Christ. His Christology advocated that Christ was Lord on a cosmic scale, and that earthly philosophies and traditions, or elemental spirits of the universe, were subject to his Lordship, including the Roman Empire. Walsh and Keemaat argue:

> The Epistle to the Colossians was an explosive and subversive tract in the context of the Roman Empire, and it can be thought to function in an analogous way in the imperial realities of our time. This letter proclaimed an alternative vision of reality, animating a way of life that was subversive to the ethics of the Roman Empire.[41]

PAUL'S PRAYER

Colossians 1: 3-4 & 9-12

> We always thank God the Father of our Lord Jesus Christ when we pray for you, since we heard of your faith in Christ Jesus and of the love that you have for all the saints. – And so, from the day we heard, we have not ceased to pray for you, asking that you may be filled with the knowledge of his will in all spiritual wisdom and understanding, so as to walk in a manner worthy of the Lord, fully pleasing to him, bearing fruit in every good work and increasing in the knowledge of God. May you be strengthened with all power, according to his glorious might, for all endurance and patience with joy, giving thanks to the Father who has qualified you to share in the inheritance of the saints in light.

THANKSGIVING SETS THE TONE

Paul and Timothy begin their prayer in Paul's customary manner, and thank God for the Colossian Christians and for the encouraging report they have received about their faith in Christ, and their love for one another. 'It is interesting to note that a characteristic feature of the ancient art of letter writing was the congratulatory thanksgiving. In Paul too it follows a regular pattern.'[42] Through this liturgical framework of prayer, formed and inspired by the Holy Spirit, Paul never tires of being full of thanksgiving and joy for those whom he intercedes. Clearly prayer requires discipline, effort and time – but here we learn that it can bring great joy and fulfilment, when it is an expression of love. A reminder that the prevailing ethos of the Christian faith, and our fellowship and worship, are also to be characterised by joy and thanksgiving.

SPIRITUAL WISDOM & UNDERSTANDING

As we know the context of Paul's letter and prayer, is the lure of the 'alternative teaching,' that is influencing the Christians and threatening to draw them away from Christ. So his petition naturally addresses this situation head on when he says, 'And so from the day we heard, we have not ceased to pray for you, asking that you may be filled with the knowledge of his will in all spiritual wisdom and understanding.' We know from 1: 6, that Paul has received a report from Epaphras about their faith, along with news about the deviant teaching which he alludes to in chapter two. Clearly then, this initial petition, refers to the 'alternative teaching' that had begun to infiltrate the fellowship and influence their faith. Here, Bishop Handley Moule is acutely perceptive about Paul's underlying concern when he says:

> For the state in which they are has inevitably with its blessings, its risks also. It is the very state in which a lack of direction may bring loss, if not disaster. The sails are set so full that the need of compass and rudder is the more pressing. Let the warm and loving community begin to live its spiritual life on the wrong line, let it go into wrong convictions about the will of God, the work of Christ, the manifestation of holiness, and it may follow those convictions to all the greater length. This noble passage, this prayer in solemn detail for these living and loving souls, is no mere exercise of sacred rhetoric. It has to do with the joy he feels over Colosse, but also the fears he has about the permanence of its blessing. He dreads the prospect of an alien teaching and influence laying hold of this fine material and moulding it all awry.[43]

R. C. Lucas also perceives, 'that there was possibly an incipient Gnosticism at Colosse, that offered a greater spiritual fullness: a new spiritual freedom: an ascetic lifestyle and also further initiation into a deeper "knowledge" of God, and a greater experience of his power – 2: 8-15.'[44] Insidious Gnostic teaching had infiltrated the fellowship and was claiming to offer a spirituality superior to what they had in Christ. Rather than being Hellenistic, F. F. Bruce highlights a definition of gnosticism proposed by G. Scholem, 'A religious movement that proclaimed a mystical esotericism for the elect, based on what he calls "Jewish gnosticism" on illumination and the acquisition of a higher knowledge of things heavenly and divine – the higher knowledge being "soteric" as well as "esoteric."'[45]

We can identify the nature of the philosophy and elemental spirits in Colossians 2: 8-10, 15, 18, 20 and 23, that threatened the church as originating from a Jewish background. Dunn says, 'To some this seemed to require a hypothesis of Hellenistic or more explicitly (pre-) Gnostic syncretism, that can be more readily seen to fit in within Judaism, including the emphasis on wisdom and fullness. And, most striking of all, several other elements are so clearly Jewish that no other hypothesis will serve 2: 11-14, 16-17, 21-22. In other words the number of distinctively and definitively Jewish features are such that it is scarcely possible to envisage the Colossian 'philosophy' as non- Jewish. The main proponents of this philosophy therefore almost certainly have to be understood as belonging to one of the Colossian synagogues.'[46]

Ralph Martin has a different perspective on this issue. He sees the false teaching as made up, 'partly of the Jewish elements already mentioned and Hellenistic religious philosophy and mysticism. Bearing in mind Colosse was pre-dominantly Greek, rather than Jewish, this is not surprising. Equally persuasive is the fact the congregation was essentially composed of Gentile Christians, who would not have been familiar with the Jewish religion and its traditions. In the church at Colosse, there appeared to be an amalgamation of the freethinking Judaism of the dispersion, and the speculative ideas of Greek religion.'[47]

PRAYER TO KNOW GOD'S WILL

Bearing in mind the threat this subversive teaching posed, Paul prayed for these Christians 'to be filled with the knowledge of God's will, in all spiritual wisdom and understanding, so as to walk in a manner worthy of the Lord.' A reminder that the Lord gives wisdom and from his mouth come knowledge and understanding – Proverbs 2: 5. Here, it is worth noting, the request is, for 'all' spiritual wisdom and understanding, and that further in his prayer Paul asks for 'all' power and 'all' endurance, and to walk in a manner 'all' pleasing to the Lord – (all is the correct translation). This is a petition that embraces the abundance and fullness of God's provision. 'The motif of fullness recurs frequently in this Epistle, and it seems that the false teachers boasted that they offered the fullness of truth and spiritual maturity.'[48]

These Christians were being pulled in two directions, and may have genuinely believed that the 'alternative teaching' was compatible and complementary to their faith in Christ. But Paul realised they needed to receive knowledge, understanding and wisdom from the Lord, in order to make an informed choice about God's will. Clearly, and unambiguously, they would have interpreted his prayer to know God's will, to be related to this 'alternative teaching.' 'The content of the petition is that God who supplies this knowledge in abundance might fill the Colossian Christians with a knowledge of his will, which consists in understanding what is spiritually important.'[49] As they were in danger of being deceived and drawn away from Christ, the apostle knows that only through persistent prayer, will spiritual light shine into their hearts so they can know God's will. And his teaching in Colossians is also designed to open their eyes to this truth.

CHRIST IS SUFFICIENT

The petition for knowledge, understanding and wisdom in the spiritual realm, is reminiscent of a similar request for the Ephesian Christians. This is a request that can satisfy our longing, to learn more of the object of our love. Paul highlights that the object of the Colossians' love was to remain firmly focused on Christ, in whom are hid all the treasures of wisdom and knowledge – 2: 3. The more they know and understand about Christ and his Lordship and his saving activity, the more their love can deepen in the knowledge that spiritually, they are not lacking any fullness. The underlying theme of Paul's prayer for the Colossian Christians, is for them to realise that Christ can satisfy the deepest longings of their hearts: and that Christ can satisfy their intellectual and spiritual aspirations, because he is God's ultimate source of knowledge, revelation and wisdom. This emphasis reflects, that 'The importance Paul gives to religious 'knowledge' – gnosis, seems to indicate that he has to deal with a situation in which the acquirement of esoteric knowledge needed to be refuted, as the apostle does in his repeated teaching.'[50]

With the issue of religious knowledge and wisdom being a key theme, it is helpful to explain this concept further, to enable us to understand how attractive it was. 'In Paul's day the Greeks elevated wisdom, because it was through knowledge that everything made sense to them. From rational intelligence they were able to deduce ultimate meaning in their lives. The relevance of this is seen in the importance they attached to the Greek word 'logos.' In philosophical terms, 'logos' denoted the creative power and intelligence behind the universe. It was the ultimate reality. The controlling power and source of the universe – but detached from it. This philosophical rational thinking described a God who was an impersonal creator and an impersonal force. However, 'Logos' is the very word which John, in the prologue to his Gospel, takes and applies to Christ in a theological sense – with the staggering claim, that this impersonal force is in fact a personal being – Christ himself.

In 1 Corinthians 1: 22-23, Paul succinctly summarises the dilemma the cross and the gospel presented to both Jews and Greeks: 'For Jews demand signs and Greeks seek wisdom, but we preach Christ crucified, a stumbling block to the Jews and folly to the Gentiles.' The death of Christ contradicted the philosophical and theological beliefs about God, which both the Jews and Greeks held.

It presented them with a dilemma of meaning and challenged their deeply held assumptions about God: for they struggled to grasp that Christ crucified was a manifestation of divine power – and did in fact bring ultimate meaning and make sense of life. But that is a response of faith not a philosophical or rational conclusion.'[51]

PLEASING THE LORD

As Paul's prayer progresses we see a connection between each request. As God gives them the knowledge of his will, this also involves receiving from him all spiritual wisdom and understanding. As a result they may walk in a manner fully pleasing to the Lord. Consequently, they will bear fruit in every good work and subsequently also increase in the knowledge of God. Clearly the opposite is equally true if they embrace the alternative teaching on offer. Presumably the emphasis on praying for the knowledge of God's will and a knowledge of the Lord, is to counteract the false knowledge associated with Gnostic teaching. Similarly, O'Brien says, 'Paul's use of knowledge here might be by way of contrast with the much-canvassed gnosis of the false teachers.'[52] R. C. Lucas also adds, 'We may surmise that an exciting promise of the visitors (false teachers), was that those willing to accept a further initiation at their hands, would come to enjoy a deeper knowledge of God.'[53] In contrast, for the Colossians to increase in the knowledge of God, also means increasing in the knowledge of Christ – because in Christ, all the fullness of God was pleased to dwell 2: 15-20.

As in his prayers for the Ephesians, here it is abundantly clear that Paul's petition for an increase in the spiritual realm of their lives, begins with the initiative of God. So he concludes his petition by saying in 1: 11-12, 'May you be strengthened with all power according to his glorious might, for all endurance and patience with joy, giving thanks to the father…' If there is one thing that is indispensable in the Christian life, it is having the power to be strengthened spiritually. In Ephesians this empowering is seen to take place in our innermost being, our inner-man. And here in Colosse they needed to be strengthened spiritually to know God's will concerning the 'alternative teaching.'

We know from Paul's previous prayers that the way to get spiritual knowledge, power, understanding, wisdom and similar virtues, is by receiving them from God – because these are not merely intellectual attributes we can lay hold of ourselves. Clearly, then, the implication of Paul's petition, is that spiritual growth and maturity in the area of Christian truth and our understanding about Christ, is inseparably linked to prayer.

PAUL'S PRAYER CONTINUED

Colossians 2: 1-4 & 6-7:

> For I want you to know how greatly I strive for you, and for those at Laodicea, and for all who have not seen my face. That their hearts may be encouraged as they are knit together in love, to have all the riches of assured understanding and the knowledge of God's mystery, of Christ, in whom are hid all the treasures of wisdom and knowledge. I say this in order that no one may delude you with beguiling speech. Therefore as you received Christ the Lord, so live in him rooted and built up in him established in the faith, just as you were taught abounding in thanksgiving.

PRAYER FOR UNITY

As Paul spoke to Epaphras, it became clear to him that the underlying danger of the 'alternative teaching,' was that it would be divisive and fracture the fellowship. So at the heart of his prayer, which he now continues after a digression, is a petition for unity. The apostle reacts in his customary manner when error is creeping into the churches. He feels compelled to use his influence to help Epaphras resolve the situation at Colosse. As is characteristic of Paul he writes to exercise his apostolic authority, in order to correct and teach the church. As he does so, he combines prayer alongside his teaching, so the two are complementary. 'As an apostle, therefore, he works energetically, seeking systematically to teach and warn everyone, with the aim of presenting everyone perfect in Christ – 1: 28-29.'[54] Here, what we have to remember, is that he has never been to Colosse and doesn't know these Christians.

Nevertheless, as an apostle with great authority and influence, he takes a personal interest in them and expresses his concern. His letter is not a matter of polite rhetoric as he is genuinely interested in their spiritual progress and welfare. He shows this by assuring them of his heartfelt prayers on their behalf.

PRAYER IS STRENUOUS

While prayer can be joyful and rewarding, there are times when it is intense because it requires a great deal of spiritual energy. On these occasions it is accurate to describe intercession as 'hard work.' In his petition Paul is using an athletic metaphor to show that prayer is strenuous when he says, 'I want you to know how greatly I strive for you.' Dunn sees this image as expressing, 'the concentrated and sustained effort that his ministry demanded.'[55] As an apostle he is the example par excellence of a minister being deeply committed to prayer. Bishop Handley Moule points out that Paul prayed for the Colossians while he was incarcerated in prison. 'Whatever he does, whatever he endures or achieves, he must do it – sitting still. It is more than ever open to him in this compulsory retirement to wrestle and to run in intercessory prayer. Prayer is now his grace and assiduous occupation: his toil, his course. He is working hard, like the wrestler on the ribbed floor of the Olympian court: he is engaged in a long indefatigable effort for the Colossian converts, and their neighbours. And it all means – prayer.'[56]

Paul unreservedly prays for unity amongst the Colossian Christians. He knows that even if only a handful of members are won over by the 'alternative teaching,' this will fracture and divide the church. He also knows this is a spiritual battle that has to be won through prayer. So his petition is that 'their hearts may be encouraged as they are knit together in love,' to counter the possibility of them being deluded or divided by plausible arguments, or deceived by philosophy. This request for encouragement is almost certainly connected to the influence the 'alternative teaching' had. It is possible this had created some difficulty in the fellowship, and some members may have been discouraged because it undermined their faith in Christ. R. Martin sees the Colossian heresy, 'as being a threat to the uniqueness of Christ and the salvation and freedom he secured.'[57]

CHRIST IS SUFFICIENT

This was an unsettling time and Paul knew that only the love of Christ would encourage and enable them to remain united. However, an integral part of this prayer for unity is also the request for them to 'have all the riches of assured understanding, that in Christ are hid all the treasures of wisdom and knowledge.' O'Brien points out that in the hymn in 1: 15-20, 'Christ has been identified with the wisdom of God. By stating that all of God's wisdom and knowledge are hidden in him, in an overwhelmingly impressive way, Christ was to these Christians all that the Wisdom of God was.'[58] We can readily imagine Paul's letter being the topic of bible study and prayer for many weeks and months, as they grappled to understand his elevated Christology and sought to resolve the issue about the 'alternative teaching.'

The Colossians would require the help and inspiration of the Holy Spirit, to give them an inner assurance that Christ could satisfy the deepest longings of their hearts: and a confidence that Christ could also satisfy their spiritual hunger for more knowledge and wisdom. Something the 'alternative teaching' could not do. R. C. Lucas captures this concern when he says: 'The apostle recognises that lasting unity depends on truth as well as love. Once it is agreed among the brethren that there are no essential truths outside of Christ, and that therefore there can be no essential insights hidden from anyone who is now in Christ, it becomes possible to maintain mutual confidence and love among themselves.'[59]

As Dunn expounds the Greek he says, ' their encouragement is one of "being held together in love." This verb is not very common, but elsewhere includes the thought of being brought together and of being reconciled. Only a love which penetrates to the heart and wells up from the heart can sustain the sort of unity that Paul sought.'[60] The use of forceful language by Paul implies strong feelings were involved in the threat from the 'alternative teaching.' He feels so strongly about this that he greatly strives for them in prayer even though they are strangers.

While his petition finishes at the end of verse three, verses four and six are almost certainly included in his prayer. He would have been praying that they would not be deceived by this 'alternative teaching' – because their allegiance to Christ was in danger of being deflected, and transferred to this alternative system of belief where Christ was relegated in importance. In effect their faith was in danger of being kidnapped – taken captive. Equally, verse six hints at another integral aspect of his intercession for them – namely that their faith in Christ would remain firm and strong. This emphasis is seen when he exhorts their faith to be rooted in Christ and built up and established in him. Something he undoubtedly and repeatedly prayed for.

CONCLUSION

I am inclined to think that at all levels in the Church we attend too many meetings and talk too much, and by contrast spend so little time in prayer and intercession in the presence of the Lord. Paul's petitions are a timely reminder of the strategic significance of prayer in the growth and maturity of the Church. As we have looked at his petitions we cannot help but conclude that he knew the importance of prayer. He is a man who prayed consistently: earnestly: thankfully: unceasingly and worshipfully. He has much to teach us about prayer. Undoubtedly, Paul would have kept the Jewish custom of praying three times a day, regardless of whether he was able to go to the local synagogue. Also, prayer would have been imbued in him from a young age, and this discipline would have been reinforced as a Pharisee and as an apostle.

In God's providence we have inherited Paul's prayers as paradigms to use today. There is a timelessness about their content, and a universal relevance, as they have intrinsic spiritual value for the Church. And his prayers are based on the paradigm of his spirituality that began at his conversion. Namely, that our life in Christ as Christians begins with God's initiative and revelation in reaching out to us and depends upon and flows from his grace: and also on God giving us understanding about himself and Christ. This is a reminder that prayer originates with the initiative of God – who gives his people the desire to pray: and through Christ we have access to the Father, as the Holy Spirit helps us in our prayers. For prayer is primarily a Trinitarian initiative and activity. Ultimately any lasting spiritual effectiveness as we serve the Lord has to be rooted in prayer.

CHAPTER FOUR

PAUL'S EXPERIENCE OF CHRIST

INTRODUCTION

Paul is one of the most striking figures in the history of the Church and has influenced a countless number of Christians down the centuries. Some like Luther have found a renaissance in their faith through his teaching, while others feel marginalized by what they perceive him to be saying. As we explore Paul's relationship with Christ and the churches, we learn more about him.

As you read Paul's letters and survey his ministry, and observe the controversies with false teachers infiltrating the churches, or the humiliating and painful encounters with the Christians at Corinth, or his considerable physical suffering, you might well recoil. To read through 2 Corinthians and his catalogue of suffering might lead to the conclusion – 'ministry can damage your health!' This raises a compelling question, 'What on earth possessed him to go through all this?' At first glance he was either an ascetic or a Stoic who courted pain. But as we shall see it was his profound experience of Christ and his intimate relationship with him, that under-girded his spirituality.

AN APOSTLE

In Paul's relationship with Christ his call to be an apostle shaped his spirituality. His astonishment at Christ revealing himself along with this call to serve him, left him with an eternal debt of gratitude and obligation to preach the gospel – Romans 1:14: 'I am under obligation both to Greeks and to barbarians, both to the wise and the foolish.' 'The root meaning of the term apostle comes from the verb "apostello" which means to send out, although the term is rare in Greek literature outside of the New Testament.'[1]

H. Ridderbos informs us, 'The apostolate – Rom. 1: 5, 1 Cor. 9: 2, Gal. 2: 8, is distinguished from all other gifts and ministries because it does not belong to the continuing, repeatedly renewed equipment of the church, but bears a foundational once-for-all character…The concept of apostle is determined first of all by the idea of appointment and authorisation. As apostles of Jesus Christ their word has absolute authority in the church, and they lay claim to obedience. They are receivers and bearers of the tradition, the foundational gospel…their writings are intended for liturgical reading in the church.'[2]

Paul's call as an apostle was not something that went unchallenged during his ministry. His critics readily argued that he did not fit the criteria that applied to the original twelve apostles, whom Christ called and commissioned to spread the gospel and who knew him personally and witnessed his resurrection. They were given authority by Christ and sent as his messengers. 'The word ''apostolos'' occurs thirty five times in Pauline literature and eighty five times in the New Testament, and was evidently an important office in the early church.'[3] There were also other leaders such as Barnabas – 1 Cor: 9: 5-7, James the Lord's brother – 1 Cor: 15: 7 and Apollos – 1 Cor: 4: 6 who were also called apostles. Paul puts himself in this category in 1 Corinthians 9: 1-2, when they questioned whether his call as an apostle was authentic. At the same time he has no illusions about himself when he says in 2 Corinthians 15: 8, 'Last of all as to one untimely born, Christ appeared also to me. For I am the least of the apostles, unworthy to be called an apostle, because I persecuted the church of God.' We clearly see Paul's humility in designating himself to be the least of the apostles, that went against all his natural instincts. This is especially striking bearing in mind his competitive nature in outperforming all his peers as a Pharisee.

2 Corinthians 11: 12-13 also raises the issue of leaders who designated themselves as apostles, but whom Paul called 'false apostles.' However, for Paul his call as an apostle by the will of God had great significance, as it was a perpetual reminder of the sovereign grace of the Lord. Clearly he knew his call could not be

attributed to any merit on his part prior to his conversion. His call to this office reflected God's providential purpose and seal on his life. O'Brien highlights this significance when he says, 'To speak of himself as an apostle of Christ Jesus not only signifies that he belongs to Christ, but that also he is a messenger who is fully authorised and sent by him to proclaim the gospel...He has been called to this ministry by the will of God.'[4]

A SERVANT

Paul's call as a servant of Jesus Christ resonates with two of the most evocative calls in the Old Testament – that of Isaiah and Jeremiah. He sees his call as being predestined when he says in Galatians 1: 15-16, 'But when he who had set me apart before I was born, and who called me by his grace, was pleased to reveal his Son to me, in order that I might preach him to the Gentiles.' His call resonates with the servant motif in Isaiah 49: 1& 6, 'The Lord called me from the womb' and 'I will make you a light to the nations,' along with Jer. 1: 5, 'Before I formed you in the womb I knew you, and before you were born I consecrated you: I appointed you a prophet to the nations.' This sense of being set apart, and apprehended by Christ to be a servant, gives Paul a compelling sense of destiny. 'As in the case of his predecessors he saw in his conversion the working out of a plan devised much earlier by God. The goal of the plan was the extension of God's grace to the Gentiles.'[5] D. Horrell also says, 'Paul does indeed speak of God "calling him" – Gal. 1: 15, and uses language highly reminiscent of the calling of Jeremiah and of the "servant" of deutero-Isaiah – Jer. 1: 5, Isaiah 49: 1-6. He was commissioned to a new task by the God whom he had served all his life.'[6]

To willingly become a servant and a slave of one's own freedom, was unheard of and radically counter-cultural in Paul's day, especially as anyone who was a slave looked forward to the day when they would be free. Yet as an apostle Paul wholeheartedly became a servant and slave of Christ, modelling himself on his example – which he captures in his awe-inspiring christological servant liturgy in Philippians 2. In his culture this was a controversial and subversive leadership style. 'It needs to be understood that this was not a goal of Graeco-Roman society. People were not eager to be others' servants: indeed they deprecated and ridiculed slavish behaviour. Humility was not seen as a virtue in Graeco-Roman antiquity...he was deconstructing certain key attitudes about status and power in his society.'[7] (On the concept of being a slave it should also be noted, 'that Plato seems to make a similar claim when he states we are owned by the gods in 'Phaedo' in 62 BC).

Paul would have been aware of the sociological status of being a servant, and of the theological implications from his acquaintance with the Old Testament Scriptures. Men like Moses, Joshua, David and the Prophets fitted this illustrious tradition. They were servants of the Lord called to serve God's people to be instruments of his salvation. M. Bockmuehl in effect perceives that as a servant, 'Christ is Paul's irreducible message and this is what made him tick. He was the slave of one who became a slave.'[8]

In Philippians, Paul portrays Christ as a servant whose example we are exhorted to follow. In this letter the English translation of 'doulos'– slave loses something of its impact. In his culture a slave belonged to another and implied humility and servitude. In this context G. Fee says:

> They (Paul and Timothy) are Christ's slaves, bound to him as slaves to their master, but whose "slavery" is expressed in loving service on behalf of Christ for the Philippians – and others...often he uses this language to designate any and all of those who 'serve' God as "free bond-slaves," that is, as those who are free in Christ Jesus, but who have used that freedom to "perform the duties of a slave" in the service of God and his people.[9]

THE JOY OF THE LORD

'Rejoice always, pray constantly, give thanks in all circumstances: for this is the will of God in Christ Jesus for you' – 1 Thess: 5: 16-17. It is a pleasant surprise as you explore Paul's experience of Christ, to discover that a central factor that inspired him in his arduous ministry, was the joy of the Lord. To overlook or miss this insight may confine him to being only an intense, passionate religious person – which on occasions he is. Through his letters we clearly see the joy that reveals Paul was a cheerful person. In them we see that one of the main things that sustained him throughout his eventful ministry was the 'joy of the Lord.' Equally, we should not overlook how much the Christians in the churches were also a tremendous source of joy to him – despite the ensuing problems. To be aware of this enables us to avoid a caricature of Paul and brings a balance to our perception of him.

After Paul was filled with the Holy Spirit when Ananias laid hands on him, the awareness that he was now united to Christ, and that he was in Christ and Christ in him, released the 'joy of the Lord' to reverberate throughout his entire being. His heart, his mind and his spirit overflowed with joy at experiencing the love of Christ. His salvation brought him the 'joy of the Lord.' When this began to sink in as Paul had a Mediterranean temperament we can imagine his joyful laughter.

We catch a glimpse of the joy the Lord brought Paul from the way he describes salvation in his benediction in Ephesians 1: 3-14. 'He predestined us for adoption through Jesus Christ, according to the purpose of his will, to the praise of his glorious grace with which he has blessed us in Christ.' Also in Romans chapter 5, his joy shines through when he speaks about being justified by faith through the Lord Jesus Christ, and God showing his love for him through Christ's death. Also in 5: 11 he says, 'we also rejoice in God through our Lord Jesus Christ, through whom we have now received reconciliation.' Again in Romans 8: 1 his joy shines through when he says, 'There is therefore now no condemnation for those who are in Christ Jesus.' Paul never lost the wonder of Christ's salvation which gave him a joyful heart.

As Paul was the apostle to the Gentiles we can imagine him being overjoyed when they responded to Christ. We catch a glimpse of this joyful fellowship with the Christians in Philippi when he says, 'I thank my God in all my remembrance of you, always in every prayer of mine for you all making my prayer with joy, because of your partnership in the gospel' – Phil. 1: 3-5. Philippians is clearly a letter that shows Paul as a man whose life is characterised by Christian joy. Even though he is in prison when he writes this, his joy in the Lord radiates throughout: and this is an extraordinary testimony to the joy that Christ can bring. M. Bockmuel perceptively says, 'The importance of this theme is not accidental. Joy in the midst of affliction is a hallmark of the churches in Macedonia. Its significance in Philippi apparently continued for some time. Joy for the biblical writers is not primarily a mood or an emotion: it is not dependent on success or well-being or outward circumstances. Instead, joy is a basic and constant orientation of the Christian life, the fruit and evidence of a relationship with the Lord…As Philippians shows joy arises from the quiet hope and confidence that the Lord will turn affliction into deliverance. Joy in the Lord is not a feeling, but an attitude…its prominence in OT restoration indicates that joy is especially characteristic of the age of redemption.'[10]

Paul learned that joy is a gift of the Holy Spirit and a Christian virtue to exercise, something he also encouraged the Philippians to do. So he exhorts them in 4: 4-5, 'Rejoice in the Lord always: again I will say Rejoice…The Lord is at Hand.' These few verses (4-7) contain the distilled wisdom of Paul's joyful Christianity. His basic premise is that joy is not conditional on our circumstances but is dependent on trusting the Lord – because he has learned that the Lord is always at hand. O'Brien in effect says, 'that the key to this rejoicing is the "governing factor in the exhortation." This signifies that the Lord is either the object of their rejoicing or the ground and the one in whom their joy thrives… Clearly, continuous rejoicing in the Lord is of great significance to Paul. It is a Christian's distinguishing mark and a characteristic of the kingdom of God.'[11]

We may perceive that another reason for his exuberant joy in writing to the Philippians, is because they have recently made contact with him again. 'I rejoiced in the Lord greatly that now at length you have revived your concern for me. You were indeed concerned for me but had no opportunity' – 4: 10. Clearly Paul interpreted their renewed interest as a sign of the Lord's answer to prayer. He was overjoyed because he had a special place in their hearts, a reflection of the Lord's love that meant so much to him. G. Fee says:

> Joy, unmitigated, untrammelled joy, is – or at least should be – the distinctive mark of the believer in Christ Jesus…Paul the theologian of grace is equally the theologian of joy. Christian joy is not the temporal kind, which comes and goes with one's circumstances: rather, it is dependent altogether on one's relationship with the Lord, and is thus an abiding, deeply spiritual quality of life. It finds expression in "rejoicing" which is not a Christian option, but an imperative. With its concentration "in the Lord," rejoicing is "always" to mark the individual and corporate life in Philippi.[12]

This joy spills over into Paul's life and he expresses this when he says, 'even if I am to be poured out as a drink offering upon the sacrificial offering of your faith, I am glad and rejoice with you all. Likewise you also should be glad and rejoice with me' – 2:17-18. I suspect that the theme of rejoicing despite suffering, is relatively alien to us in the West – as institutional Christianity is a sanitised faith that represents nothing worthy of persecution in society. But for Paul and the Macedonian churches he founded, joy was an experiential reality in the midst of affliction. 'What Paul describes is a joy in spite of suffering not because of suffering – Christian joy in affliction takes its source and occasion in the example from Christ.'[13]

As Paul works towards a conclusion in his letter to the Philippians he says, 'Therefore, my brothers, whom I love and long for, my joy and crown, stand firm thus in the Lord my beloved' – 4: 1. This is a further reminder to them not to be discouraged by his imprisonment. And in 4: 4 he also exhorts them to, 'Rejoice in the Lord always: again I say rejoice.' Unmistakably, Paul's life is marked by the joy of knowing Christ – and is Christian joy. He also expects this to be true for the Philippian Christians.

THE LOVE OF CHRIST

The transforming factor in Paul's life was his experience of the love of Christ, and for him this love was at the heart of preaching the gospel. We glimpse his perspective on this when he says in Galatians 2: 20, 'And the life I now live in the flesh I live by faith in the Son of God who loved me and gave himself for me.' He was profoundly touched by his love after the encounter with Christ on the Damascus road: and he never stopped being amazed at the love of Christ because, he knew only too well that he was undeserving of it. Dunn reflects this when he says, 'To take the "me" here as a generalised "I" retains the sense of an immediate relationship between Christ and the believer: but it loses too much of Paul's own sense of wonder and gratitude so clearly evident. The thought, of course, is not "only me," but even me.'[14]

Paul understood Christ's love to be very costly and supremely sacrificial, and although there is a universality about the love of Christ, he discovered it also has a compelling personal attraction. He learned that it is a love that seeks to draw us to himself, something that is echoed in John 12: 32 when Jesus says, 'And I, when I am lifted up, will draw all men to myself.' But for Paul this love was not just an intellectual or theological equation, to be incorporated into his new spirituality. While he could speak 'theologically' about Christ's love, it was an emotional experience that flooded his heart and life – and a love that he felt deeply and keenly.

Paul was to discover that the love of Christ was also a reflection of God's love for him. He echoes this in Ephesians 2: 4, 'But God being rich in mercy, because of the great love with which he loved us, even when we were dead in our trespasses, made us alive together in Christ – by grace you have been saved.' O'Brien says, 'In the Old Testament God is frequently characterised in this way: he abounds in mercy. Indeed he delights in it. "Mercy" often represents the Hebrew term "hesed," which has been taken to refer to Yahweh's steadfast covenant loyalty and love, especially when Israel was unfaithful…God's love is conjoined with his mercy as another motivation in the divine initiative in saving his people. That love is emphatically underscored by the adjective great and the cognate expression "the great love which with he loved us." As Paul has stressed the riches of God's mercy, so he now asserts the greatness of his love.'[15]

Paul was staggered to learn that Christ's love existed before time and history. It was a love he describes as our destiny in Ephesians – 'In love he predestined us for adoption (as his sons and daughters) through Jesus Christ' – 1:5. In the Epistle as he continues to describe this divine love of God and Christ he speaks of it in terms of being 'lavish' and 'immeasurable' – the riches of his grace. To speak about our adoption by God as an expression of this immeasurable love is an important truth we are likely to overlook, because we do not understand the significance Paul attached to it. 'Adoption was understood in Graeco-Roman law as referring to the adoption as sons of those who were not so by birth. It signified entry to a privileged position. Paul applies this to the special relationship which believers have with God. And he asserts that adoption as sons was one of the particular privileges of belonging to Israel. Now it belongs to Christians.'[16]

A MUTUAL LOVE

For Paul his experience of the love of Christ was an influential factor in shaping his personality and spirituality. Yet we can easily miss this integral aspect of his ministry that shows him to be extremely loving. This may surprise us depending on our preconceived image of him. At some stage presumably he became acquainted with Jesus' command 'to love one another as I have loved you' – John 17: 3, as this is a hallmark of his ministry as an apostle. Perhaps the Lord revealed this to him or possibly this was a tradition passed on to him by other Christians soon after his conversion. Perhaps Peter would have also passed this on to him, when he met him in Jerusalem after his conversion, as it was a pivotal command of Jesus' last supper.

As you read Paul's letters he comes across as a very loving man, who endeared himself to his converts (despite the relational difficulties he had to resolve with the Corinthians). We first glimpse this from Acts 20, when he calls the Ephesians elders to meet him at Miletus, so he can say farewell to them as he knows he is not going to see them again. In 20: 31 he says, 'for three years I did not cease night or day to admonish everyone with tears.' This is a very moving encounter and verses 36-38 record how it ended: 'And when he had said these things, he knelt down and prayed with them all. And there was much weeping on the part of all: they embraced Paul and kissed him, being sorrowful most of all because of the word he had spoken, that they would not see his face again.' The Jewish culture and temperament is naturally very loving and warm, and Paul is no exception as he shares the love of Christ with these Ephesian elders.

Despite the admonishing tone of his letter to the Galatians, this gives us an insight into the mutual affection that existed between them. He says, 'Brothers...You did me no wrong. You know it was because of a bodily ailment that I preached the gospel to you at first, and though my condition was a trial to you, you did not scorn or despise me, but received me as an angel of God. What then has become of the blessing you have felt? For I testify to you that if possible, you would have gouged out your eyes and given them to me. Have I then become your enemy by telling you the truth?' – 'My little children for whom I am again in travail until Christ is formed in you' – 4: 12-15, 19. Dunn points out, 'The meaning, then, is clear enough to the extent that Paul's physical condition had been such as would normally occasion contempt or scorn or revulsion.'[17]

J. Stott adds, 'Their behaviour towards him had been exemplary. Whatever the disease was, it evidently had unpleasant and unsightly symptoms. It seems to have disfigured him in some way. The Galatians had been tempted to despise and reject Paul, to treat him with what Bishop Lightfoot calls "contemptuous indifference" and even 'active loathing.'[18] Clearly, and conclusively, despite his obnoxious ailment, Paul's endearing terms suggest they were very close to one another when he was with them. And when he addresses them as 'My little children' – Gal. 4: 19, this reflects a warm fatherly tone, full of concern for them still, despite his sharp reproof.

Paul's letter to the Philippians, also give us a good example of the warmth of his inter-personal relationships, and his love for them reflects the love of Christ in a tangible way. He very much writes with his heart on his sleeve when he addresses them by saying, 'I thank God in all my remembrance of you, always in every prayer of mine for you, always making my prayer with joy – it is right for me to feel this way about you all because I hold you in my heart...For God is my witness how I yearn for you all with the affection of Christ Jesus' – Phil. 1: 3, 7-8.

Paul's loving reference to the Philippians is also seen in 2: 12,'Therefore, my beloved,' in 3: 1 'Finally, my brethren' and especially in 4: 1 'Therefore, my brothers whom I love and long for, my joy and crown.' He unashamedly expresses his Jewish temperament that has been tempered by the love of Christ. This is why he says earlier, 'I long for you all with the affection of Christ Jesus' – 1: 8, because he wanted them to unmistakably know his love was not just a human bond. It was an attachment formed through Christ.

TOUGH LOVE FOR CORINTH

2 Corinthians it is a painful account of how the church's relationship with Paul has deteriorated, yet the letter is permeated with the love of Christ shining through Paul. A number of problems have arisen that he has attempted to resolve, by replying to the letter the church sent him, and by his personal visits. But some outsiders whom he calls 'superlative apostles' – 2 Cor. 12: 11, have influenced the church to challenge his authority as an apostle, something he is seeking to re-establish through his correspondence and visits. He has to exercise a 'tough love,' as there are many ethical and spiritual issues to be resolved. The discipline of his 'tough love' is mentioned in 2 Cor. 2: 1 where he says, 'For I made up my mind not to make another painful visit to you.' The same discipline is referred to in 7: 8 when he says, 'For even if I did make you grieve with my letter...'

G. Fee comments on the occasion of Paul writing 1 Corinthians, 'Given the combative nature of so much of his response, it seems likely that in their letter they have taken exception to several of his positions.'[19] Quite possibly he embarrassed the Christians by what he said, and as a result had been humiliated by the conflict that ensued. O'Connor says, 'The Corinthians were the "most exasperating church" he had to deal with' and he also speaks of "an extremely turbulent relationship" between them.'[20]

From this we could conclude that Paul was a difficult person and his inter-personal relationship skills were somewhat deficient. But a careful look at 1 and 2 Corinthians in particular, shows how much Paul loved the church. This love for the Corinthian Christians was a reflection of the love of Christ for them. There are allusions to the 'good shepherd' and the 'prodigal son' – in Paul's relationship with the church at Corinth. Clearly the love of God and Christ resonates through the apostle towards them. Presumably, the Holy Spirit filled him with their love, that enabled him to resolve the problems there. It is certainly to Paul's credit that he did not blank them out, or switch off his affection for them, or wipe his hands of these immature Christians.

In 1 Cor. 4: 14-15 he says, 'I did not write these things to make you ashamed, but to admonish you as my beloved children. For though you have countless guides in Christ, you do not have many fathers.' Here we detect a tender attachment to them, which is not surprising as he founded the church and led them to Christ. He also echoes his love for them in 2 Cor. 2: 4, ' For I wrote to you out of much affliction and anguish of heart and with many tears, not to cause you pain but to let you know the abundant love that I have for you.' A love which is transparent throughout this letter as is evident in 7: 2-3, 'make room in your hearts for us. We have wronged no one, we have corrupted no one, we have taken advantage of no one. I do not say this to condemn you, for I said before that you are in our hearts.' We cannot fail to see the tender love of the Lord for his wayward Corinthian children through the apostle.

2 Cor. 11: 1-2 reveals Paul's jealous attachment to them. 'I wish you would bear with me in a little foolishness. Do bear with me! I feel a divine jealousy for you, for I betrothed you to one husband, to present you as a pure virgin to Christ.' He wants them to grasp how genuine his love for them is, in comparison to the false

superlative apostles who are taking advantage of them. He expresses his heartfelt concern for them when he says in 2 Cor. 12: 15, 'I will most gladly spend and be spent for your souls. If I love you more am I to be loved less?' P. Hughes elaborates on this:

> Those who stress the severity of the final four chapters of our Epistle, as evidence for the hypothesis that these chapters belong elsewhere, seem predisposed to overlook the great tenderness and affection which time and again shine through so brightly as we have already seen at 11: 3. What could be more genuinely tender and loving, what could be less austere, than the sentiments Paul expresses at this point? Justin Denney has described this as "one of the most movingly tender passages in the whole Bible." It breathes the spontaneous spirit of dedicated love that we have previously encountered in 6: 11-13 and 7: 1-4.[21]

C. M. Martini in his insightful book, 'In The Thick Of His Ministry'– a very appropriate title for Paul's relationship with the Christians at Corinth, mentions that he had to clear up misunderstandings between him and the church. In his opinion this was one of the greatest challenges of his ministry. He shows acute perception as he comments on the nature of Paul's love in resolving the situation, a love that reflects the love of Christ, for these young immature Corinthian Christians when he says:

> From the many pages of the letter it stands out that all this is going on (the problems), while at the same time he feels an unshakeable love for his community. We see that people who are rather unkind and hostile to Paul, are constantly loved tenderly and constructively. The community has tried to push him out, to smear his name, and he is struggling to present himself as a loving father who is neither indignant nor bitter. He greets his community with authority and with almost violent affection. There is something extraordinary in Paul's love when we consider how easily we can close up if we are not welcomed, or only by some when others remain cold, critical and reserved. In the letter we feel Paul's suffering but we do not find a single sentence which can be called withdrawal.[22]

ETHICAL & RELATIONAL LOVE

Paul's letters are written 15-30 years after his conversion and they represent the maturity of his ministry, his spirituality and his theology. This is especially true of his emphasis on love that was based on the example of Christ, and also on his experience of this love in his relationship with him. He understood that Christians showed their Love for the Lord, by extending that love towards one another: and this love was to be shown in the areas of ethics and morality – that is how Christians should live which his letters expound. Equally, this love was to be shown in the relationships Christian have with one another, that his letters also expound.

In 1 Corinthians 13 Paul describes the love of Christ, to help them to understand that it is the characteristic quality Christians are to have in their relationships: and to see that this love is also the quality that brings intrinsic value, to gifts and ministry in the body of Christ. The emphasis on love was the underlying solution to the problems raised in 1 Corinthians. The stunning simplicity of Christ's love he describes in this chapter, is that primarily it displays the right attitudes towards others. M. Hooker reiterates this when she says, 'The appeal to love is an appeal to have certain attitudes…This passage (1 Cor. 13) does not appear by accident. A close re-examination of the letter will show how relevant this chapter is to the letter's concerns, and will give us some insight into how Paul dealt with the day-to-day problems that arose in one of his churches.'[23]

The Christ-like attitudes Paul mentions are to characterise their inter-personal relationships. Love therefore is the solution to their jealousy and division in ch. 3. Love is the solution to taking out lawsuits against each other in ch. 6: love is the solution concerning food offered to idols in ch. 8: and love is the solution to their separate fellowship meals when they celebrate communion in ch. 11. We know that for Paul love was a fruit produced by the Holy Spirit. as Christians walked in obedience to the Spirit and not the flesh – Galatians 5: 22. The Corinthians were clearly going in the wrong direction and ironically thought they were being 'spiritual.'

Similarly, G. Fee has this to say about love in 1 Cor. 13, 'much of the language suggests Paul is picking up on some of the differences between himself and them, that have emerged throughout the letter...At issue have been opposing views of "spirituality." They speak in tongues, to be sure, but at the same time they tolerate, or endorse, illicit sexuality, greed and idolatry...Finally, he includes examples of self sacrificial deeds. It is not a matter of these things or love, or even these things motivated by love, but these things by a person whose whole life is otherwise also given to love. If not, that person's life before God adds up to zero.'[24] The simple yet sublime exposition of Christian love by Paul, leads to a shocking conclusion when this is missing.

T. Schreiner also highlights the centrality of love in Paul's theology, when he says, 'We must still insist that love is the heart and soul of the Pauline ethic. All the exhortations are expressions of love. All the commandments of the Law can be summed up in loving one's neighbour – Rom 13: 8-10, Gal 5: 14. The whole Christian life can be summed up in the admonition to "walk in love" – Eph 5: 2, a love that is patterned after Christ's love for his people, which is demonstrated in the giving of his life.'[25] What may be helpful to remember is that from Paul's Jewish background and culture, love is expressed in an open and affectionate manner. Love was something he was familiar with, but the love of Christ adds a new dimension and transforms it into Christian love.

CONTENTMENT

Scholars believe Paul wrote his letter to the Philippians in prison, in Rome around 60 AD when he was chained and under house arrest. The truths he shares have an autobiographical slant, that reflect what he learned during 30 years as a Christian. This apostle who was an action-orientated Christian, may have felt frustrated at having his ministry curtailed. Perhaps, initially, his instinctive prayer was – 'set me free Lord, quickly!' But Paul learned that the Lord has a habit of answering his prayers, in ways he didn't anticipate or expect – (as when he prayed for his thorn in the flesh to be removed). In God's providence his captivity resulted in him writing four of his Epistles. Also he shared the gospel with all the imperial guard, and others knew he was in prison for Christ.

Here in his confinement, he discovered that Christ enabled him to find contentment through his indwelling presence. Here he has learned the secret of contentment, even in unfavourable circumstances. So he writes to the Philippians saying, 'I have learned in whatever situation I am in to be content. I know how to be abased and I know how to abound. In any and every circumstance I have learned the secret of facing plenty and hunger, abundance and need. I can do all things through Christ who strengthens me' – Phil 4: 11-13.

Markus Bockmuehl in his incisive commentary says, 'As for Paul himself, his joy in the Lord does not depend on his "needs" being met: he has learned to be content in all his circumstances. The Greek word for contentment is used, to describe the classic Stoic and Cynic ideal of independent self-sufficiency and serene contentment with one's circumstances, whatever they might be…In the wider context of this letter it is at any rate clear Paul intends not Stoic self-sufficiency based on one's own resources, but a Christian 'God-sufficiency' supplied by Christ…He closes verses 11-13 with a statement that has had a wide-ranging influence on later Christian history, in which it has often been cited out of context. Here is not a general affirmation that "I can do anything." In this context **I have the strength to do everything** refers in the first instance to the apostle's needs, to God-given contentment in both want and plenty. The power to cope resides in his union with Christ, rather than in Paul himself.'[26]

'I can do everything through Christ who gives me strength' – G. Fee in effect says, 'Christ is the basis and source of everything for Paul. This sentence spells out at the practical level the slogan of his life, expressed in 2: 21, "For me to live is Christ."…this passage is not an expression of Stoicism, not even a christianised version of the Stoic ideal: rather, it is but another of scores of such passages that indicate the absolute Christ-centredness of Paul's whole life. He is a "man in Christ." As such he takes what Christ brings. If it means "plenty" he is a man in Christ and that alone: if it means "want" he is still a man in Christ, and he accepts deprivation as part of his understanding of discipleship.'[27]

Ministers are faced with a diversity of situations many of which they cope with exceptionally well, but they also encounter difficult circumstances and people. I am inclined to think that one of the most fundamental truths relevant in ministry is, 'I can do all things through Christ who strengthens me.' One of the crucial lessons in ministry, is finding contentment in the midst of this diversity and difficulty. It is a challenge to put our faith in Christ and trust him to strengthen us, as we learn to live with the people and situations we face on a daily basis. A. Motyer highlights the significance of the phrase 'in Christ.' He speaks about the necessity, 'to preserve a living relationship with Christ, which is something we consciously enjoy by attending to it.'[28] This is an exhortation to remember that Christ not only resides in our hearts by his Spirit, but is also with us as we serve him. It is also a call to spend time in communion with the Lord so that he may 'serve us.' In this way we can rely on Christ and trust him to give us contentment.

Here O'Brien says, 'Paul eloquently describes what it means for him to have learned contentment in every situation. He thus further explains why he has not written to the Philippians out of a sense of need. In other words he was relying on Christ! Consequently, the apostle is not simply stating that he has experienced life at both ends of the scale, though this was true enough. Rather, as an amplification of verse 11b, he is explaining that he knows how to live in an appropriate manner under contrasting circumstances... Because he has the right attitude he has learned to cope in a positive way.

He has learned the secret of being content because of the enabling power of Christ...In well known words that. climax his personal confession, Paul affirms with assurance and humility, that he is able to be content in all things, because of his relationship with Christ who gives him strength.'[29]

GRACE

When Paul says, 'I can do all things through Christ who strengths me,' clearly he had 2 Corinthians 12: 9 in mind: 'My grace is sufficient for you for my strength is made perfect in weakness. Therefore, I will boast all the more gladly of my weaknesses, so that the power of Christ may rest upon me.' As this letter was written around 55-56 AD, between writing this and Philippians, Paul has had ample opportunity to experience Christ's sustaining grace. Paul knew that his life in Christ began with the initiative of God's grace, in calling him and drawing him to Christ: depended on his grace and flowed from Christ's sustaining grace.

At the heart of Paul's ministry and spirituality is Christ's grace. Clearly, and unambiguously, since the Lord gave him his thorn in the flesh, this led to a deeper experience of Christ. But we know it is not a path he chose of his own will, as three times he asked the Lord to remove it. R. Clements says, 'God would not take the risk of removing the thorn. It had a vital purpose in Paul's life. What he did do was to assure Paul, that no hindrance would be suffered in his ministry as a result of it: on the contrary, he would be all the more effective. Others would become Christians not because they saw Paul as some impressive, dynamic, supernatural hero, but because the grace of God could be seen at work in him, despite his natural weakness.'[30]

'The Greek word for thorn is "skolops" which translated means either a "stake" which pegged him to the ground or a "splinter" (or thorn) which constantly irritated him. The word was employed in both senses. H. Minn contests that it conveys 'the notion of something sharp and painful which sticks deeply in the flesh and in the will of God defies extraction.'[31] D. Carson sees this as, 'something substantial and not some mere irritation. An apostle who could willingly put up with the sufferings and deprivations listed in 2 Corinthians 11, would not beseech the Lord so strenuously and repeatedly, for the removal of some minor problem that could easily be borne. Paul's thorn was something very painful or extraordinarily embarrassing, and perhaps both.'[32]

It is striking that this thorn was given to him, after the abundance of revelations the Lord also gave him. In 2 Corinthians 12: 1-7, he describes his thorn as a messenger of Satan to harass me, to keep me from being too elated. In his providence the Lord give him this thorn, when he could have merely commanded him not to become conceited or proud. This is striking as we may feel Paul is unlikely to be a boastful person, as he is aware how unworthy he is to be an apostle. Hughes touches the heart of the matter when he says, 'Every believer must learn that human weakness and divine grace go hand in hand together. Hence Paul's thorn in the flesh is by definition, a type of every Christian's ''thorn in the flesh'' not with regard to externals, but by its spiritual significance.' It was for Paul, and also is for us, a salutary lesson that the power of Christ is shown through our weaknesses, rather than our strengths.'[33] This highlights the fact, that an emotional (inner) weakness or a physical (outer) weakness, that may constitute a thorn – may be interpreted as having an underlying spiritual significance.

Hughes also clarifies that the correct interpretation of what Paul says in Greek, is literally, 'there was given to me a stake for the flesh.' Whereas in the flesh indicates some physical affliction ''for the flesh'' leaves this an open question…This stake for his flesh is further described as a ''messenger (or angel) of Satan.'' This as we have seen, has been understood by some to signify that Paul is speaking of a person rather than a thing. It need indicate no more, however, than that this stake for the flesh was satanic in origin, attributable to the demonic agency, though permitted by God and overruled by Him, for his servant's good. As was the case with Job (Job 2: 1ff), God's gracious and restraining hand is never removed. And as always the heavenly chastening is ''for our profit that we may be partakers of His holiness'' – Hebrews 12: 10.'[34]

The Lord can allow us to have a 'thorn in, or for the flesh' that may constitute a weakness temperamentally or psychologically. This may well have evolved through what we have been through, or how we have been treated. As a result, Satan plays on this, and through it can assault our emotions and minds for a prolonged period of time. From my experience, the ensuing pain can be described as, 'the internal horrors' of our thorn, as such is the strength of its impact.

Our weaknesses or thorn in, or for the flesh, can be used by the Lord, to teach us to rely on him and to keep us humble. When we feel helpless or incapacitated by these things, this is an opportunity to experience Christ's sustaining grace. The difficult thing to learn is to embrace our weakness or thorn, and be at ease and peace with our painful affliction – once the Lord has shown us they originate from him. It is also a challenge to live with them in the knowledge they are also conspicuous to others. But, ultimately, we know that through these things, Christ's grace can be even more conspicuous in our lives.

JESUS IS LORD

In his relationship with Christ in Philippians 3: 8, Paul speaks about 'the surpassing worth of knowing Christ Jesus my Lord.' This closeness did not suddenly occur overnight after his conversion. It is the outcome of his dedication in serving Christ and his desire to know him intimately. At the heart of Paul's ministry and spirituality, is the truth that Jesus is Lord. F. W. Beare aptly remarks:

> Here and here alone in his writing, do we find the intensely personal "Christ Jesus my Lord" – and it would be a dull reader indeed who did not mark the warm and deep devotion which breathes through every phrase....This same person Paul remarkably calls "my Lord." In using the singular pronoun rather than the plural "our" – the apostle is in no way suggesting that his relationship to Christ is exclusive. Rather, the wonder of this knowledge of Christ Jesus as his Lord is so great, and the relationship so intensely personal that he focuses upon it in his testimony.[35]

The centrality of Jesus as Lord in Paul's experience of Christ and in his theology, is seen from his letters, whose introduction always includes a reference, to 'our Lord Jesus Christ' or 'the Lord Jesus Christ.' 'The earliest Christian writings are Paul's letters and they provide evidence for the origin of a practice of referring to Christ as "Lord," that antedates the apostle. From his earliest letters onwards he applies "kurios" – "Lord" to Jesus without explanation or justification, suggesting that his readers were familiar with the term and its connotation...The frequently occurring references to Jesus simply as "the Lord'– 1Thess. 1: 6, shows how the term had acquired such a familiar usage for Christ that no further identification was necessary. Paul's letters presume a familiarity with the term as a christological title from the earliest stages of his ministry.'[36]

In Paul's day, in Aramaic in Hebrew and in Greek, the term for master or lord was used in two ways. This could be used when addressing persons who were socially superior and also when addressing deities. Equally, there would have been political overtones associated with this title, as Caesar would have been addressed as lord. The use of lord in these ways made its application to Christ striking, and to address Christ as Lord may well have been interpreted as subversive and a challenge to Roman rule. M. Hooker says, 'In the Roman Empire, emperors came to claim divine honours, and as a result there was a growing emphasis on the imperial cult. Though Paul himself did not challenge the claims made by the state of his day – Rom. 13: 1-7, he would certainly have refused to acknowledge Caesar as kurios had that been demanded of him. By the end of the first century AD, the confessions that "Jesus is Lord" and "Caesar is Lord" were recognised as expressing conflicting loyalties, and the proclamation of Christ was seen as subversive.'[37]

Paul would have known that the use of the term Lord, also had a religious association in the life of Israel. The Jews did not actually pronounce the name of God-Yahweh – but instead, used other forms by which to address him. In Hebrew God was often referred to as 'adonay'- 'the Lord.' In the first century this could be used as a substitute for the name of God. So in effect addressing Christ as 'Lord' conferred on him the status of God. Anyone who was familiar with the O. T. would not fail to recognise the allusion of 'Lord' to Isaiah 45: 22-23:

> Turn to me and be saved all the ends of the earth! For I am God and there is no other. By myself I have sworn, from my mouth has gone forth in righteousness a word that shall not return. To me every knee shall bow and every tongue swear allegiance.

Dunn says, 'What is astonishing, however, is that these words in Isaiah are spoken by God, and in one of the most unyielding monotheistic passages in the whole Bible. At the very least we have to recognise that the Philippian hymn – 2: 6-11, envisaged acclamation of and reverence before Christ, which, according to Isaiah, God claimed for himself alone. On any count that is an astonishing transfer for any Jew to make.

Even as Lord, Jesus acknowledges his Father as God. Here it becomes plain that "kurios" is not so much a way of identifying Jesus with God, but if anything more a way of distinguishing Jesus from God. We may note also from 1 Cor. 3: 23, 'you are Christ's and Christ is God's' and in 11: 3, 'the head of Christ is God.' And again in 1 Cor. 15: 24-28, 'the Lord of all.' Christ has been given his lordship by God. And it is a lordship which will in the end be wholly subject to God.

The only obvious resolution of the tension set up by Paul's talk of Jesus as Lord, then, is to follow the logic suggested by his reference of Yahweh texts to Jesus as Lord (as above). That is, that Jesus' lordship is a status granted by God, a sharing in his authority. It is not that God has stepped aside and Jesus has taken over. It is rather that God shared his Lordship with Christ, without it ceasing to be God's alone.'[38]

In Paul's letter to the Philippians in 2: 6-11, Christ is exalted as Lord by his Father because of his obedience, and is commonly known as the 'Philippian hymn.'

> Christ Jesus who, though he was in the form of God, did not count equality with God a thing to be grasped, but emptied himself, taking the form of a servant, being born in the likeness of men. And being found in human form he humbled himself and became obedient unto death, even death on a cross. Therefore God has highly exalted him and bestowed on him the name which is above every name, that at the name of Jesus every knee should bow, in heaven and on earth and under the earth, and every tongue confess that Jesus Christ is Lord, to the glory of God the Father.

Commenting on Christ's exaltation as Lord, O'Brien sees, 'God the Father as decisively intervening and acting on Jesus' behalf. Jesus' self-humbling reached the absolute depths in his most shameful death, a death on a cross. But now, by way of vindication and approval of Jesus' total self-humbling, the Father has magnificently exalted his Son to the highest station and graciously bestowed upon him the name above all other names, this is, his own name, Lord (Yahweh), along with all that gives meaning and substance to the name. In his exalted state Jesus now exercises universal lordship…It is not implied that Jesus' eventual exaltation was the incentive for his temporary humiliation: otherwise the humbling would have been no true humiliation at all, and as such would have been self-regarding, not self-denying.'[39]

There is also a liturgical, as well as an eschatological nuance implied, in the exaltation of Jesus as Lord. In 1 Corinthians the references to Jesus as Lord, indicate that this title was an integral aspect of their worship – for example in 10: 21 & 11: 17-38. Also in 16: 22, we have 'Maranatha' – 'Come Lord Jesus.' For Christians in Paul's day the emphasis on every 'knee shall bow' expressed submission in worship to Jesus, worship that previously had been directed only to God. But, now, God has conferred on Jesus divine status that qualifies him to be the recipient of worship too. In the early church there was a political cutting edge to the acclamation 'Jesus is Lord' and 'bowing the knee to Jesus' – as this was a contrast to the homage Caesar demanded. Similarly Fee says, 'We should note finally that this declaration of Jesus as 'Lord,' would probably not be lost on believers in a city whose inhabitants are Roman citizens and who are devotees of "lords many," including "lord Caesar." Paul well knows to whom he is writing these words, especially since he is one of the emperor's prisoners and the Philippians are suffering at the hands of Roman citizens as well.'[40]

As well as having a contemporary relevance in Paul's day, 'Jesus is Lord' also has perennial significance, as Christians down the centuries have offered worship to their Lord. Equally, there is an eschatological dimension to the acclamation Jesus is Lord, because at the 'parousia' – the second coming, every knee shall bow at Jesus' feet. Because God has given Jesus the name that is above every name, he exercises authority and power on a universal scale. Therefore, Jesus' lordship has a cosmic and an eternal dimension to it. 'There is in this language no hint that those who bow are acknowledging his salvation: on the contrary they will bow to his sovereignty at the end, even if they are not yielding to it now.'[41]

The universal lordship conferred on Jesus by God, is something O'Brien comments on when he says, 'This bestowal by God is the rarest of all honours, in view of his assertion in Isaiah 42: 8, 'I am the Lord, that is my name, that is mine and no one else's...God not only gave Jesus a designation which distinguished him from all other beings, a title which outranked all other titles. He also conferred on him all that coincided with that title, giving substance and meaning to it. In his exalted state Jesus has a new rank involving the exercise of universal lordship...All authority in heaven and on earth were his by nature as well as by gift.'[42]

The challenge for Paul and the churches he founded was to live in submission to Christ as Lord. In our era it is rare to hear ministers and the Church advocating publicly that Jesus is Lord. As a result this acclamation has lost its cutting edge in the West. In carrying out their responsibility, politicians have been subversive in asserting a psuedo - lordship to achieve their own agenda. More often than not they serve their own ends rather than the people they represent. The dilemma the Church faces, is how to proclaim the lordship of Christ in a way that challenges political structures or other equally subversive lords, such as technology, sexuality, or the acquisition of finance or property. Perhaps the starting point for the Church, is to begin to reflect how Christ can be Lord of the Church – in contemporary matters of doctrine and church politics: and indeed how the Lordship of Christ challenges our sociological and political ideals and structures too.

CHAPTER FIVE

WHO WANTS A THORN?

My instinctive reaction to this heading is – 'Not me thank you. I've already got mine!' If the Lord was handing out 'thorns in the flesh,' I wonder how many ministers and Christians would volunteer to accept one? Not many I guess. We may think we have enough challenges without adding to them. It may surprise us to discover the Lord not only gives us spiritual gifts as a blessing, but complements these with thorns that are also counted as a blessing. Identifying our thorns in the flesh and understanding why the Lord gives them to us, helps us to realise it is possible to integrate our strengths in ministry with our weaknesses.

DAVID'S THORN

In the Old Testament David must surely rank as one of the most attractive, charismatic and successful leaders. He was an extremely handsome young man, courageous in battle and successful in his exploits against the enemies of Israel. Musically talented, emotionally rich in character and with just under half of the 150 Psalms attributed to him, he loved to praise the Lord and worship him. A man whom God described as, 'A man after His own heart' - 1 Samuel 13: 14, and whom the Lord drew into an intimate relationship with him in his youth.

We may be excused for thinking David was always ministering from a position of strength, as he had so much going for him. However, a look at the early years of his life, along with a closer look at many of the Psalms he wrote, reveals a more complex character than at first is apparent. From these we discover that the Lord allowed the circumstances of his life to evolve in a way, that left him with the equivalent of a thorn in the flesh. A psychological weakness that was acutely painful to him.

The foundation of David's weakness can be traced by looking at the early years of his life. The first significant occasion is when

Samuel arrives at the household of Jesse, to anoint the King God has chosen to replace Saul. 1 Samuel 16, clearly shows that on this important event David is absent when he arrives. As the youngest he is looking after the sheep, and it doesn't occur to anyone in his family to go and get him. After meeting Jesse's seven sons Samuel is somewhat perplexed, as the Lord has not identified any of them as the king. So he asks, 'Are all the young men here?' – 1 Samuel: 16. At this he is informed the youngest is looking after the sheep. So Samuel asks for David to be fetched before him.

We know that David turned out to be God's choice to replace Saul as King, and as we explore his family background we can perceive the roots of his thorn in the flesh. Was it an oversight that everyone forgot to call him to the anointing of the new king – or is it an indication that he was on the fringe of family life? Equally, the silence of scripture about his brothers' reaction to his anointing is intriguing. It is also left to us to speculate what David's response was to his anointing. W. Brueggemann perceptively says:

> The story draws our attention to the one outside the completed number, the one who surely is an outsider. The eighth son is the youngest, surely unimpressive, with no claim to make and no credentials to present...There is a central incongruity in the selection of David that is surely intended by the narrator. The one anointed is qualified by his "right heart." He needed nothing more...David is one of the marginal people. He is uncredentialed and has no social claim to make.[1]

The striking irony is that David having just been anointed king has gone back to looking after the sheep. And shortly after this occasion in 1 Samuel 17, we find that David is indeed on the edge of family life. His brothers have joined Saul's army to fight the Philistines, yet as the future king of Israel he is too young to go to battle with them. However, his father calls him and asks him to take some provisions to his brothers and their captain and to see how they are.

The following day he takes the supplies to the battle and greets them. At the same time Goliath comes and issues his challenge to the army of Israel – if anyone kills him then the Philistines would serve Israel, but if he wins Israel must serve them. At this David engages some of the soldiers in conversation about this challenge. When Eliab his eldest brother overhears he is angry with him and says, 'Why did you come down here? And with whom have you left those few sheep in the wilderness? I know your pride and the insolence of your heart, for you have come down to see the battle.' David replies, 'What have I done now? Is there not a cause?' – 1 Samuel 17: 28-29. Brueggemann says:

> David is too young to fight the battle he is at home still tending the sheep. His menial task at home is matched by his menial task with the troops...David is rebuked by his older brother Eliab and is generally ignored and disregarded. His treatment by his brothers and their resentment of him is parallel to that of Joseph by his brothers. David's brothers have witnessed his anointing but they do not recognise that he is the wave of the future. They wish to dismiss him to the margin of the narrative.[2]

David's reply to Eliab, 'what have I done now?' indicates that his brothers were usually finding fault with him and that he couldn't do anything right in their eyes. They probably picked on him being the youngest and may have been jealous of him. Perhaps this was because he was so handsome and had been singled out in a strange ceremony by Samuel. This incident gives another insight into the fact that David was on the edge of family life and was picked on by his brothers. We can perceive he had become sensitive to the way they treated him.

The way David was treated by his brothers contributed to his sensitive temperament, which was to develop into his weakness. To further trace how this evolved, we must look at his relationship with Saul (the current king of Israel), that began after he accepted Goliath's challenge to fight him (which reveals his mighty anointing with the Holy Spirit). Having defeated Goliath in chapter 17, he is invited to live in the king's house by Saul himself – 18: 2. David is then put in charge of the men of war – 18: 5. In 18: 7-9 on returning from the slaughter of Goliath, 'the women came out of all the cities of Israel, singing and dancing, to meet king Saul, with tambourines, with joy and with musical instruments. So the women sang as they danced and said: 'Saul has slain his thousands and David his ten thousands.' Then Saul was very angry and the saying displeased him and he said, 'They have ascribed to David ten thousands and to me they have ascribed only thousands. Now what more can he have but the kingdom?' So Saul eyed David from that day forward. Jealousy found a deep root in his insecure heart.

Unfortunately for David, this incident set in motion events that were ultimately to result in his thorn in the flesh, and from that day onwards he inadvertently became Saul's enemy. Saul not only became jealous of him but paranoid about him too. He sensed without knowing of David's secret anointing by Samuel, that one day he would inherit his kingdom and become king. 1 Samuel chapters 18 – 26, record ten specific incidents where Saul attempts to kill David.

* 18: 11 Saul tries to kill David with a spear.

* 18: 20-30 Saul's daughter Michal is to be given in marriage to David. But first he has to kill 100 philistines and bring back their foreskins. Saul's intention is that he will be killed in the attempt.

* 19: 1 Saul speaks to all his servants that they should kill David.

* 19: 10 Saul attempts to kill David with a spear for a second time.

* 19: 11-17 Saul sends messengers to David's house to kill him.

* 20: 30-32 Saul says to his son Jonathan, 'Send and bring David to me for he shall surely die.'

* 23: 14-18 David is in the wilderness of Ziph. Saul sought him every day to kill him.

* 23: 19-27 Saul pursues David in the wilderness of Maon: but has to return as the Philistines are invading the land.

* 24: 1-22 David is hiding in a cave in the wilderness of En Gedi. Saul uses this cave to relieve himself. Instead of killing him David cuts off a corner of his robe. A moving dialogue then takes place between them.

* 26:1-25 David spares Saul's life a second time. He goes into Saul's camp, into his tent, and takes his spear and jug. Again there is a moving dialogue between David and Saul, with David protesting his innocence.

For a number of years as Saul hunted David to kill him he lived in fear of his life. His temperament was now acutely sensitive to his enemies, and we see his fear and sensitivity expressed in half of David's Psalms (appx 37). Although he always defeated his enemies, paradoxically he had a temperamental weakness at the thought of them trying to kill him. This was the equivalent of his thorn in the flesh and continued to trouble his heart and mind throughout his life. While David the King was successful in defeating his enemies, they also constituted his psychological weakness. Many of his Psalms reveal that at times he was oversensitive in his reaction to his enemies: and as you read them at times he sounds paranoid, as if they are hiding in the palace grounds waiting to pounce on him and kill him. His psychological weakness concerning his enemies was a reminder to him of his Achilles heel.

A brief look at some of David's Psalms enables us to see the extent of his fear and sensitivity towards his enemies. Psalm 31: 11-13, 'I am a reproach among all my enemies, but especially among my neighbours, and am repulsive to my acquaintances: those who see me outside flee from me. I am forgotten like a dead man, out of mind: I am like a broken vessel. For I hear the slander of many: fear is on every side: while they take counsel against me, they scheme to take away my life.' Psalm 55: 2-6, 'I am overcome by trouble. I am distraught by the noise of the enemy, because of the oppression of the wicked. For they bring trouble upon me and in anger they cherish enmity against me. My heart is in anguish against me, the terrors of death have fallen upon me. Fear and trembling come upon me, and horror overwhelms me. And I say, 'O that I had wings like a dove! I would fly away and be at rest.'

Psalm 55: 15-18, 'Let death come upon them, let them go down to sheol alive: let them go away in terror into their graves. But I call upon God: and the Lord will save me. Evening and morning and at noon, I utter my complaint and moan, and he will hear my voice. He will deliver my soul in safety from the battle that I wage, for many are arrayed against me.' Psalm 69: 1-4, 'Save me O God! For the waters have come up to my neck. I sink in deep mire, where there is no foothold. I have come into deep waters and the flood sweeps over me. I am weary with my crying: my throat is parched. My eyes grow dim with waiting for my God. More in number than the hairs of my head are those who hate me without cause: mighty are those who would destroy me, those who would attack me with lies.'

Of course David's enemies were real and not a figment of his imagination. And although he was invariably victorious against them in battle, they still constituted his thorn in the flesh – his psychological weakness, that preyed on his mind. We may well ask, 'Was David's weakness fortuitous and due to his circumstances, or did the Lord deliberately allow this to happen?' This also begs the question, 'If the Lord allowed this to happen what was his purpose behind it?' Discerning the reasons why the Lord allowed this to happen, may reveal why he also allows our particular thorn in the flesh to take root.

One of the main reasons the Lord gave David a thorn was to teach him to rely on him. The irony and paradox is that this great man of war, victorious over Goliath, mighty in battle, finds his enemies to also be his psychological weakness. This was a reminder to him that the Lord was behind his success. It was the Lord who strengthened him and who protected him. And it was the Lord who gave him victory over his enemies.

The second reason the Lord allowed David's weakness to develop, is that he used this to mould his character and to stretch and test his faith. Through his adversity in his own family life and through the adversity over a number of years with Saul, the Lord was laying foundations in David's character. He was forming, chiselling if you like, qualities of patience, perseverance and trust: and also the quality of integrity before God and loyalty to Saul as King. As a result he resisted the temptation to kill Saul and take the crown in his own strength: so the discipline of waiting for God's perfect timing to replace Saul was forged in his life. (Although, sadly, later in his life his integrity was compromised because of his adultery with Bathsheba).

The third reason the Lord allowed his weakness to develop, was because David had triumphed over Goliath as a teenager, an extraordinary event that could easily have led him to becoming a precocious young man. One who was full of himself and puffed up with pride. This would not have been surprising, as not even the mightiest man of war in Israel had the courage to challenge Goliath. Instead, David's adversity because of Saul, prevented him from becoming arrogant or proud.

The fourth reason the Lord allowed David's weakness, was to remind him of his humble beginnings. It was the Lord who took him from being a shepherd boy to being the King of Israel. It was a sobering lesson for David to learn how God mightily used him to slay Goliath, and then allowed Saul to try and kill him over many years. The paradox is that Saul who was afraid to slay Goliath – wanted to slay his conqueror. His feelings of insecurity and inferiority, plagued his imagination as he pursued David. Sadly for Saul and Jonathan his son (David's covenant friend) and for David too, he wasted all his energy in hunting him like a fugitive. Instead of enjoying his companionship and friendship and sharing together in the victories over their enemies. It is indeed difficult to perceive whether this is what the Lord had intended, or whether this just happened to be the choice Saul made. But, David shepherd boy with humble origins, giant slayer, anointed future king and innocent fugitive on the run, finds himself in a long drawn out drama that shaped his character and moulded his faith. And which resulted in his thorn in the flesh.

JESUS' THORN

While we are aware of Jesus' dual nature of being both divine and human, it is possible that many Christians do not consider Jesus had any weaknesses: after all he was God incarnate. The Messiah endued with supernatural power. He had power over nature, power over demons, power over disease. Jesus perfect

God and man and sinless, appears to have no weakness
whatsoever. While Jesus' divinity was perfectly clothed in our
humanity, we may perceive areas that may have constituted his
thorn in the flesh. Areas of weakness that were painful
emotionally, psychologically and spiritually. While it is
speculative, perhaps Jesus' divinity clothed in our humanity left
him open to the limitations of his human nature. This may have
been one aspect of his thorn in the flesh, as he lived in the tension
of being both divine and human.

Jesus' controversies with some of the religious leaders, the
Scribes and the Pharisees, along with their hostility and hatred and
their jealousy and opposition towards him, may well have been an
aspect of his thorn. He probably didn't anticipate these painful
encounters and he may well have expected to be welcomed by
them. Another aspect of his thorn may have been that the religious
leaders, failed to recognise him as the Messiah prophesied in the
Old Testament. He may have expected them to positively respond
to the revelation that he had come from God, and was a prophet in
the tradition of Moses. Their rejection was undoubtedly a painful
aspect of his public ministry.

Alongside their failure to recognise Jesus as the Messiah was
the failure of his own people to respond to him. His disappointment
is echoed in Matthew 23: 37- 38, 'O Jerusalem, Jerusalem, killing
the prophets and stoning those who are sent to you! How often
would I have gathered your children together, as a hen gathers her
brood under her wing, and you would not! Behold your house is
forsaken and desolate.' He probably had high expectations that the
people of Israel would rejoice in his ministry, and in the salvation
he announced as the Lord's Servant. Subsequently, it would not be
surprising if the peoples' failure to recognise and accept him as the
Messiah was another aspect of his thorn.

I wonder to what extent the death of John the Baptist affected
Jesus? John had fulfilled the prophecy in Isaiah 40 by preparing the
way of the Lord, and acting as a sign confirming to Jesus that this
was the fullness of time for his ministry to begin. John had been
recognised as a prophet in the tradition of Elijah, and had

challenged the nation spiritually in a bold way. John was someone with whom Jesus felt an affinity and who was spiritually a kindred spirit. Was his death tantamount to being part of his thorn in the flesh?

Another aspect of Jesus' thorn, may have been the disciples constant inability to understand his teaching about the Kingdom of God and himself. Along with their failure to grasp that the Kingdom was not going to be a territorial one, and that he was not going to overthrow the Romans as a political Messiah. There may well have been times when he agonised about their level of spiritual comprehension, no matter how hard he tried to clarify his teaching on these issues. Although towards the end of his earthly ministry Jesus did all he could to explain his death to them and to prepare them for his departure, ultimately he had to entrust the outcome of the disciples' ministry in the future into his Father's hands.

During the last year of his ministry when Jesus became fully aware of his imminent death on the cross, the temptation to avoid the cross may have been another aspect of his thorn in the flesh. And whether the cross really was the will of God probably preyed on his heart and mind. What if he made a mistake – what were the implications for him? What would be so untimely as to cut short Jesus' spectacularly successful ministry? What difference would a few more years make? Quite possibly for Jesus these doubts and temptations troubled him. The prospect of death and the possibility of annihilation, for Jesus who had existed before time and history, may well have been one of the most painful aspects of his thorn.

PAUL'S THORN IN THE FLESH

As we know the phrase 'a thorn in the flesh' originates with the apostle Paul in 2 Corinthians 12: 7-11:

> To keep me from becoming conceited because of these surpassingly great revelations, there was given me a thorn in the flesh, a messenger of Satan, to harrass me. Three times I pleaded with the Lord to take it away from me. But he said to me, "My grace is sufficient for you, for my power is made

perfect in weakness." Therefore I will boast all the more gladly about my weaknesses, so that Christ's power may rest on me. That is why for Christ's sake I delight in weaknesses, in insults, in hardships, in persecutions, in difficulties. For when I am weak, then I am strong.

P. Hughes says, 'Every believer must learn that human weakness and divine grace go hand in hand...although it – the thorn, involved a messenger of Satan, it was permitted by God and overruled by him for his servant's good. As was in the case of Job.'[3] B. Witherington 111 also has this to say on this issue:

Paradoxically enough, Christ's power is completed or comes to fullness in the midst of human weakness. When it is evident that Paul is weak, it will be equally evident that the power and miracles and conversions could not be coming from a human source: but from Christ working in and through him. Thus weakness makes Paul most translucent so that one can see the source of the real power and light.[4]

Paul refers to his thorn in the flesh as a messenger of Satan to harass him. As we attempt to understand this it would appear that this messenger was fully acquainted with his weakness. It was within the power of this servant, this adversary, to assault Paul on a regular basis through his weakness. The attacks may have embraced three dimensions in his life. The emotional level, the physical level and the psychological dimension. Clearly, this caused him considerable discomfort and suffering on a regular basis. This constituted his thorn in the flesh and weakness, that the Lord in his wisdom gave him.

'An interesting verb is used in 12: 9. Paul says, the power "made its home" in him or "came to rest" on him. He is probably drawing on the image of the Shekinah (glory) coming down, the divine presence that conveys power. Because it has come on him, he is content with whatever weaknesses or verbal or physical abuse he has to undergo, because Christ is better revealed when it is apparent that the power and help are not coming from a human source (V10). When he is weak it is then that he is strong because he must rely totally on the Lord. Paul hopes by the material in the

"Fool's Discourse" – 2 Cor. 11-12, to bring about a transvaluation of the Corinthian values and of their criteria for apostles. This required him to use irony, parody, invective and paradox, to make clear to his converts this message: 'things are not what they seem.'[5]

WHAT WAS PAUL'S THORN?

There has been a great deal of speculation as to what this might have been, but ultimately we do not know. However, we may surmise and make some suggestions. The earliest reference may be found in Tertullian, who thought this might have been headache or earache. Chrysostom also considers it to have been headache. A more recent suggestion is that Paul suffered from a severe form of ophthalmia. This inference can be deduced from Galatians 4:13-15, where Paul has been speaking of 'an infirmity of the flesh.' It was because of a body ailment that he first preached the gospel to them. Although his condition was a trial to them they did not scorn or despise him, but received him as an angel of God, as Christ Jesus. Moreover, if possible the Galatians would have plucked out their eyes and given them to him. Further hints of defective eyesight are discerned from chapter 6:11, where Paul says, 'See with what large letters I am writing to you with my own hand.' That this was his thorn is not stretching our imagination too far. He may have contracted a disease some years later, as there is no mention of any debilitating impact on his eyes, from the vision on the Damascus road.

The correct meaning of the Greek word translated thorn, is 'stake' or a sharpened wooden shaft. In Hellenistic Greek the modified meaning of thorn or splinter is found, though not to the exclusion of the original meaning. P. Hughes says, 'no recent conjecture has aroused greater interest than that of Sir William Ramsay. He strongly advocated a form of recurrent malarial fever. Known in the Eastern Mediterranean, particularly in Pamphylia and satisfying every symptom of Paul's infirmity, deducible from the New Testament. In some constitutions, malaria fever tends to recur in very distressing and prostrating paroxysms, whenever a person's energies are taxed a great deal. A strong corroboration is found in the phrase, "a stake in the flesh." which Paul uses about his illness.'[6]

One indicator of what Paul's thorn may have been comes from 2 Corinthians 12 itself. Perhaps the constant opposition he encountered from the Judaizers accounted for this. They persistently pursued him from city to city as he preached the gospel determined to stir up trouble. O'Connor also identifies, 'the 'spirit-people' in Corinth as opponents. These were the Christians who considered themselves "truly spiritual" probably because of the ecstatic use of the gifts of the Spirit, such as speaking in tongues and prophecy. They were publicly humiliated by Paul writing 1 Corinthians, (which would have been read out aloud to the church and naturally sought revenge). They may well have formed an alliance with the Judaizers, in challenging Paul's authority and undermining his influence.'[7] This may tie in with the clue to Paul's thorn in the flesh that he shared quite openly, when he speaks of his thorn as being a 'messenger of Satan.' The implication is the devil attacks him spiritually and psychologically, causing him the most acute pain. Perhaps there was an opponent, or opponents, who Paul identified as his thorn. Jews who followed him around (perhaps a certain leader or ring leader was involved) and undermined his ministry and authority as an apostle. Something the messenger of Satan used to his advantage.

As Paul's ministry evolved because he did not circumcise Gentile converts, this became a key issue for the Judaizers who opposed him, as they insisted the Law of Moses had to be observed. This developed into a crisis as they were going around the churches he established, questioning his status as an apostle, undermining his authority and teaching the necessity of circumcision. Moreover, as is evident from 2 Corinthians they were coming with letters of recommendation, probably from Jerusalem or Antioch, that validated their authority and ministry. F. B. Meyer says, 'this was an important crisis and led to the breaking out of a controversy, which embittered many succeeding years in the apostle's life. Great questions were at stake. This for instance: 'whether Christianity was to be a sect of Judaism? Whether adhering to the Law of Moses and insisting on circumcision was necessary for salvation?'[8]

Clearly they perceived that Paul was a severe threat to the Jewish faith and the traditions of Moses. So we should not be too surprised by their opposition, that challenged and undermined his authority as an apostle. F. B. Meyer called this, 'the conflict of Paul's life. From this moment a relentless war broke out which followed the apostle for the next ten years of his life and cost him many bitter tears. Every church he planted was visited by the emissaries of his virulent opponents, who were not content with insisting on the necessity of circumcision, but asserted that Paul was no apostle, because he had only seen Christ in a vision, and had never accompanied him during the days of his flesh. They trashed his personal character, misrepresented his reluctance to take the (financial) gifts of his converts (as was the custom), dwelt with cruel animosity upon his personal defects, and in many cases succeeded in alienating the love and loyalty of his converts. This cruel persecution is constantly alluded to in the Epistles to the Galatians and Corinthians, and cut Paul to the quick.'[9] By no stretch of the imagination is it difficult to identify these opponents – the Judaizers and their emissaries as Paul's literal and metaphorical thorn in the flesh. They were indeed messengers – but could have been the messengers of Satan he alludes to.

In drawing a conclusion about Paul's thorn in the flesh, E. Best reminds us of what is there for all to see. He says, 'Whatever aggrieved him he clearly thinks of it as beginning at the time of his vision – in 2 Cor. 12, or as a consequence of it. It cannot then have been something to which he was always subject, for example, persecution or temptation. Equally it cannot have been a congenital physical illness or handicap, like a speech impediment for that would always have been there. Some physical ailments also seem highly unlikely because no one who suffered from them could have accomplished Paul's missionary work or endured the sufferings he listed in 2 Cor 11. Whatever or whoever it was, it continued with Paul at least up to the time of writing 2 Corinthians. The "this" of v. 8 can equally be, probably ought to be, rendered "him" and the "it" rendered "he" both referring to the 'messenger.'[10]

Despite E. Best's suggestion that the thorn clearly has to begin at the time of Paul's revelations, it is possible of course that his eyes which flared up occasionally, (as is evident in the letter to the Galatians), may have become the permanent feature that constituted his thorn. This would have regularly been a painful physical symptom, that the messenger of Satan tormented him about as well, by insinuating the Lord could not heal him, and was deliberately causing him unnecessary debilitating suffering.

THE PURPOSE OF A THORN

Reflecting on the painful issue of the thorn in the flesh, we may discern that this spiritual affliction can contradict our image of Christian leadership. We may well expect our leaders to be attractive charismatic personalities, well educated, impressive speakers and very gifted with people. We do not usually include in our list of qualities, a specific or particular weaknesses. When we look carefully at 2 Corinthians we must re-evaluate our outlook and expectations. Clearly, from God's perspective, weaknesses that he gives or allows to develop are integral to leadership.

I suspect this is not an easy concept and truth to embrace, although the over-riding truth is, that through human weakness the power of God is revealed. When we discern a weakness we should not be too surprised to discover, a very powerful anointing of the Holy Spirit in a person's ministry. Yet some leaders appear to have weaknesses and other do not. Or is it only leaders who have had particularly profound experiences of the Trinity, who are blessed with their particular thorn in the flesh? Alternatively, do some leaders know their specific weakness and live in denial of it, or try to keep it hidden? Are others blind to them? On the other hand does God allow everyone in leadership to have their thorn in the flesh? Or is it only those who are called to significant areas of ministry, who are deliberately given a thorn by God? This is not an easy matter to discern. Equally, we may try to distinguish between a weakness the Lord has allowed to develop into a thorn and between a natural weakness. Of course a natural weakness in an area of ministry or temperament, is to be worked at until it overcome.

Ultimately, we do well to take care when assessing our leaders if we see an obvious weakness we are tempted to despise, especially if it is our particular strength. Also we should tread carefully, because this may be holy ground to the Lord, that he has allowed to develop at great pain to his servants who live with them.

R. Clements in 'The Strength of Weakness,' raises similar insights about Christian leaders and our perception of them. In effect he says, 'we are wrong to base our models of Christian leadership on secular models. In St. Paul's day the Greeks were characterised by huge admiration for success, and at the centre of their philosophy and religion was the cult of the hero. Moreover, they despised any physical defect in a person. If you wished to advance in Hellenistic culture you had to have and project a high powered image. You had to be eloquent, confident, achieving, strong and indeed successful. These appear to be the kind of Christians who had turned up in Corinth and were criticising Paul, insisting to the Corinthian Christians that in many ways he was not a very impressive man. Consequently, they ridiculed and despised Paul. So much so, that he had to make at least one painful visit to them, where we discern there was a confrontation about the issue of leadership. As a result he wrote 2 Corinthians, to correct the Christians about the impressive and seemingly superlative apostles, who were despising him.'[11]

R. T. Kendall in 'The Thorn in The Flesh,' also makes some perceptive comments about this issue. In this he devotes a number of chapters to possible thorns in the flesh that Christians may have. One insight of his is worth mentioning and concerns God's purpose for allowing this. He believes that the thorn is actually, 'a manifestation of God's glory and it may also be a severe form of chastening or discipline.' He also says that,'God's power flowing abundantly through his servants with weaknesses glorifies God. For it is abundantly obvious that he is working through that individual.'[12]

In conclusion, having a thorn in the flesh may well be reassuring, because it prevents us from thinking that we have to be spiritually invincible. Whether we are in the early days of ministry and seeking to lay the right foundations, or whether we are already established, this issue directs our gaze firmly to the grace of Christ and his power and strength. While we aim for excellence in whatever we do, ultimately this is a reminder that it is God who gives the growth – 1 Corinthians 3:6. It certainly does not depend on us. It is God through the Holy Spirit who empowers us. This enables us to relax as we seek to hone our gifts, in the knowledge that ministry does not depend on us, because it flows from the initiative of the Trinity. Ultimately, we are likely to have the thorns and the Trinity the power! This paradox is often what God ordains. One of John Newton's lesser known hymns perfectly sums up the topic of a thorn in the flesh.[13]

> I asked the Lord that I might grow
> In faith and love and every grace:
> Might more of His salvation know
> And seek more constantly His face.
>
> 'Twas He who taught me thus to pray
> And He I trust has answered prayer:
> But it has been in such a way
> As almost drove me to despair.
>
> I hoped that in some favoured hour
> At once He'd answered my request:
> And by His love's constraining power
> Subdue my sins and give me rest.
>
> Instead of this He made me feel
> The hidden evils of my heart:
> And let the angry powers of hell
> Assault my soul in every part.
>
> Yes more with his own hand He seemed
> Intent to aggravate my woe:
> Crossed all the fair designs I schemed
> Blasted my gourds and laid me low.

'Lord why is this?' I trembling cried
'Wilt thou pursue thy worm to death?'
'Tis in this way' the Lord replied
'I answer prayer for grace and faith.'

'These inward trials I employ
From self and pride to set thee free:
And break thy schemes of earthly joy
That thou mayest seek thy all in Me.'

CHAPTER SIX

PAUL'S PHILOSOPHY OF MINISTRY

It may seem surprising to think about Paul having a philosophy of ministry, but most ministers whether they realise it or not also have one. It may be that they have never articulated it, and simply have a way of doing things based on certain assumptions and beliefs. The idea of this concept occurred to me a few years ago when I was part of a ministry team. Paul's philosophy of ministry essentially reflects the foundations that his ministry was based upon, and which are still relevant in the 21st century.

KNOWING CHRIST

It is not surprising that Paul's ministry is comprehensively Christological. One or two aspects of this are straightforward and others are more challenging and complex. Yet they can still provide us with a paradigm of ministry even in the 21st century. The essence of his ministry is found in Philippians 3: 5-10:

> circumcised on the eighth day, of the people of Israel, of the tribe of Benjamin, a Hebrew born of Hebrews: as to the law a Pharisee, as to zeal a persecutor of the church, as to righteousness under the law blameless. But whatever gain I had, I counted as loss for the surpassing worth of knowing Christ Jesus my Lord. For his sake I have suffered the loss of all things, and count them as refuse, in order that I may gain Christ and be found in him, not having a righteousness of my own based on the law, but that which is through Christ Jesus, the righteousness from God that depends on faith, that I may know him and the power of his resurrection.

Clearly Paul is contrasting his faith in himself through keeping the law and his faith in Christ after his conversion. His confidence in his spirituality as a Pharisee was based on his religious heritage and also his achievements. His credentials as a religious leader prior to his conversion were very impressive, and you could not emulate his achievements that gave him supreme confidence in himself. But, after he encountered Christ his outlook completely changed. Of course he didn't suddenly relinquish his religious heritage, or stop being a well qualified religious leader. The difference now was that he had a new perspective on these things. His faith no longer rested on his religious inheritance and achievements – but in Christ. M. Bockmuehl says, 'Paul's wholesale rejection applies not to the qualities and achievements listed, but the value he had attached to them. In contrast knowing Christ is incomparably more valuable than anything else.'[1]

We may see also a comparison between Christ having suffered a loss in becoming a servant, and Paul willingly suffering the loss of all things to gain Christ. As we know it is possible for people to be 'in Christ' and gain a foothold in him by becoming Christians. Yet, sadly, they may not make any further progress in 'gaining more of Christ.' The language of loss and gain is used in sacrificial terms by Jesus, when he says in Luke 9: 23, 'If anyone would come after me, let him deny himself and take up his cross daily and follow me.' This is a call to give up or sacrifice something in order to gain Christ. Also, the image of gain and loss is disturbing, because it challenges us to weigh up if our church is gaining more of Christ. Equally, a church may have Christ but not perceptively gain more of him. The inference is unmistakably clear. You can gain more of Christ, but the opposite is also true. Here, A. Motyer speaks about, 'Paul's progressive nature of gaining Christ as he made progress from his conversion, to increasingly knowing more of Christ as he become more consecrated to him.'[2]

For Paul knowing Christ in a personal relationship far outweighed the advantages he previously considered valuable, and his philosophy of ministry after his conversion was radically transformed. He echoes this when he speaks of the surpassing worth of knowing Christ Jesus my Lord. 'Here and here alone in his writings do we find the intensely personal "Christ Jesus my Lord:" and it would be a dull reader indeed who did not mark the warm and deep devotion which breathes through every phrase.'[3] Paul's relationship with Christ far outweighed the previous advantages of his religious framework, and his confidence as a religious leader was now firmly in Christ. His aim, his ambition, his heart's desire – was to 'know Christ Jesus my Lord.' This is the foundation on which his ministry was established. G. Fee also eloquently captures the essence of knowing Christ:

> This is one of the truly "surpassing" moments in the Pauline corpus: it would be a tragedy if its splendour were lost in analysis. Finally, therefore, one should go back and read it again and again, until what one learns in the analysis is absorbed in praise and worship over the "surpassing worth of knowing Christ Jesus our Lord."[4]

In his ministry as an apostle Paul's focus and defining factor was 'knowing Christ.' Everything he did was subordinate to this aim. No aspect of church life or ministry was allowed to challenge or take priority over Christ. He had discovered that religious traditions did not compare with knowing Christ, not just on a personal level, but also for the churches he founded and continued to pray for. Bockmuehl echoes this when he says, 'Knowing Christ Jesus then, describes the fundamental reality of Paul's life, the relationship that suffuses, empowers and motivates all that he is and does…Just as the christological passage of Philippians 2: 6-11, presented the objective theological reality of Christ as the "kurios" – the Lord who bears the divine name YHWH, so this verse makes the astonishing claim that this same Christ is "my" Lord. In other words, the great doctrinal affirmations of 2: 6-11, are here seen to shape the deepest realities of Paul's own life and self-understanding.'[5] Moreover, they shaped the formation of his ministry as it evolved.

TO LIVE IS CHRIST

This is probably one of Paul's best known sayings, and as we know he shared this with the Philippian Christians when he was in jail in Rome. In 2: 19-25 he writes reflectively, uncertain of whether he will be officially released or executed:

> Yes, and I shall rejoice. For I know that through your prayers and the help of the Spirit of Christ Jesus, this will turn out

for my deliverance, as it is my eager expectation and hope that I shall not be at all ashamed, but that with full courage now as always Christ will be honoured in my body whether by life or death. For me to live is Christ to die is gain. If it is to be life in the flesh that means fruitful labour for me. Yet which I shall chose I cannot tell. I am hard pressed between the two. My desire is to depart and be with Christ for that is far better. But to remain in the flesh is more necessary on your account. Convinced of this I know that I shall remain and continue with you all, for your progress and joy in the faith. So that in me you may have ample cause to glory in Christ Jesus, because of my coming to you again.

It is certainly outside of our experience to identify with Paul's joyful confidence, when he is imprisoned and in imminent danger of being executed. Even in this vulnerable situation he views everything through Christ. For him Christ is the lens that brings a fresh perspective, on any and every situation he encounters. He can be joyful if he dies because he will go to be with the Lord. He can be joyful if he lives because once again he will see the Philippians for their benefit. 'Again, one can hardly miss the three-way bond – between him, them and Christ – that informs every part of this letter.'[6]

Paul has had ample time to weigh up what will happen to him. He is faced with one of two choices that are out of his hands. He can live. Or he can die. Yet he is confident that the Lord will deliver him, because of the prayers of the Philippian church and the intervention of the Holy Spirit. A combination of human and divine initiative, that is reminiscent of Peter's deliverance in prison when his life was in danger in Acts 12. Such assurance seems extraordinary and perhaps astonishing, but then we are dealing with the irrepressible apostle. Commentators tend to see a link in his hope of deliverance with that of Job in 13: 18: 'I know that I shall be vindicated.' Here O'Brien comments, 'one learns a great deal about Paul's own spiritual life and his understanding of the role of the Spirit in that life. He does not simply think of Christian life as lived in isolation from others. He may be the one in prison and headed for trial: but the Philippians – and others – are inextricably bound together with him through the Spirit.'[7]

Despite his conviction that he will be released, Paul has had time to think through his attitude towards dying and he freely and frankly shares this with the Philippians. Not only because he is on intimate terms with them, but, because he wants to set them an example and so he says: 'for me to live is Christ to die is gain.' Bockmuehl says: 'As the emphatic first word suggests, Paul's tone becomes even more personal, as he affirms what is clearly one of his most deeply felt convictions, palpably forged on the anvil of doubts and trials. But, although he knows something of the human struggle with death, it is not an experience he faces with fear or despair…If to live this present life is already 'Christ' to join him more fully in the life to come, can only be a further advantage.'[8]

Paul set the Philippians an example about how to face dying for Christ, something he knew they may possibly face in the future. While he assures them it is better to be with Christ in glory, he then thinks out loud so to speak and shares how he arrived at his decision. Clearly he is torn between the choice he has to make, as he is not certain which will advance the cause of Christ and the gospel. 'While Paul's preference is to be with Christ immediately, remaining alive on earth is more necessary for the sake of his continued ministry to the Philippians and others. For the advance of the gospel, Paul gladly postpones his personal desire on behalf of his vocation to bring the gospel to the Gentiles.'[9]

Commentators tend to see a complexity in some of the Greek in this passage, and G. Fee comments on this. 'Because of its complexity, one can easily overlook the theological thrust of the whole, namely Paul's unshakeable confidence in the living God…That Paul will turn to momentary soliloquy over the prospect of life and death, does not indicate doubt or anxiety on his part, quite the opposite. The whole passage breathes with confidence that God will fulfil Paul's "eager expectation and hope." Indeed the Trinitarian substructure of the whole exudes another reason for existence: to encourage the Philippians regarding the certainty of their own future, as long as for them, too, "to live is Christ." The heart of everything, of course, is Paul's utter devotion to Christ, and his desire that Christ alone be "magnified' in his life, however present circumstances turn out.'[10]

Clearly, and unambiguously, Paul's motivation in ministry was to live for Christ. This may be an obvious point to make, but, it can seem attractive to be a minister, or a leading lay-person, because of the influence and prestige this brings. The temptation here is the desire to lord it over others as we serve Christ and to seek affirmation and praise. It is also possible to be serving our own ambitions and aspirations as we serve the Lord. But Paul would have none of that. Without being self-conscious he transparently declares his philosophy of ministry. His sole purpose was to live for Christ and to honour and glorify him. And his underlying motive in serving the Lord, was his attitude to be a servant to others. Long ago he had grasped that living for Christ was characterised by sacrifice. He inevitably knew there was a personal cost involved, regardless of whether this was internal suffering or physical hardship. His outlook on ministry embraced these things, without a second thought and without even flinching.

SUFFERING TRANSFORMED

As you read the catalogue, or if you like curriculum vitae, of Paul's suffering in the book of Acts and in his letters, this can easily be mistaken for a film script of a gladiator or soldier, whose enemies were determined to kill him. This may sound far-fetched but ultimately this is what happened. Clearly for us in the West this scale of suffering is alien territory, and we might understandably flinch from it. Yet from the outset of his ministry, Paul anticipated suffering and embraced and welcomed it. He understood this as a characteristic sign of being an apostle that authenticated his ministry, as the Lord informed him through Ananias how much he must suffer for his sake – Acts 9: 15-16. So his perspective on this issue was that it was an inevitable part of his ministry. It was a dimension of his philosophy of ministry, that could not be laid aside. It was a given that could not be avoided.

Acts provides us with a good idea of the suffering Paul encountered as an evangelist, 13: 7-12 opposition in Cyprus: 13: 45 & 50 persecution by Jews in Pisidian Antioch: 14: 2 & 5 opposition and an attempted stoning in Iconium: 14: 9 Paul was stoned at Lystra and left for dead: 16: 19-24 attacked and beaten with rods and imprisoned at Philippi: 19: 23-34 the crowd cause an uproar and a riot in Ephesus: 21: 27-36 the crowd cause an uproar and are violent: 23: 12-14 a plot to kill Paul. Having survived all these incidents Paul obviously had a strong constitution and seemed to revel in adversity. He was going to preach even when there was a riot in Ephesus – but the other disciples wouldn't let him! It was too frightening for them – but not for Paul the extrovert and fearless evangelist. Life didn't sound dull with him around – just precarious at times.

We cannot help but admire Paul's resilience and single-mindedness, in his attitude and response towards suffering. Writing to the Philippians about his imprisonment in Rome, reveals a passage rich with meaning for comfortable Christians in the West. And in a way that he never anticipated, he speaks prophetically to those who have suffered after him. As we think about suffering in Paul's philosophy of ministry, this issue that has been outside our experience in the West, may be one we have to embrace in the future.

From Acts we have seen that Paul was no stranger to suffering, and this is by no means an exhaustive list – wait until you get to 2 Corinthians 11: 23-27! So to end up in prison and suffer for being a Christian was not entirely unexpected. His outlook on suffering for Christ stood him in good stead to respond positively to this. We can perceive that the point of transition in his situation, was his attitude about being imprisoned for Christ. Had he reacted negatively and become despondent, word would have quickly spread about this, and it would have had a negative knockon effect on the other Christians in Rome.

However, when Paul is in prison, as we have seen from Acts 16: 23, he is likely to burst into praise and worship the Lord. Although that was a long time ago, Paul's habit of always rejoicing in the

Lord was so strong, he continued this practice even in prison. After all the Philippian jailer came to know the Lord, so who knows what might happen here. Also, he is wise enough to know that he doesn't want the Christians in Rome or anywhere else, to be discouraged by his response. He cannot change his circumstances but he can rise above them. He cannot miraculously change his situation, but his spirit can remain buoyant.

Paul knew the Lord was with him to strengthen him and bring good out of his situation. What he can do is to pray for opportunities to share the gospel, with the soldiers who take it in turn to guard him. As they enquired what he had done to be put in prison, he had endless opportunities to share that it was for preaching about Christ. 'It has become clear to all who have had any association with him, that his imprisonment has to do with his Christian faith, with his "gospel." This at least means that they have come to know that it is a religious matter: but for Paul it surely means as well, that he has tried to evangelise "the palace guard" itself. That Paul was 'in chains for Christ' also became known to 'everyone else.'[11] We see a double testimony to this, when firstly the Christians from Caesar's household send greetings to the Philippian church in 4: 22. And secondly in 1: 15-17, when Paul alludes to the Christians who preach Christ out of rivalry. Presumably he is referring to the Christians in Rome, who may have different views on certain aspects of doctrine.

We can imagine the Lord reminding Paul he particularly wanted to preach the gospel in Rome and here was his opportunity. Now, he could see the Lord's irony and sense of humour in this situation. Here he was a prisoner and his captors were a captive audience for Christ. He was probably overjoyed at this prospect. Moreover, the Christians who visited found him rejoicing in the Lord and were tremendously encouraged by him. In turn they themselves witnessed for Christ with greater boldness and confidence. As O'Brien observes, 'Paul wanted to show the Philippians that the majority of the believers in Rome, having had their confidence in the Lord strengthened by his example, have been encouraged to set forth the apostolic message more boldly.'[12] In the not too distant future, 'Such fearlessness and courage would be increasingly necessary in the deteriorating political climate and growing hostility to Christians in Rome during the early 60's under Nero.'[13] And as O'Brien comments, 'An intensifying force appears here…the point is not that the majority had been unduly timid before this, but that their courage had risen to new heights, when they might have been intimidated.'[14]

Instead of stopping Paul in his tracks and preventing the gospel from spreading, his imprisonment and suffering have actually advanced and promoted it. 'What Paul wants the Philippians to know is that "what has happened to me" has really served to advance the gospel. They are to understand that its effect has been quite the reverse of what they might have expected. He wants them not to be anxious about him…"To advance the gospel" has been his life long passion: he has thus ordered his life so that nothing will hinder, and everything advance, the message about Christ.'[15]

Bockmuel perceives the underlying significance of Paul's suffering and imprisonment, that initially seemed the opposite of how it turned out. 'Even at a time of hardship for him and persecution for them (the Philippians), the gospel's progress continues into the very seat of imperial power…Nevertheless, his fellow Christians are encouraged by the fact that his imprisonment is "in (and for) Christ:" his present circumstances serve to advance the gospel by carrying it into the very heart of secular political power. This is why in 1: 18 he shows himself rejoicing.'[16]

PAUL'S VICARIOUS SUFFERING

At the heart of Paul's philosophy of ministry was the concept of sharing in Christ's sufferings. He knew that serving others as Christ served us inevitably involved some aspect of sacrifice, as Christian ministry reflects the example of Christ – who gave himself for us. He also knew that invariably there is a cost involved – but for Paul this concept developed further. We not only reflect Christ's example in some measure, we also replicate his ministry by sharing in his sufferings. But there is also a sense of identification and solidarity with Christ as we serve him, because he is alongside us –

as he is in and with us by his Spirit. So as his representatives, as and when we suffer, this is a participation in the sufferings of Christ.

This theme of sharing in the sufferings of Christ on behalf of others, for their benefit, (vicarious suffering) echoes that of the suffering servant in Isaiah 53: 4-5:

> Surely he has borne our griefs and carried our sorrows: yet we esteemed him stricken, smitten by God and afflicted. But he was wounded for our transgressions, he was bruised for our iniquities upon him was the chastisement that made us whole, and with his stripes we are healed.

This theme is also echoed by Paul in 2 Corinthians 1: 5-6:

> For as we share abundantly in Christ's sufferings, so through Christ we share abundantly in comfort too. If we are afflicted, it is for your comfort and salvation: and if we are comforted, it is for your comfort, which you experience when you patiently endure the same sufferings that we suffer.

Here Hughes points out, 'Christ's work of redemption is unique, complete, once-for-all...For the Christian, however, as Paul explains elsewhere, there is such a thing as the fellowship of Christ's sufferings – Phil: 3: 10 & I Peter 4: 13, that is a sharing or partnership with Christ in suffering. To follow Christ is to follow him into suffering. In this also the disciple must expect to be identified with the master. It is important to observe here that the apostle is speaking of the sufferings of Christ, and not sufferings in general. Suffering which is the consequence of disobedience and selfishness has no blessing in it, and cannot possibly be described as of 'Christ.'[17]

A divine balance is brought into the equation when Paul speaks about sharing in Christ's sufferings, because suffering with Christ also results in sharing in his comfort too. And that comfort is likely to come through the body of Christ – other Christians. Here suffering and comfort are not seen on an individual level. There is a sense of identification and solidarity with other Christians, by a mutual sharing in suffering and a mutual exchange of comfort. E. Best echoes this when he says, 'What Paul does is to associate comfort with salvation (v 6). The God of comfort is also the God of mercy (v 3) and because he is a God of mercy he saves…The point he makes here is not the nature of the comfort, but the way it can be transferred form one person to another within the church. When Paul says here that he is comforted, it is not to express his self-satisfaction that God has comforted him. He affirms instead that through his sufferings, and the comfort he received, the Corinthians have been comforted (v 4).'[18]

The concept of mutuality in sharing suffering and comfort is not just confined to Christians. We all probably know a group of people who have shared someone's suffering and comforted them at the same time too. We can only speculate how much the church at Corinth grasped what Paul was saying, about sharing in the mutual concept of suffering and comfort. This radical concept challenged their individualistic, elite spirituality, as they failed to identify with Paul and stand alongside him in his suffering – a great deal of which they had caused.

The theme of suffering for Christ is taken a stage further by Paul when he says in Colossians 1: 24:

> Now I rejoice in my sufferings for your sake, and in my flesh I complete what is lacking in Christ's afflictions, for the sake of his body, that is the church.

At first glance this does seem an extraordinary and unusual statement, as it advances the concept of vicarious suffering a stage further. However, Paul is consistent in his customary manner of 'rejoicing always.' God's people were a great source of joy for him and we see his generosity of heart in willingly suffering on their behalf. Here, D. Dales says, 'The word he uses to describe this "filling up" or "completing" is unique here, though the conviction is echoed elsewhere in the Pauline writings – 2 Tim. 2: 10 & Eph. 3: 13. It indicates how deep in his mind was the link between the sacrifice of Christ on the cross, the experience and the work of an apostle, and the meaning of the church's life as the Body of Christ. So at the end of the same chapter in Colossians, Paul concludes that his own labour in the power of the Spirit, is to enable people to grow in their perfection in Christ. His toil is life-giving.'[19]

R. Martin informs us about the background of the concept of completing what is lacking in Christ's afflictions. He believes, 'there were some insinuations at Colosse that because of Paul's sufferings and being in jail, his claims as an apostle were dubious. This entire section is a sustained statement of "apology," explaining that his ministry amongst the Gentiles was one that involved suffering. A parallel passage is 2 Cor. 1: 5-7, and in both instances the most likely idea is taken from Jewish apocalyptic teaching, that Israel's chosen ones will have to suffer a quota of afflictions before Messiah comes. Paul takes over this concept of vicarious suffering and bends it to his purpose...he is called upon to represent his people as a martyr figure and to perform a vicarious ministry on their behalf. In this way he fills the still deficient tally of sufferings, that God's new Israel has to endure before the end of the age.'[20]

A few years ago, in the early days of his ministry at St. Barnabas in Cambridge, in the early 1990s, I perceived that the Vicar Leonard Browne, had a 'big heart for God and a big heart for people.' This description sums up Paul perfectly. He too had a 'big heart for Christ and a big heart for people.' How else can we make sense of his willingness to rejoice in his sufferings for the sake of others? It just doesn't add up to think he was having some mystical spiritual experience. F. F. Bruce clarifies the issue for us:

> He realised that by bearing hardships on behalf of the people of Christ, he was entering into the fellowship of his sufferings – a fellowship which, as he told his friends at Philippi, he desired to know more fully – Phil. 3: 10. This remarkable statement – I complete what is lacking in Christ's afflictions – can best be understood, if we bear in mind the oscillation in Hebrew thought between individual and corporate personality. The portrayal of the Isaianic servant of Yahweh presents a relevant instance. In one place at least the Servant is a corporate entity, the Israel of God – Isa. 49: 3: 'You are my servant Israel, in whom I will be glorified.' In the N. T. this person is identified with Jesus...But the servant's identity which narrowed in scope

until it was concentrated in our Lord Jesus alone, has since his exaltation broadened out again and become corporate in his people.[21]

Dunn further expounds the subject of 'completing what is lacking in Christ's afflictions,' when he says, 'Colossian 1: 24 is clearly building on this theme. In particular, the thought that Paul by sharing in Christ's death was essential to the well-being of his converts, is already present in 2 Cor: 4: 10-12. But Paul here has also made a unique addition to the theme, by adding the (implied) thought that Christ's afflictions lack something and need to be completed in Paul's flesh, literally 'fill up the place of'…For at its heart (of this line of thought), is the double claim that the suffering and dying of Christ, provides a key insight into the way the cosmos is constituted and into its reclamation – Col: 1: 15-20: and that it is only by identification with Christ in the way of suffering that those who serve the church can help it to truly be his body, the body which mirrors the cosmos as it was intended to be.'[22]

SHARING CHRIST'S SUFFERINGS

When Paul speaks about vicariously sharing in Christ's sufferings, as an apostle on behalf of others we probably have no problem with that. That is how he interpreted and understood his calling, but when he says that Christians also have a share in Christ's sufferings this might be problematic. I am aware of my tendency in the past to think of my emotional or psychological suffering as a minister often as an irritation. Something that at times was avoidable and unnecessary. After all there is no relative value in suffering just for the sake of it. Despite this, at times I embraced my suffering as 'a familiar companion.' Now as I learn about sharing in Christ's sufferings, I am not certain how much of my affliction these past few years was the wrong type of suffering, and how much was for Christ's sake. The wrong type occurs when we are struggling with what the Lord wants to do in our lives. However, Paul viewed his robust acceptance of sharing in Christ's sufferings in a positive light, because of what he believed it accomplished. This challenges our perspective, on what part suffering has to play in our philosophy of ministry, as we serve the Lord.

Clearly for us in the West suffering for Christ because of physical persecution is virtually unheard of. Also I suspect we are not very well informed about this important subject. However, in his correspondence to the Philippians Paul introduces them to a new perspective in his philosophy of suffering. He teaches them that it is their privilege not only to believe in Christ, but also their privilege to suffer for him. Presumably the same is true for us. We read in Philippians 1: 29-30:

> For it has been granted to you that for the sake of Christ you
> should not only believe in him but also suffer for his sake,
> engaged in the same conflict that you saw I had and now
> hear that I still have.

N. Walter has recently argued, 'The believers at Philippi were drawn mainly from a Gentile and pagan background, and for them the idea of suffering "for one's god" was entirely new. This explains Paul's references to his own example in 1: 12-26, and why he warns the Philippians of the impending necessity of suffering…Certainly their trials were not due to some accident. Nor were they a mark of divine punishment as though God was angry with them. Quite the reverse. Their suffering had been freely bestowed on them as a gracious gift. In verses 29-30 Paul's comparison has symbolic significance. Not only do he and the Philippians share the same "aywv" (struggle): they are both involved in suffering for Christ's sake as well… The sufferings and persecution that believers endure, whether difficult to bear or not are endured for the sake of Christ, and the apostle desires that his example may encourage them to bear them with equanimity, even joy.'[23]

Suffering on behalf of Christ as a gift of grace is also echoed by Bockmuehl when he says, 'These verse (29-30) offer a surprising explanation of why Paul thinks that Christian steadfastness in adversity is God's proof of salvation. It is because the suffering of Christians is inherently, indeed almost by definition, related to that of Christ. The passive "it has been granted" (echaristhe) suggests that both "to believe in Christ and to suffer" as a result of it, are in fact the gift of God's grace (charis)...The Greek here shows quite emphatically, if somewhat clumsily and untranslatably, that this gift of grace is profoundly related to Christ: literally 'it has been granted to you on behalf of Christ, not just to believe in him but also to suffer on his behalf.'[24]

There may be no intellectual difficulty accepting the concept that Christ's sufferings are something we also share, but to embrace this truth inwardly in the spiritual dimension, may require asking the Holy Spirit for help. Verses 29-30 provide us with a theological explanation for the Philippians' suffering, that hinges around their relationship with Christ and with Paul. The idea of conflict and struggle is integral to sharing in Christ's sufferings and a fairly common theme in the N. T. 'The picture of a struggle is again taken up, this time with the Greek term "aywv," so that the whole phrase characterises the nature of God's gracious gift of suffering for Christ. "aywv" (struggle, fight) appears in the N.T. at Col. 2: 1, 1 Thess. 2:2, 1 Tim. 6: 12, 2 Tim. 4: 7, Heb. 12...This describes Paul's conflict for the gospel or the faith. It involves untiring toil and labour, an intense wrestling and struggle for the spread, growth and strengthening of the faith as the goal of his mission. Further, the thought of a continual struggle against opposition is not too far distant when Paul speaks of his "aywv." Suffering is often involved, as here, so that when, for example, he refers to his struggle on behalf of the Colossians – 2: 1, this is akin to his statement about his sufferings for their sake – 1: 24.'[25]

FORMATION IN CORINTH
INTRODUCTION

It is impossible to comprehend Paul's philosophy of ministry that he shares with the Corinthians, without a background knowledge of Corinth and it's cultural and religious influences: because these formed an integral part of the expectations and outlook of the Corinthian Christians, and influenced the way their spirituality developed. Something G. Fee echoes when he says, 'As much as for any other document in the N. T. – and more so than for most – the various sociological, economic and religious factors that make up the environment of the city of Corinth, have a profound influence on one's understanding of Paul's letters to the church there.

As a Greek city-state, Corinth flourished both before and after the golden years of Athens (5th c. BC), but as leader of the Achaean League in the mid 2nd century BC it came into conflict with Rome and was destroyed by the Roman consul Lucius Mummius in 146 BC. The city lay dormant for one hundred years until it was refounded in 44 BC by Julius Caesar. Corinth was repopulated by freedmen from Rome.'[26]

'Corinth had long been visited by religious pilgrims coming to see the famous temple of Aphrodite on the mountain overlooking Corinth, the Acro-Corinth. Aphrodite was the goddess of love, beauty and fertility and prostitutes considered her their patroness. She was also a goddess of seafaring. Strabo informs us that in classical times this temple had many sacred prostitutes, but it is not at all clear that the practice of sacred prostitution was revived on the same scale in Roman Corinth.

Nevertheless, one should not underestimate the place of sexual expression, not only in some pagan religious festivals, but also in some pagan temple precincts. It would be surprising if such activities did not take place in Corinth, especially in connection with the dinner parties that were often held in these precincts. Corinth was a bustling and prosperous metropolis of perhaps 70-80, 000 inhabitants in Paul's day. It was primarily a service city, one that derived its wealth from the goods and services it provided to visitors, including religious pilgrims, sailors, merchants, soldiers, salve traders and those who were in town for the games.

SOCIOLOGICAL BACKGROUND

Paul worked with his hands and would have been seen by many as an artisan. Well-to-do or aristocratic Romans, like Greeks, often had a low opinion of those who practiced a trade, and many of his problems seem to have been caused by the wealthy and the social climbers among the Corinthian Christians, who were upset at him for not meeting their expectations as a great orator and teacher. Corinth was a place where an enterprising person could rise quickly through the accumulation and judicious use of newfound wealth. It seems that in Paul's time many in Corinth, were already suffering from a self-made-person-escapes-humble-origins syndrome. It was also a magnet for the socially ambitious, since there were many opportunities for people to gain higher social status and accumulate a fortune, in this city re-founded by freed slaves.

The Corinthian Christians and Paul's opponents, observed that his letters were weightier than his bodily presence and his oral rhetoric – 2 Cor. 10: 10, which was hampered by some physical disability. They also cared little for his deliberate self-humiliation and his servant role. This was an attitude in violent reaction to much that was central to the classical way of life, not excluding the smooth doctrines of moderation. In a city where social climbing was a major pre-occupation, Paul's deliberate stepping down in apparent status, would have been seen by many as disturbing and even provocative.

The evidence is that Paul was well educated and in this regard he would have been identified with and received by the well-to-do. His Roman citizenship would have worked in the same direction. In Corinth that he was an artisan who practiced a trade, not a teacher or philosopher who accepted patronage, would have worked against his social status. The status opportunities Paul declined remain the measure of his potential professional standing, and of the expectation of his supporters for him. The extent of his renunciation explains his intense consciousness of debasement. He was stepping down firmly in the world. An apparent result was that some considered him unsophisticated and unworthy of the status of an "apostolos."

Some, though few of the Corinthian Christians apparently were members of high status groups. This group seems to have included one or two government officials. Although there were according to Paul's testimony few wealthy people amongst the Corinthians, their influence among the converts was probably well out of proportion to their numbers, since they could provide meeting places for the Christians in their homes –1 Cor. 16: 15,19. That there were significant numbers of poor or relatively poor people among the converts, is suggested by 1 Cor. 1: 28 and 11: 22. And there were domestic slaves in the congregation as well – 1 Cor. 7: 21-23. 1 Cor. 16: 22 & 2 Cor. 8-9, suggest that Paul believed there was disposable income or assets among the Corinthians. So their social strata varied from the quite poor, to the rather well-off.

Those whose status depended on newfound wealth, played prominent roles not only in society at large, but undoubtedly also in the Christian assembly. Paul's words in 1 Cor. 1: 26 would have been a pointed reminder to such status-hungry people of their origins, and this was at the root of the attraction that Christianity had for some Corinthians. This new religion gave them status in their own eyes, that they had been unable to obtain in the larger society.'[27]

SPIRITUAL BACKGROUND

One of the major concepts and problems Paul had to tackle head on at Corinth was the issue of what it meant to be 'spiritual.' The other concerned his authenticity as an apostle which they questioned. G. Fee says, 'That for Paul these two crises overlap. It is not his own person that is at stake in their denial of his authority, but the gospel he preaches. To deny the one is to deny the other. Most likely the key issue between them is a basic theological problem – what it means to be "pneumatikos" – spiritual. The problem is that they think of themselves as "pneumatikos" but are not so sure about the apostle Paul – 1 Cor. 14: 37, and some unkind comparisons may have been made between him and Apollos...although one cannot be sure, their understanding of being "pneumatikos" is most likely related to their experience of Spirit inspiration, especially their overemphasis on the gift of tongues.

This in turn is probably related to their interest in "sophia" and "gnosis"– wisdom and knowledge...Both of these "gifts" have become their special possession by means of the Spirit. They are spiritually endowed hence they have special wisdom and superior knowledge. It is probably no accident that that the statement, "if anyone thinks that he/she is?' – is found in the three major sections of the letter in chapters 1-4, 8-10, 12-14: and reflect these three crucial Corinthian terms wisdom: knowledge: and spiritual...related to this is their apparently "spiritual" understanding of the sacraments, whereby the one who has been baptised and partakes of the "spiritual food" of the Lord's Table also finds security – 10: 1-5, so that behaviour in this present life has little or no effect on one's true spirituality.'[28]

AN UNCOMPROMISING MESSAGE

1 Corinthians 1: 17-18 & 22-24:

> For Christ did not send me to baptise but to preach the gospel, and not with eloquent wisdom, lest the cross of Christ be emptied of its power. For the word of the cross is folly to those who are perishing, but to us who are being saved it is the power of God. For Jews demand signs and Greeks seek wisdom, but we peach Christ crucified, a stumbling block to Jews and folly to Gentiles, but to those who are called, both Jews and Greeks, Christ the power of God and the wisdom of God.

From these verses, we can immediately see the relevance of the sociological and spiritual background of the Church at Corinth. The Christians were naturally drawn to a spirituality that was aesthetically attractive and impressive, as this added 'kudos' to their status. So they liked to boast about how 'spiritual' they were. However, Paul refuses to compromise the centrality of Christ crucified in his preaching of the gospel. He also refuses to indulge in what they considered 'skilled rhetoric' to pander to their impressionable egos. C. K. Barrett says:

> Paul represents himself as a preacher not an orator. Preaching is the proclamation of the cross: it is the cross that is the source of its power. The convincing power of the cross could not be fully manifest if preaching shared too evidently in the devices of human rhetoric. Hence Paul rejects wisdom "sophia" as a rhetorical device. [29]

D. Dales says, 'The way in which Paul sets about puncturing the spiritual complacency and pride in the Corinthian church in his first letter, is precisely to emphasise that, "the foolishness of God" is wiser than men and the weakness of God is stronger than men.'[30] The fact that the Jews were attracted by powerful displays of signs and Greeks by impressive displays of wisdom, is not something Paul would go along with. He faithfully preached the cross of Christ, that to the Jews and Greeks was a sign of powerlessness and weakness, qualities they could not identify with God and which were unattractive to them. As Paul deflates their pride by reminding them of their Christian roots in the preaching of 'Christ crucified,' C. K. Barrett says:

> This is Paul's most brilliant epigrammatic description of the world in which the Gospel is preached and of the Gospel itself. Religious egocentricity will inevitably find Christ crucified a scandal, for in the cross God does precisely the opposite of what he is expected to do: the intellectual egocentricity of wisdom-seeking Gentiles finds the same theme folly, because incarnation crystallised in crucifixion, means not that man has speculated his way up to God but that God has come down to man where he is. What God has done in Christ crucified is a direct contradiction of human wisdom and power, yet it achieved what human wisdom and power failed to achieve.[31]

Paul is intransigent about his philosophy of ministry, to faithfully preach 'Christ crucified' as the way of salvation, because he sees this as the hallmark of true spirituality. The challenge of preaching the paradox of the cross (God's power manifested through Christ's weakness), is to trust God to touch peoples' hearts and draw them to Christ. It demands conviction and courage to speak about Christ crucified and salvation even in the 21st century. D. Prior addresses this issue when he says, 'It is important, therefore, for Christians today to appreciate the ways in which our thinking has been influenced by the secularism of our own age, in the same way as Paul found it necessary to uncover for the church at Corinth the emptiness and folly of contemporary thinking.

In uncovering the empty foolishness of worldly wisdom, Paul in no way underestimates its significance or impact. The essential characteristic of worldly wisdom is that it can empty the word of the cross of its power –1: 17. That is the measure of its serious threat to the gospel and the church. We are dealing, therefore, not with anything peripheral or superficial, but with a subtle enemy that strikes at the very heart of our message. If we cannot identify it and isolate it, our gospel will be puny and empty.'[32]

PAUL'S PERSPECTIVE ON POWER

In 1 Cor. 1: 18-25 Paul reminds the Corinthian Christians of the power of preaching Christ crucified, in contrast to their inclination to be attracted to the rhetoric of human wisdom. He continues to elaborate on this theme in 2: 1-5:

> When I came to you brethren, I did not come proclaiming to you the testimony of God in lofty words or wisdom. For I decided to know nothing among you except Jesus Christ and him crucified. And I was with you in weakness and in much fear and trembling and my speech and message were not in plausible words of wisdom, but in demonstration of the Spirit and power, so that your faith might not rest in the wisdom of men but in the power of God.

Here, we are confronted with the truth that God's power accompanies preaching that faithfully proclaims Christ crucified, and this power is manifested through the Holy Spirit. It is essential to grasp that this is God's perspective. He will endorse preaching about Christ crucified with his power, as preaching the cross of Christ is the channel through which God's power is released. God's power does depend on our eloquence or being impressive speakers – although we may be. C. K. Barrett emphasises this truth when he says, 'The theological principle Paul has stated at the end of chapter 1 (that your faith might not depend on men's wisdom but on God's power) has practical implications, for example for his own ministry...In his proclamation Paul placed no reliance upon eloquence or wisdom.'[33]

There is an obvious contrast between Paul's preaching and his writing. He himself admits to the Corinthians he is not a notable speaker, 'even if I am an unskilled speaker' – 2 11: 6. Yet, clearly, he is obviously an eloquent writer and a theologian of considerable ability, so we can hardly imagine that he was a useless speaker or a bad preacher. He also says in 2: 11: 6 'he was skilled in knowledge' – so the inference is that he deliberately did not use the rhetorical speaking style of his day, to make his message about Christ sound sophisticated, or appear attractive for the wrong reasons. We also have to remember that a crucified Christ was not an attractive Saviour. This was a humiliating death reserved for the worst criminals. The heart of the matter is that he was not out to impress them as a speaker, by altering the content of his message about Christ. This was powerful precisely because he refused to adopt the style the orators of his day used. Nevertheless, this is not an invitation to be careless in our presentation of Christ. Nor do we have to suppress our personality when we preach about Christ – which we may eloquently do. The heart of the matter lies in our motivation. To what extent are we pointing people to Christ without subtracting from the message of the cross: and without seeking to impress our audience as a speaker? C. K. Barrett reflects Paul's outlook as a speaker when he says:

> Even had he been able to do so, however, he had no intention of using human powers or oratory, whatever they may have been, and his confidence in the power of Christ and the Spirit could not conceal from him that Christ was Christ crucified.[34]

What is striking in the context of 2 Cor. 2: 1-5, is that Paul draws attention to how inadequate and vulnerable he felt when he first preached Christ crucified to them. We may discern two reasons for this. Firstly, we learn from Acts 18, that in Corinth he was sharing the gospel with the Jews who opposed and reviled him, and he may have been sensitive about encountering the same response from the Gentiles in Corinth. Secondly, he may have felt intimated by the reputation of the city and its emphasis on rhetoric and wisdom. Consequently, he was with them 'in weakness and in much fear and trembling.' This reflects how much this affected him emotionally and psychologically.

Here Paul elaborates once again on his philosophy of ministry. He reminds the Corinthians how utterly reliant he was on God, because he felt so vulnerable and weak when he first preached Christ to them. His confidence was completely in Christ crucified and not in his skills as a speaker. He also reminds them that the impact of his message about Christ, was accompanied by the power of God's Spirit. Here D. Prior draws our attention, 'to the close relationship between the cross and the Spirit: and that the work of the Spirit is stressed repeatedly in chapter two.'[35]

A. Thiselton highlights, 'the gospel's obvious independence of human intelligence: the lowly character of those called: and the manner in which Pàul consistently introduces the gospel at Corinth not humanly and self-confidently, but in an effacement of himself. This released the Spirit to indicate his presence and power effectively.' He also provides some illuminating background that explains Paul's perspective on preaching Christ crucified. He quotes M. Bullmore, who contends that 'Paul uses and opposes rhetoric in these verses: it was against a particular strain of Graeco Roman rhetoric that he set forth his own statement of rhetorical style. The specific style that Paul opposed and disowned is described by Bullmore, as "public display oratory" associated with the second Sophistic. Stylistic virtuosity won audience approval, in contrast to Paul's conscious choice of a simple and unaffected style which draws no attention to himself.

There were "sophistic conventions" regarding the initial visit to a city by an orator, seeking to establish acceptance as a professional speaker, and who would be escorted with much enthusiasm...Paul repudiated the Sophist method of "presenting himself" when he came to Corinth. He renounces preaching for effect in the sense of parading cleverness in the eyes of the audience.'[36] The pressure on Paul to conform to the contemporary paradigm as a public speaker must have been considerable. But he remained unflinching in his conviction that to compromise the gospel in this way, would have capitulated to the prevailing spirit of his age. To do so would have disarmed the gospel and robbed it of its distinctive saving power.

At the beginning of the 21st century we can see that something more insidious has disarmed the saving power of the gospel. But in this instance the disarmament has come from within the church. By failing to faithfully preach Christ crucified as the heart of the gospel, there is no cutting edge to the Church in the life of the nation. The Church has been relegated to the status of a religious club or cult that only appeals to its members. We have diluted the message of Christ crucified and anaesthetised the gospel. It is as if Christ crucified is in suspended animation, having been deposed of his saving power. We have dis-empowered Christ crucified so extensively, that if Paul was here today he might well not recognise our anaemic gospel.

FOOLS FOR CHRIST'S SAKE

Paul's sober perspective on his ministry comes in 1 Cor. 4 where he speaks about being a 'fool' for Christ's sake. The context finds the Corinthian Christians comparing him with Apollos and Peter (ch. 3), where judging Paul is a sign of their inflated pride. Along the way they have become anti-Paul and have been influenced by the false apostles – 2 Cor 11, to reject his teaching and his authority. Although he does not use the word pride, arrogance and pride jump out from the text to describe them. And in ch. 4 he uses powerful irony and devastating sarcasm, to challenge their perspective on being 'spiritual' and how they view him – and just as importantly themselves. 'With rhetoric full of sarcasm and irony he goes for the jugular.'[37]

Paul begins ch. 4 by informing the Corinthians that the right attitude to have towards him, is that he is a servant of Christ and a steward of the mysteries of God. He then challenges their view that they have spiritually arrived, while in comparison his is a 'fool' for Christ. It may be reading it into the text, but, perhaps he perceived this is what they really thought of him. Even if this is wide of the mark this is certainly how Paul saw himself. Here, he is out to puncture their pride and deflate their inflated opinion of themselves: and as is apparent from the text he perceives they think they have arrived. D. Dales eloquently comments on this:

> With consummate irony he debunks the worship of visible success by the leading Corinthian Christians, by indicating how genuine apostles have to endure becoming 'fools' for the sake of Christ: he lists the depth of humiliation which is his lot as the only proof of his genuineness as an evangelist.[38]

In this context in 4: 7 Paul makes what is almost an immortal statement, that challenges Christians down the centuries – 'What have you that you did not receive?' This is a rhetorical question that clearly only has one answer, and it is designed to stop them in their tracks – and it still has the same impact on us today. G. Fee sees the profound challenge this question imposes on us when he says, 'If the first question in 1: 4: 7 marks the Corinthians conceit as presumptuous, the second marks it as ungrateful and is singularly devastating. This is an invitation to experience one of those rare, unguarded moments of total honesty, where in the presence of the eternal God one recognises that everything – absolutely everything – that one has is a gift. All is of grace: nothing is deserved, nothing earned.'[39]

From Paul's letters to the Corinthians, we see the extraordinary irony that he was considered to be an unimpressive speaker. Yet the paradox in chapter four, is that we have a masterful piece of rhetorical writing. Skillfully and with consummate ease, like a master tactician, he pulls his opponents to pieces as he reveals the flaws in their spirituality. Only of course they are not his opponents – but his 'beloved children'– 4:14. 'In some ways this is one of Paul's finest hours.'[40] Yet clearly he will only consider it his finest hour, if he succeeds in persuading them to embrace his perspective. Because he is not out just to win an argument – he has their best interest at heart.

Paul has concluded the best way to correct the Corinthians is by comparing their behaviour with his, something he does in 4: 8-13:

> Already you have arrived! Already you have become rich! Without us you have become kings! And would that you did reign so that we might share the rule with you! For I think

> that God has exhibited his apostles as last of all, like men sentenced to death, because we have become a spectacle to the world, to angels and to men. We are fools for Christ's sake, but you are wise in Christ! We are weak but you are strong. You are held in honour but we in disrepute. To the present hour we hunger and thirst, we are poorly dressed and buffeted and homeless, and we labour working with our own hands. When reviled we bless, when persecuted we endure, when slandered we entreat. We have become and are still, the scum of the world, the refuse of all things.

It may be reading it into the text, but Paul's description of the Corinthians' exalted status is likely to reflect their own perception. It would not have been surprising if they had treated him with great respect and esteemed him highly as an apostle, this would have been natural as he was their 'father' in Christ. Instead, in their pride, they have exalted themselves and looked down upon him. He wants to pierce their pride when he says, 'Already you have arrived! Already you have become rich! Already you have become kings! Here, he might merely have drawn a contrast between them and himself as a servant, but his exaggerated use of hyperbole guarantees this confrontation is intensified. They have assumed a spiritual arrogance, whereas Paul presumed only to follow the example of Christ, so he is willing to be a 'fool' for Christ's sake. He has embraced derisory humiliation, 'we have become like the scum of the world, the refuse of all things.' In effect he sees himself as worthless. 'The sandal of the cross is written large over Paul's vision of his own apostleship. For him it truly was 'like master, like servant.'[41]

This is a pivotal text because it portrays Paul's philosophy as a servant of Christ. He is not just writing for effect or using rhetoric to correct the Corinthians. Here we not only see his humility, we get a glimpse into the heart of the apostle. It portrays how he accepted humiliation, deprivation, being despised and considered to be worthless. This is the theology of the cross indelibly sealed on his heart.

A MATURE PHILOSOPHY

To understand Paul's ministry in 1 & 2 Corinthians, it is essential to have some background information about these two Epistles, as this also helps us to understand what was going on between him and the church. During this period we can perceive that Paul's philosophy of ministry deepened. While this is speculative it may not be far of the mark, as we see many signs that shape the formation of his ministry in 2 Corinthians. After 1 Corinthians there followed a particularly painful visit, and this almost certainly influenced the way he wrote to them in 2 Corinthians.

Paul's relationship with the church spans a period of around 6-7 years, and in 50-52 AD he spent 18 months in Corinth establishing the church – Acts 18. Some time in 55 or 56 he made a second visit – 2 Cor. 13: 2, which he calls a painful visit to deal with an emergency disciplinary problem. In 56 or 57 he visited the church for the third time – 13: 1 staying for three months. He wrote 2 Corinthians from Macedonia after his second visit, to prepare the church for his third and final visit. This is a letter written with his heart on his sleeve. In the section on 'Tough Love In Corinth,' we saw how much he loves the Corinthians, something we must take care not to overlook.

Paul writes with complete openness, and shares how he feels without holding anything back. He mentions their mutual pain on his second visit when they were all deeply hurt, and also shares his vulnerability with them too. He wants them to understand his integrity and to see that he is being authentic, so that they may see how genuine his love and concern for them is, in contrast to the 'false apostles.' They had obviously been out to impress them, and had succeeded, and were benefiting from their financial support. We may speculate that Paul hoped his letter would enable them to see through these 'false apostles.' And despite its loving atmosphere, it challenged them considerably.

R. Martin informs us, that by the time Paul wrote 2 Corinthians, 'he had been deeply concerned with the church for a number of years. He stayed 18 months after founding the church, and after he left wrote to them on several occasions. Not all of this correspondence survived, and 1 Cor. 5: 9-11 shows that even prior to that letter, he had already written to them. He wrote 1 Corinthians because of information he received from 'Chloe's people' – 1 Cor. 1: 11, who had travelled to see Paul in Ephesus and inform him about the problems in the church. The Corinthians themselves had also written seeking his advice on problems facing them – 1Cor. 7: 1. In 1 Cor. 4: 18-21, Paul said he hoped to visit them again in the near future. He later changed his plans, hoping instead to visit them twice – 2 Cor. 1: 15-16, once on his way from Ephesus to Macedonia and again on his way back to Ephesus. He never made this double visit and was accused of indecision – 2 Cor. 1: 15-22. However, he did pay a single visit – 2 Cor. 13: 2, 2:1, but it was not a happy occasion either for him or the Corinthians. After this he wrote a strong and angry letter – 2 Cor. 2: 3. This is variously known as the intermediate, severe, painful, or tearful letter. It is not our 2 Corinthians. This came later, though not necessarily all at once (it may be an amalgam of letters). While he was writing these letters, his assistants Timothy and Titus were also going back and forth there – 1 Cor. 16: 10, 2 Cor. 2: 11: 3, 7: 6-7. These visits and letters took place within five or six years of his original mission in Corinth.'[42]

RELYING ON THE LORD

An important lesson in understanding Paul's letters, is to pay close attention to how he begins them, as these tend to focus on key themes that will appear later. At the beginning of 2 Corinthians, he shares with them an integral aspect of his philosophy of ministry – learning to relying in his weakness on God's power. This theme of weakness will recur throughout this letter, and is contrasted with their paradigm of triumphant spirituality, that has been influenced by the false apostles he refers to. We may discern that Paul's ministry in dealing with the Corinthians, has been honed, refined and transformed in the process. We can perceive that his model of ministry has undergone a painful period of formation, through the severe letter he wrote and through his very painful visit – which may have further matured his philosophy of ministry. Previously he may have been authoritarian and confrontational, when he mentions the painful visit in 2 Cor. 2: 1. In the process he almost certainly had to defend himself, and justify his stance concerning the issues of conflict.

In contrast, his approach in 2 Corinthians is not authoritarian, but one of mutuality and partnership. He shares openly with them about his affliction and suffering, and also alludes to their sufferings. In 2 Cor. 1: 8 he openly shares about the frightening experience he had been through, which was so extreme he feared for his life and wondered if he would survive. In the opening chapter suffering is referred to in one way or another 17 times. P. Barnett says, 'Paul had in mind, in particular, what he called in 1: 4 "troubles." The Greek word contains the idea of "pressure," the pressure which he felt as a result of his ministry. Paul's challenge to idols and idolatry in Ephesus (Asia -Acts 19), brought upon him such an oppressive sense of burden, that he expected to die as a result of the experience 1: 8-9.'[43]

Paul wants to share with the Corinthians that the Lord allowed this to happen, in order to teach them to rely on him and not on themselves. This may contain a veiled reference to their 'triumphant spirituality,' where they think they have arrived and are above such experiences. This suggests that prior to this, his philosophy of ministry had been too self-reliant, as he was trusting in his own resources. However, through this 'near death experience,' the Lord taught him a lesson, that would shape the formation of his ministry in the future. A lesson he would never forget. This reminds us that it is wise to reflect on what the Lord allows us to go through, as we serve him, as what happens to us is not just coincidental or fortuitous. The Lord is using our difficulties and acute suffering, to not only transform our ministry, but also to mould and shape us as for our future ministry. This may be scant consolation when this is happening, but this perspective of faith reflects our trust in how the Lord deals with us. This transforming experience that Paul went through, was equivalent to an 'epiphany' that shaped his ministry. D. Dales has this to say about it.

The "extraordinary" nature of this onset of "affliction" is stressed, and frequently in this letter the word "extraordinary" or "exceedingly" marks the initiative of divine grace. The situation he faced was overwhelmingly burdensome, oppressive beyond normal conditions and virtually unsupportable by natural resources. Paul admits that despair set in…He is now looking back at a moment which proved a spiritual turning-point: a real whiff of death itself with a finality comparable to an execution, so that thereafter a whole way of living, naturally self-reliant, was jettisoned…He communicates an ultimately indescribable moment: a furnace of suffering in which trust towards God was forged, in a radically new and lasting way.[44]

THE FRAGRANCE OF CHRIST

In 2 Corinthians 2: 14: 3:5, Paul is contrasting the impact of his ministry, with that of the false apostles in Corinth.

But thanks be to God who in Christ always leads us in triumphal procession, and through us spreads the fragrance of the knowledge of him everywhere. For we are the aroma of Christ to God among those who are being saved and among those who are perishing: to one a fragrance from death to death, to the other a fragrance from life to life. 'Who is sufficient for these things?' For we are not, like so many, peddlers of God's word, but as men of sincerity, as commissioned by God, in the sight of God we speak in Christ. Are we beginning to commend ourselves again? Or de we need, as some do, letters of recommendation to you, or from you? You yourselves are our letter of recommendation, written on our hearts, to be known and read by all. And you know that you are a letter from Christ delivered by us, written not with ink, but with the Spirit of the living God, not on tablets of stone but on tablets of human hearts.

The first metaphor Paul uses is that of a 'triumphal procession.' This would have evoked the image of a victorious general, riding into Rome with the vanquished foe marching behind him. Here, however, this image is not used in exactly the same way. R. Martin says, 'The Greek word rendered "leads us in triumph" is often used without any idea of triumph, as meaning, "display publicly, make known." With this meaning the first picture joins up neatly with the second. 'Thanks be to God who displays us publicly in Christ and makes known the fragrance of the knowledge of Christ.'[45]

If we apply this image of triumphant entry to Paul, he is almost certainly referring to the effectiveness of his ministry in Asia, where he has preached the gospel. While the Corinthians and the false apostles saw him as 'a loser,' his perspective is different. In contrast his opponents thought of themselves as triumphant because of their superior spirituality. While they basked in the glory of being self-sufficient, Paul draws their attention to his outlook as an apostle when he says: 'Who is sufficient for these things?' A reminder of his inadequacy and weakness, but also of the power of God.

The use of the metaphor, 'the fragrance of the knowledge of Christ,' is a striking image that describes the ministry of Paul. However, there is a double meaning concerning 'fragrance.' 'Paul spells this out in the words which literally mean "a stench from death itself to the dying, and a fragrance from life itself to the living." The tragedy of the gospel is that it is both attractive and repulsive.'[46] The fragrance of Christ is an evocative metaphor, that is an integral aspect of Paul's philosophy of ministry.

As I look back on my early days as a young teenager, the 'fragrance of Christ' evokes happy memories of our Christian leaders at All Souls Clubhouse, affiliated to All Souls Church, Langham Place, in the west end of London. Their love and friendship was infused with the fragrance of the personality of Christ. There was something attractive about them – it was the fragrance of Christ. We could sense the presence of Christ that filled their lives, and which permeated the atmosphere of our youth club. I cannot pay a higher compliment to them, because the 'fragrance of Christ' they were sharing with us was transparent and contagious.

Following on from Paul's image of the fragrance of Christ, he alludes to the fact that the false apostles came with letters of commendation that impressed them, from the Jerusalem church. This enabled them to exact a fee for the ministry they performed. The inference here is that they were taking advantage of the Corinthians, and although they may have been preaching about Christ, to a greater extent they were commending themselves. But Paul does nothing of the sort. The implication is that appearances can be deceptive, and ministry can be superficial, when it is not flowing from a deep commitment to exalt Christ.

TREASURE IN EARTHEN VESSELS

At the beginning of 2 Corinthians 4, Paul continues to defend his ministry, and at the same time draws attention to the philosophy of ministry the 'superlative apostles' practice. He does this by stating the principles on which his ministry is based: 'We have renounced disgraceful, underhanded ways: we refuse to tamper with God's word, but by the open statement of truth we would commend ourselves to every man's conscience in the sight of God' – 4: 2. Here he draws attention to the importance of the character and integrity, that is required in Christian ministers. They are not to abuse their privilege of serving the Lord and his people. To fully appreciate the impact this passage and 2 Corinthians made as a whole, we have to remember that Paul's letter was read out aloud to the entire church, when they assembled to worship. So not only are the Corinthians being corrected and rebuked, the false apostles are hearing the same message as well. This was unquestionably a challenging message, to the entire Christian community at Corinth.

Paul's continues his policy of being open with the Corinthians, and expands on the theme of ministering from a position of weakness. So he says in 4: 7-12:

> But we have this treasure in earthen vessels to show that the transcendent power belongs to God and not to us. We are afflicted in every way, but not crushed: perplexed but not driven to despair: persecuted but not forsaken: struck down but not destroyed: always carrying in the body the death of

Jesus, so that the life of Jesus may also be manifested in our bodies. For while we live we are always being given up to death for Jesus' sake, so that the life of Jesus may be manifested in our mortal flesh. So death is at work in us but life in you.

This is a magnificent passage of sublime rhetoric, as well as the most profound theology of ministry. Here we need to pause, and reverently grasp, that this is a paradigm of ministry, that replicates the pattern of the cross of Christ. Paul wants the Corinthians to realise, that authentic ministry is not only self-effacing and from a position of weakness – but cross-shaped too. This is the pattern of ministry that points people to Christ, that glorifies God and is empowered by the Holy Spirit. R. Kent Hughes says:

> This is one of the grand rhetorical moments in Paul's writings. Each paradox is smooth in its polish and balance and follows the same pattern hinging on the identical emphatic adversative 'but not.' And the paradoxes together present an ascending intensity of weakness countered with power.[47]

M. Harris comments on Paul's afflictions, in a way that helps us to identify with them in contemporary ministry. 'This can refer to physical, psychological, or spiritual pressure or affliction. Perhaps it occurs first in the list, precisely because it is the most comprehensive term available, to denote any type of distress or tribulation. Although troubles pressed on Paul from every quarter, he never found himself crushed or cornered...Because the power of God was active in preserving his life and spirit.'[48]

Once again in these verses Paul wants to reiterate the basis of his ministry. He clearly, and unambiguously, wants them to grasp what the essence of a Christ centred ministry is, so he categorically and unapologetically keeps on making the same point. In our weakness God will manifest his power. In our afflictions, in our perplexity, in our despair and in our persecution, the resurrection life of Jesus will deliver, renew, strengthen and uphold us. Here Hughes says, 'The extent of God's power is such that it overcomes and transcends all of man's weakness: the former is not merely sufficient to counter-balance the latter, but also goes beyond and far exceeds it. Indeed, as Paul perceives, there is a particular purpose behind the almost incredible contrast between the brilliance of the treasure and the meanness of the vessel, namely, that the surplus or excess of power may be, that is, may be apparent as being of God and not from himself,'[49] These truths also speaks to ministers and Christians down the centuries, and are also the touchstone for our ministry.

Our frailty, our inadequacy and our weaknesses as servants of Christ, allow the Lord to manifest his power and strength through us. We have this 'treasure in earthen vessels,' shows that the transcendent power belongs to God. The treasure is the knowledge of Christ. The truth is we are fragile, we are vulnerable, we are weak. The truth is the power that raised Jesus from the dead, is the very same power that resides in us. The life of the risen Jesus is our source of deliverance and spiritual renewal, time and time and time again. M. Harris says, 'Such vessels were regarded as fragile and as expendable, because they were cheap and often unattractive. So the paradox Paul is expressing, is that although the container is relatively worthless, the contents are priceless...It is precisely because the proclaimers of the gospel are in themselves frail and fragile, relatively insignificant and unattractive, that people clearly recognise the transforming power of the gospel is God's alone...Because the gospel treasure has been entrusted to frail mortals who lack inherent power, the power displayed through preaching and in suffering, is demonstrably divine and not human.'[50]

Possibly some confusion may arise from Paul's emphasis on being fragile, vulnerable and weak. Clearly he is not advocating that we are to be whimps. He is not saying that we have to be insipid spineless Christians. Rather, he shares his weaknesses in this passage, to help us to have the right foundations for ministry, and in effect he challenges our philosophy of ministry. How self-reliant are we? How do we cope when we face insurmountable problems? What do we when we feel inadequate and vulnerable? Is our trust in ourselves and our ability, or are we relying on and trusting the Lord?

Paul wanted to teach the proud Corinthians, who liked to impress others with how deeply spiritual they were, that their attitude and outlook on ministry was un-Christ like. He wanted them to realise that from God's perspective, it was acceptable to be vulnerable or weak, or even not very impressive. Because that allowed the Lord to demonstrate his power more effectively through them. The same is true for us. When we are afflicted in every way – we will not be crushed. When we are perplexed – we will not be driven to despair. When we are persecuted – we will not be forsaken. When we are struck down – we will not be destroyed: because the life of Jesus renews, strengthens and sustains us. Our difficulties are God opportunities to manifest his power. M. Harris has this to say about these four contrasting examples:

> When these four pairs of antithesis are read, as they might be, as illustrations of the thematic statement in v. 7, it is clear that in Paul's estimation, this 'hardship catalogue' demonstrates, not his virtuous character or his buoyant self-sufficiency or his steadfast courage amid adversity, but his utter dependence as a frail human being in the superlative excellence of God's power. Also it was not a case of divine power revealing itself as a weakness transcending and replacing human weakness, but of divine power being experienced in the midst of human weakness.[51]

D. Dales also perceives God's perspective on Paul's afflictions, and what he accomplishes through them. 'The frailty of human life indwelt by the Spirit is emphasised. So too is the "power of God" at work through a Christian flowing out of the vessel in weakness. For through man, God reaches out to man, and the reaction is that which assailed the true Light when he came into the world…The assault is relentless – perplexity may obscure one's vision of faith, hope and love, and of the will of God in a situation, but it will not end in utter despair though it may drive one very near to it…Things may happen which throw a person and strike him down physically or emotionally, by way of circumstances or relationships, or by some subtle means of spiritual opposition, but the outcome will prove in the end not to be destructive, despite the clear intention of the antagonist.'[52] We will not necessarily have to go through the extreme difficulties or suffering Paul went through, although on occasions we will invariably face situations that stretch us to the limit and beyond. The challenge is to tenaciously put our trust in the Lord – and not in ourselves. And through our strengths and our weaknesses, the lesson is to rely on the Lord and his power, and to ensure that our philosophy of ministry is firmly rooted in God and Christ.

THE LIFE OF JESUS IN US

The allegorical concept, of 'always carrying in the body the death of Jesus so that the life of Jesus may also be manifested in us,'– 2 Cor. 4: 10 is connected to all the afflictions Paul has just been describing. This also alludes to a mystical union with Christ, and he uses this imagery to show that as a servant there is a participation in the ongoing ministry of Christ. His afflictions are an extension of the sufferings of Christ, and his ministry reflects Christ's, because it is sacrificial in the sense he is giving of himself: and giving involves dying to oneself on behalf of those he is serving. This is a paradigm of ministry modelled on the theology of the cross. The outcome is that the Corinthians benefit from this – 4: 12, 'so death is at work in us but life in you.'

This union with Christ, can also be seen from the perspective, that Christ shares our afflictions and hardships. Through being united to him by his Spirit, Christ manifests his resurrection life and power in our lives and bodies. 'Paul is speaking of something more than example. Between master and follower there is a certain unity of experience and destiny. There is an inclusiveness in the latter of the former.'[53] M. Harris sees this from a slightly different perspective, when he says, 'In this verse then – 4: 11, Paul is making two important affirmations regarding Christian experience. First, the resurrection life of Jesus is evident at precisely the same time, as there is a "carrying around" of his dying. Indeed, the very purpose of the believer's identification with Jesus in his sufferings, is to provide an opportunity for the display of Jesus' risen life. Second, one and the same physical body is the place where the sufferings of Jesus are repeated, and where his risen power is manifested.'[54]

This implies that we are doing something on Christ's behalf by identifying with him in his suffering, so that he can manifest his life and power through us. This stops short of emphatically stating that it is precisely because we are united to Christ that this happens. The stronger interpretation of the text is that there is an indissoluble union between Christ and his servants. Christ is in us and with us and united to us by his Spirit. Through this mystical union we are partakers of the death and resurrection of Jesus and all that means: and through our union with Christ, he also shares in all our afflictions and hardships. Although the text does not specifically say this, D. Dales perceives, 'Paul's belief is that despite appearances and feelings at the time, behind the blows of evil (afflictions), lies the burnishing and transforming hand of God himself, bringing the full weight of his own glory, to bear on the person whom he is refashioning after the likeness of his Son.'[55]

Commenting on 4: 10-11, M. Hooker speaks of an 'interchange' of experience amongst Christians, when she says, 'Dying with Christ involves real suffering. But this "dying" leads not only to a future life with Christ, but to an experience of life in the present also – a life which, though revealed through Paul's dying, is being experienced in the lives of the Corinthians. Once again, we see that the pattern of "interchange" between Christ and the believer, is extended to include an interchange between the apostle and his converts. How can this be? It is because Paul and his co-workers are conformed to the pattern of Christ, and are "your slaves for Jesus" sake (4: 5). It is because, like Christ, they are prepared to die in order that others may live. Sharing daily in Christ's sufferings, they bring life – his life – to the Corinthians.'[56]

Paul's writes on this theme, to counter the pseudo-superficial and triumphant spirituality of the false apostles, that had influenced the Corinthian church. They interpreted their life in Jesus – the life of Jesus the vine that flows through us – John 15, in the wrong way.

He shows them that the life of Christ that flows through us and that nurtures and sustains us, is earthed in the reality of our afflictions and hardships. The life of Jesus does not elevate us to an esoteric triumphant dimension, that is disconnected from the reality of everyday life.

'For while we live, we are always being given up to death for Jesus' sake, so that the life of Jesus may be made visible in our mortal flesh' – 4: 10-11. O'Connor has this to say about this text:

> This extraordinary statement is the summit of 2 Corinthians, and the most profound insight ever articulated as to the meaning of suffering, and the nature of authentic ministry. Death shadowed Paul's every step, he could die at any moment. As he headed towards a fate which seemed inevitable, he saw his life as "a "dying," which he identified with that of Jesus, who had also foreseen his death." Paul also accepted the responsibility of being Jesus for his converts. The explicitness of this presentation of the minister as an "alter Christus" – is unique in the New Testament. It was forced on Paul by the spirit-people/Judaizers' denial of the reality of Jesus' terrestrial existence, and their disappointment of Paul's ministry.[57]

THE MINISTRY OF RECONCILIATION

The heart of Paul's ministry in 2 Cor. 5: 11-20, is 'reconciliation.' Unquestionably, this is another skillful and sublime piece of rhetoric, that displays a masterful summary of the heart of Paul's gospel and his philosophy of ministry. These verses also contain subtle nuances, that draw a comparison between his ministry and that of the false apostles – his opponents. Moreover, this text shows the apostle's genius of succinctly summarising, complex theological truths.

The train of Paul's thought in these verses, is the comparison he makes between himself and his opponents. In verse 11 he shares the motivation of his ministry – 'the fear of the Lord' and seeking 'to persuade' others. He renounces the ulterior motives of his opponents, who boast about outward appearances whereas the Lord looks at the heart – verse 12. He clearly states that his motives are controlled and shaped by the love of Christ, and that his spirituality is christocentric rather than self-centred.

Paul's opponents have influenced the Corinthian Christians to view him from a human perspective. He challenges this when he says, 'From now on therefore we regard no one from a human point of view. Even though we once regarded Christ in this way' – 5: 16. He now has a new perspective on Christ – because he is a new creation in Christ – 5: 17. Paul then states the heart of his gospel, 'All this is from God who through Christ reconciled us to himself and gave us the ministry of reconciliation: that is, in Christ God was reconciling the world to himself – Therefore, we are ambassadors for Christ, God making his appeal through us. We implore you therefore on behalf of Christ, be reconciled to God' – 5: 18-20. Paul's skillful use of language draws the Corinthians' attention to the divisive ministry of his opponents, who had succeeded in alienating them from the apostle. Whereas authentic Christian ministry bears the hallmark of reconciliation. In effect, Paul hits the Corinthians and his opponents, with the equivalent of a 'theological sledge hammer'– 'We implore you on behalf of Christ be reconciled to God.' Here, he stops them in their tracks, because they thought they had arrived spiritually and were reigning. But, once again they need to be reconciled to God, because their arrogant spirituality has alienated them from him. This is clearly a bold and challenging exhortation that reflects his authority.

In this context Paul's easiest course of action was arguably to let the Corinthians get on with it. He could have left them to it, and saved himself a considerable amount of heartache by saying, 'When you've had enough of these superlative apostles look me up.' But it was not his style of ministry to ignore problems or live in denial of them. He accepted his responsibility as a minister, and was aware that one day he would appear before Christ (verse 10) and give an account of his ministry. In this context his underlying motivation was 'the fear of the Lord. 'Along with 5: 8-9, this verse illustrates the fact that Paul's actions were guided and his ambitions moulded by doctrinal convictions.'[58] Hughes further elaborates on this theme, 'Paul himself has a deep consciousness of the awe which should be inspired in the heart of every servant, who will be required to give an account of his stewardship to his master. The recollection of this fact fills him with a wholesome reverence for his divine Master.'[59]

Paul states his genuineness in God's sight and says the Corinthians should be proud of him and his associates. With a clever linguistic tack, he suggests that they should boast about him to his opponents, who pride themselves on how outwardly impressive they are. Then he deftly adds, 'For if we are beside ourselves it is for God: if we are in our right minds it is for you. For the love of Christ controls us' – 5: 13-14. This acts as a parody that contrasts the ecstatic spirituality of his opponents, and their use of spiritual gifts and speaking in tongues. This elucidates his philosophy of ministry that bears the imprint of the love of Christ – and insinuates that his opponents' ulterior motives are purely self-centred.

The implication is that the love of Christ is such an irresistible force, that those who experience it have their motives transformed. M. Harris says, 'the love of Christ has a sense of compulsion and constraint. It is a love that completely dominates and overwhelms. It is a love that restrains us from self-seeking…The rendering that best captures this dual notion of constraint and restraint is 'controls us.'[60] In verse 15 in contrast to this love, Paul draws attention to the selfish motives of his opponents, and asserts that because Christ died Christians are no longer to live for themselves. 'The intended result of the death of Christ was the Christian's renunciation of self-seeking and self-pleasing, and the pursuit of a Christ centred life filled with action for the benefit of others, as was Christ's life.'[61]

Towards the end of chapter five, almost halfway through his letter, Paul shares with the Corinthians the heartbeat of his ministry as an apostle. After his conversion he was a 'new creation.' His life was 'made new' by Christ, and he now viewed Christ and others in a new way. Christ was now the lens of a new perspective that shaped his ministry. He shares this at a strategic point with his opponents' ministry in mind and says, 'From now on, therefore, we regard no one from a human point of view. Even though we once regarded Christ in this way, we regard him thus no longer' – 5: 16. A clear implication that the Corinthians' perspective about Paul has been faulty, ever since his opponents arrived on the scene. But he, of all people, understands their faulty perspective, because he himself once viewed Christ in exactly the same way. Paul's new outlook flowed from the truth, 'if anyone is in Christ he is a new creation' – 5: 17. 'A new attitude towards Jesus Christ, prompts a new outlook on those for whom Christ died. When we come to share God's view of Christ, we also gain his view of people in general...Paul implies that a change of attitude towards Christ brings about a change of attitude towards other people – when a person becomes a Christian they experience a total restructuring of life.'[62]

Therefore, at the heart of Paul's gospel and his philosophy of ministry, is the message of reconciliation. This is a predominant concept and truth in his theology. Like much of his theology, it was formed in the crucible of his own personal encounter and experience of Christ. He clearly sees God's perspective on this issue, when he says, 'God took the initiative to reconcile man to himself' – 5: 18-19. In Pauline theology, reconciliation reveals how God's relationship with humanity is possible. God accepted Christ's death and shed blood as the way of reconciliation. Our sin cut us off and alienated us from God and Christ's death was his means of reconciling us to himself. P. Barnett helpfully shares two ideas, that appear to be in Paul's mind in relation to Christ's death for others – representation and substitution. 'In 5: 20 "ambassadors for Christ" points to the image of representation, whereas in we "beseech you on behalf of Christ," the stronger concept is substitution. When he says in 5: 15, "Christ died for all" – he is portrayed as our representative. When he says in 5: 21, "God made Christ to be sin who knew no sin" – the image is of substitution.'[63]

Reconciliation is the heartbeat of the apostle's gospel. 'This is one of Paul's greatest passages in which after affirming what Christ means to him – 5: 11-15, he goes on to trace out the nature of his ministry. Seeing Christ in a new way has given him a new understanding of ministry. "As a Christian, Paul sees everything from a new angle, and in particular, he so sees Christ. This new vision has worked itself out since his conversion... Those who preach reconciliation must themselves practice it.'[64] This is precisely what Paul was doing in his relationship with the Corinthian Christians. Again we see a contrast between his authentic ministry and that of his opponents. Their ministry was characterised by pride, division and fragmentation, and their concern to make a name for themselves. In these verses Paul skillfully and succinctly summarises his gospel, and shows that his opponents message is false. His bold assertion about reconciliation in 5: 20, 'We implore you on behalf of Christ be reconciled to God' – may well have been greeted with stunned silence by the Corinthians, as its implication began to dawn on them.

At this stage in the life of the Church of England, the ministry of reconciliation has a defining role in shaping the direction and formation of the Church, in the 21st century. Especially when we reflect upon the controversial and divisive issues of homo-sexuality and women priests, and their becoming bishops in the future. Many antagonistic, unchristian and contentious things have been said by both sides, who understandably have strong feelings and deep seated beliefs about their opposing convictions. It appears that these issues cannot be resolved at the level of church politics, because peoples' beliefs and their wounds are too deeply ingrained, for these things to be resolved in this way.

The heart of the matter is theological, and the twin themes that dominate these issues, are the authority of Scripture and what people believe God's Word, and hence God himself say about these things. The other truth that affects how these issues are approached, debated and resolved, is that of the ministry of reconciliation. This challenges peoples' opposing attitudes and beliefs, strongly held convictions and feelings. Reconciliation is a neglected truth at the heart of the gospel, and of the ministry of Christ and the Church. The challenge for our leaders, is how to authoritatively declare God's truth on these issues: and to do so in a manner that is shaped by the challenge of the cross of Christ crucified – that still sounds forth the clarion call of reconciliation. This undoubtedly demands of everyone, a greater degree of spiritual maturity and meekness, than has previously been displayed. In this light, I have reproduced some of what I shared in my first book in 2003 in, 'The Priest & The People Of God' about the ministry of reconciliation.

M. Volf points out, 'Christ's stance on the cross is not to let humanity remain an enemy, but creates space in himself for the enemy to come in. The cross says despite humanity's vast enmity towards God, we still belong to God, and the cross is a symbol of God's desire to break the power of human enmity without violence: and to receive human beings into divine communion – reconciliation.'[65] He sees the divine initiative and willingness to embrace the enemy, on and through the cross, as undoubtedly a scandal.

> For the cross offers us outstretched arms. A naked body with a pierced side. Christ is the victim who has refused to be defined by the perpetrator, who forgives and makes space in himself for the enemy.[66]

Volf roots this inclusive embrace of reconciliation for humanity, 'as now being inseparably joined to the Trinity in the Eucharist. This ritual time when we celebrate this divine "making-space-for-us-and-inviting-us-in." He believes that we would profoundly misunderstand the Eucharist, if we thought of it only as a sacrament of God's embrace, of which we are merely recipients. Instead, written on the very heart of God's grace, is the rule that what happens to us must be done by us, and therefore having been embraced by God we must make space for others in ourselves and invite them in, even our enemies. This is what we enact when we celebrate the Eucharist.'[67]

The formation of the people of God as ministers of reconciliation, flows from the grace of God and is a gift of the Trinity. For most people reconciliation goes against their natural tendency for revenge, and too often Christians have attitudes and prejudices, which exclude rather than include others. Wound rather than heal. Divide rather than reconcile. The first step in becoming ministers of reconciliation is the conviction by the Trinity of our own need of reconciliation, with one another, and with God. Only then can we be ministers of reconciliation in the Church, and in the local community. The joy of being reconciled to the Trinity and others, is indeed at the heart of the gospel, and at the heart of being an authentic Eucharistic community.

STRENGTH IN WEAKNESS

In 2 Corinthians 11-12, Paul embarks on what is commonly referred to as 'the Fool's Discourse.' This reaches its climax when he shares the Lord's perspective on his weaknesses: 'My grace is sufficient for you for my strength is made perfect in weakness' – 12: 9. Chapters 11-12 are a complex and skillful passage of rhetoric and it is almost impossible to interpret these accurately, unless we are familiar with the rhetorical style of secular boasting that was used in Paul's day.

B. Witherington helpfully points out – 'throughout chapters 10-13, Paul is attacking the conventions of self-advertisement, for which the Sophist speakers of rhetorical wisdom were noted. As he believed his converts were endangered by his opponents, it was obligatory for him to resort to pathos, irony, invective, sarcasm and parody to make an impression on them. Ancient conventions involving matters of honour and shame, boasting and self-promotion necessitated this approach.

Self-admiration and self-praise, were de rigeur in Graeco-Roman Society, especially for those who wanted to raise their social status and social evaluation in the eyes of others. More to the point, self-praise was a primary characteristic of popular teachers of the day… In chapter 10, Paul is attacking those who use Sophistic rhetoric and its methods of evaluating speeches and people, and he is using rhetoric to do so. The opponents had put him in a difficult position. As E. A. Judge puts it, Paul "found himself a reluctant and unwelcomed competitor in the field of professional sophistry and…he promoted a deliberate collision with its standards and values.'

The key to grasping the real character of his argument, is recognising Paul's anti-Sophistic approach to self praise. He is attempting to follow the conventions in regard to inoffensive boasting, so that his audience will understand that he was not boasting beyond limits, indeed that he is boasting tongue-in-cheek. He follows the basic rule, that he will only boast of what God has done in and through him, and not of his own personal accomplishments...Throughout this whole section Paul is answering his opponents, but addressing the answer to the Corinthians because he cares about them...He is saying that his opponents have been building up a wall between himself and his converts, and that he must now demolish it. This fits with the idea that that this letter's function, is to remove obstacles to reconciliation between Paul and his people, and so between the Corinthians and the truth of God.'[68]

In chapters 10-11, Paul is writing tongue-in-cheek and mocking the claims of his opponents. In this context he is defending his philosophy of ministry that is 'servant shaped' like Christ's. One that is marked by afflictions and suffering, that was incongruous to the triumphant style of ministry, the false apostles boasted about. 'In chapter 10 Paul established his "bragging rights" – the issue is fundamentally theological. In whom does one place one's trust and confidence? In whom may one properly boast? Now the characteristic feature of this discourse is its irony. However, A. B. Spencer suggests, "that one should be careful not to characterise Paul's tone here as sarcastic, but rather as sardonic, for it is not sneering, caustic, or taunting but full of pathos over the apparent inconsistencies in his life.'[69]

Paul begins chapter 11 by saying, 'I wish you would bear with me in a little foolishness. Do bear with me!' Instead of turning out to be the fool, they and his opponents made him out to be, the irony that will dawn on them is that they are the ones who have been foolish – because they have been duped by his opponents. He says in 11: 2-4:

> I feel a divine jealousy for you, for I betrothed you to Christ
> to present you a pure bride to her one husband. But I am
> afraid that as the serpent deceived Eve by his cunning, your
> thoughts will be led astray from a sincere devotion and a

pure devotion to Christ. For if someone comes and preaches another Jesus than the one we preached, or if you receive a different spirit from the one you received, or if you accept a different gospel from the one you accepted, you submit to it readily enough.

Without realising it, the Corinthian Christians have been deceived, and fooled by the prospect of a more triumphant interpretation of the gospel. The prevailing Corinthian spirit of self-advancement and self-glorification was much more appealing to them. So subversive had the false apostles been, that the Christians had been fooled into believing, that Paul was the one who was being cunning – 2 Cor. 12: 16. D. A. Carson concurs and says:

> Christians are especially open to the kind of cunning deceit that combines the language of faith and religion, with the content of self-interest and flattery…We like to have our Christianity shaped less by the cross than by triumphalism, or rules, or charismatic leaders, or subjective experiences.

Paul feared that through Satanic deception the Corinthians would fall to three delusions: 'another Jesus' a 'different spirit' and a 'different gospel.'[70] Displaying all his rhetorical skill, once again he cannot contain his comments about them readily changing their allegiance to a false Jesus – a false Spirit and – a false gospel.

When we reach 11: 19 Paul sarcastically says, 'Since you are so wise, you will no doubt gladly put up with fools.' They will soon realise just how foolish they have been, by allowing these false apostles to take advantage of them and exert control over them. In this context he defends himself, by boasting-tongue-in-cheek about his catalogue of impressive afflictions – that they would have sneered at. Paul then compounds his apparent foolishness, by going over the top in what he boasts about in chapter 11.

P. Barnett points out, 'It is probable that Paul's speech in the "Fools Discourse," mirrors, so at to parody and also correct, the claims of the newly arrived false apostles. From what appear to be his responses to them, his opponents "boasted of:" (1) their Jewish heritage – 11: 22, (2) their accomplishments that accredited them as ministers of Christ – 11: 23, and (3) extraordinary "visions and revelations" – 12: 24. It is quite likely that they pointed to Paul's evident misfortunes and humiliations, in the pursuit of his ministry, as signs of inferiority and incompetence.'[71]

Paul compares his array of suffering, to that of his opponents, and insists he has emulated them. He concludes his unorthodox reason for boasting, by alluding to his abundance of visions and revelations, he then chooses not to boast about – ch. 12. Then he completes his catalogue of afflictions, by making his thorn in the flesh his supreme boast. This was tantamount to ridiculing his opponents. Although what they may have found even more foolish, was that Paul welcomed his suffering when he says in 12: 10:

> For the sake of Christ then, I am content with weaknesses, insults, hardships, persecutions and calamities. For when I am weak then I am strong.

We can imagine that his opponents found his reasons for boasting were absurd, and they may have felt he was mocking them. They may have been caught off guard, and perplexed by his claims, being convinced that he was after all a fool. Quite possibly he may have outmanoeuvred them, by his outrageous tactic to boast about his weaknesses. Clearly, what they and the Corinthians failed to comprehend, is that God's wisdom is at odds with the world's perception of what is considered wise. They failed to grasp the implications of Paul's theology of the cross – that God's saving power was manifest through the apparent helplessness, humiliation and weakness of the death of Christ. And that the power of the gospel, was also demonstrated and revealed through human weakness – especially his.

We have already seen in a previous chapter, that there is a diversity of opinion about what Paul's thorn in the flesh was. However, whatever it was is not the most important thing. P. Barnett echoes this when he says, 'The very anonymity of this particular affliction, has been productive of far wider blessing than would have been the case, had it been possible to identify the specific nature of the disability.'[72] What is important, is that when Paul asked the Lord on three specific occasions, to remove this thorn, he accepted without reservation his refusal to do so. He didn't ask for an abundance of visions and revelations. He certainly didn't ask for a thorn. He didn't ask for it to remain. He also didn't ask for grace to cope with it. But God in his wisdom – chose to give him all of these.

What aligns our afflictions and our thorns with Paul's is that we also can choose to serve the Lord. The bottom line is we can also place ourselves in God's hands, as his servants, for him to use as he so chooses. As we submit to Christ's Lordship and the afflictions that may well result in our thorn, in turn Christ will sustain us through his grace and empower us in our weakness. This reflects Paul's view on the matter, which E. Best expresses. 'Paul realised its (his thorn's) true purpose, and he was now able to see his "rapture" in a truer perspective. There was nothing in it to boast about for he had no way earned it, God had given it, just as he had given the thorn…It was Paul's weakness in respect to the thorn in the flesh, about which he could do nothing, that led him to allow God in with his strength. Once he had learned, that the weakness which came from the messenger of Satan could be born with God's strength, he learned something he could apply to all the weaknesses which afflicted him.'[73]

In recent years, as I have looked back on one or two weaknesses the Lord has allowed to evolve in my life, I am aware that the Lord could have easily prevented them from developing. But, as we know, the Lord uses what we go through to mould us and prepare us for what is ahead. Moreover, through them the Lord can draw us closer to himself and teach us to rely on him in a much deeper way, as we avail ourselves of his grace in our lives. Hughes similarly echoes the profound work of God's grace in Paul's life, when he says, 'The weaknesses which Paul welcomed were not self-induced: they were given to him, and with them was given also grace sufficient for him to triumph through a power not his own, and to rejoice, because Christ instead of self was being glorified. The apostle seems to have in mind a picture of the power of Christ descending upon him, and taking its abode in the frail tabernacle of his body.'[74]

A focus on Paul's thorn in the flesh and Christ's strength shown through his weakness, captures the essence of Paul's philosophy of ministry. This challenges Christians down the centuries, to have a ministry that is Christ centred and cruciform. Just as the Corinthians were inclined to impress others and longed for others to be impressed by them, Christians are often similarly inclined. But, we like them also have a choice to make. The choice is Christ's way – the way of the cross and weakness – or our own way. The paradox we are confronted with, is that Christ's power is most fully evidenced through weakness – not through our own self-sufficiency and strength. M. Harris echoes a similar sentiment when he says:

> It is 'in the midst of "weakness" that Christ's power reaches its plentitude: "weakness" is the sphere where his power is revealed. It is precisely when or whenever Paul is weak that he experiences Christ's power. His enabling strength cannot operate without a prior confession of weakness and need. If self-sufficiency is claimed, Christ's power will be neither sought nor experienced. But if weakness is recognised, his power will be sought and granted. Then it will operate at the same time as the weakness, and find unhindered scope in the presence of that weakness.[75]

The theme of power in weakness is raised by Paul throughout 2 Corinthians, and this is something that R. Kent Hughes comments on: 'Power in weakness therefore' runs like a thread throughout the letter, reaching its most powerful expression here – 2 Cor 12: 9-10 – power in weakness is shorthand for the cross of Christ. In God's plan of redemption, there had to be weakness (crucifixion), before there was power (resurrection). Paul came to understand and embrace the fact that his thorn in the flesh, was essential to ongoing weakness and the experience of Christ's ongoing power.'[76]

P. Barnett has the last word on strength in weakness, and in effect he says, 'Paul shared with them a revelatory story – without a revelation, and a healing story – without a healing...The verses about Paul's thorn express a supreme paradox. A painful "skolops" whatever it actually was, was "given" to Paul, and that by God!

Paradoxically, God is the invisible source of this suffering in the life of Paul his child and minister. The words of the Lord spoken to Paul then are universally applicable. They do not, however, call for resignation which is passive and impersonal, but for acceptance which is active and obedient to the Lord.'[77]

CHAPTER SEVEN

PASTOR AND THEOLOGIAN

BACKGROUND TO THESSALONICA

'Thessalonica was a well-established city with a long history, founded in the 4th century BC by Cassander. He was an officer in Alexander the Great's army, and named it after his wife who was Alexander's half-sister. This influential city was situated on what is now the Gulf of Salonica, and built in the form of an amphitheatre, on the slopes at the head of the bay. It was also the largest and most important city in Macedonia where many roads met, and occupied a strategic position, as it boasted a good natural harbour at the head of the Thermaic Gulf. The great Via Egnatia, the Roman highway to the East passed through it. This was the main route between Rome and the East, and Thessalonica became the capital of the Roman province of Macedonia. Lightfoot described it as, "the key to the whole of Macedonia" and added that "it narrowly escaped being made the capital of the world." Today as Thessaloniki, it is the second most important city in Greece.'[1]

As a result of the vision of the man from Macedonia in Acts 16, Paul turned his back on Asia, and concluded the Lord had called them to preach the gospel there. With his companions Luke, Silas and Timothy, he preached the gospel at Philippi and established a church there, but their mission ended abruptly with a public flogging and a near riot and imprisonment. Having arrived at Thessalonica, as was his custom, Paul went to the synagogue and reasoned with the Jews, that Jesus was the Christ – Acts 17. Some believed and among them were a great many devout Greeks and some leading ladies – 17: 4. However, some of the Jews were jealous of Paul's success, formed a mob and dragged the Christians before the city authorities. As a result he had to leave the city.

Paul then goes to Berea and speaks about Christ in the synagogue, where the Jews were more noble and eagerly received the word of God – Acts 17: 11. But when word got back to Thessalonica about his success, Jews came from there and created a disturbance. Again he had to leave and from there went to Athens and then to Corinth. L. Morris says, 'We have every reason for thinking that Paul was a discouraged man when he came to Corinth. Fanatical opponents had brought about his forcible ejection, from three successive preaching places. In each case just when it seemed he had met with success. After that he had gone to Athens the capital of Greece, and had been met by mockery. In later days he recalled that he had arrived at Corinth, "in weakness and in much fear and trembling" – 1 Cor. 2: 3. But not long after this, Silas and Timothy came to Paul from Macedonia bringing news of his converts there. They told him that despite all the difficulties, the new believers were standing firm and their good reports encouraged him. "He saw his setbacks in the right perspective, and realised afresh that God was with him – and he received new strength.'[2]

D. Wenham adds, 'Paul had been very anxious for the Thessalonian Christians having founded the church there, but having had to leave these young Christians because of fierce and violent opposition. Not surprisingly he was anxious for his children in the faith hoping that they were surviving. He had wanted to return to them, "but Satan stopped us" – 1 Thess. 2: 18, (presumably it just wasn't safe). So when he could bear the suspense no longer Paul sent Timothy to find out how they were. Now Timothy has returned with good news.'[3] The pastoral heart of Paul shines through in these verses, along with the fact that he is also somewhat of a 'soft touch' when it comes to these young Christians. J. Stott also perceives this human side to him when he says, '1 & 2 Thessalonians reveal the authentic Paul. Not that he is ever inauthentic. But sometimes the human Paul is obscured by his apostolic office and authority.'[4]

Paul was moved as he remembered how the Thessalonian Christians accepted the gospel of Christ, and despite opposition they received the word 'in much affliction with the joy of the Holy Spirit'– 1 Thess. 1: 6. W. Hendriksen says, 'they had welcomed the word with Spirit-wrought joy.'[5] There had been considerable opposition to Paul's preaching about Christ crucified, but the Holy Spirit honoured this so much, that the new converts were overjoyed and thoroughly impervious to the antagonism that followed. So it is not surprising that they had a special place in the apostle's heart. R. Mayhue says, 'Paul makes a point to describe the pressure as intense and frequent. Apparently, these assaults increased with the passing of time 2 Thess. 1: 4-6.'[6]

Paul combines the rare gift of writing his theology through the lens of his brilliant mind, that is tempered by his pastoral heart. He has achieved a harmonious balance between his emotions and intellect. (This is something the Old Testament prophets accomplished, when they combined God's truth with the passion of their hearts, for the Lord and his people). As we see Paul had a very rich emotional life, that was complemented by a theologically creative intellect. Here he gets carried away and writes with an adolescent eagerness, and a tender attachment for the Thessalonian Christians.

TENDER LIKE A MOTHER

In Paul's first letter to the Thessalonians, in 2: 7-12, he uses the image of mother and father to describe his ministry, and that of Silvanus and Timothy. These two images describe their relationships with these Christians, in terms of affection and close familial bonds. In this maternal and paternal manner, they were able to nurture the young Christians' faith at Thessalonica. C. Cocksworth, mentions Gregory the Great's, 'On The Pastoral Charge,' in which he also uses the images of mother and father for the priest - minister. 'Gregory talks of the capacity of mothers to give birth and to nurture life.'[7] An appropriate analogy for Paul and his associates, in their relationship with the Thessalonian Christians. He also points out that Gregory the Great, 'Speaks of the priest – minister, as someone who has a mother's bosom, and who can "wash away by the comfort of exhortation and the tears of prayer," the troubles that overwhelm their charges.'[8]

In 1 Thess: 2: 7-8 we read:

> But we were gentle among you, like a nurse taking care of her children. So being affectionately desirous of you, we were ready to share with you not only the gospel of God but also our very own selves, because you had become very dear to us.

Clearly, one of the characteristic features of the ministry of Paul and his associates, was gentleness. Knowing how aggressive he was before his conversion, we can only marvel at this Christ-like quality that he now displays. For all his stridency in defending Christian truth from false teachers, he shows the ability to conduct affectionate and tender relationships with the Thessalonians, as indeed he also did with the Philippian Church. Moreover, in writing to correct the Christians at Galatia we see Paul's maternal instinct when he says, 'My little children with whom I am again in travail, until Christ is formed in you' – Gal. 4: 19. As we see how these young Thessalonian Christians were very dear to Paul and his associates, we can discern that this was a reflection of how precious they were to the Lord. In effect they were reflecting the Lord's heart towards them. J. Stott comments, 'It is a lovely thing that a man as tough and masculine as the apostle should have used this feminine metaphor. Some Christian leaders become both self-centred and autocratic...We all need to cultivate more in our pastoral ministry, the gentleness, love and self-sacrifice of a mother.'[9]

In this context, Paul was aware of the great pressure there was on the new Christians, to return to their old way of life. His wholehearted devotion was clearly an encouragement to them to continue in their faith. And when he says, 'being affectionately desirous' of you' – 1 Thess. 2: 8, this indicates that a close emotional bond had formed between them. Just as it is normal for a mother who gives birth to her child to have a strong emotional attachment to it, so too the apostle and his companions had a similar attachment to the Thessalonians. It naturally follows that they had become very dear to them, because they were their 'spiritual children.'

The close parental bond established between these Christians, Paul and his associates, is reflected by their dedication to them in 1: 9, 'We worked night and day that we might not burden any of you, while we preached to you the gospel of God.' C. Cocksworth says, 'the energy of motherhood and the willingness of mothers to risk their lives in the giving of life are strong and powerful pictures of the calling of a priest – minister.'[10] D. Tidball also quotes John Calvin on motherhood, 'A mother in rearing her children reveals a wonderful and extraordinary love, because she spares no trouble or effort, avoids no care, is not wearied by their coming and going and gladly gives her own life blood to be drained.'[11] Similarly, Paul and his associates gave themselves unreservedly to these young Thessalonian Christians, much like a mother would in nurturing her children.

D. Tidball compares the motherly devotion of Paul and his associates, to that of a 'mother wet nursing' her own children.'[12] This motherly image is also a reflection of God's feminine qualities, which we see in Isaiah 49: 15-16, 'Can a woman forget her suckling child, that she should have no compassion on the son of her womb? Even these may forget but I will not forget you. Behold I have graven you on the palms of my hands.' We also glimpse this in Hosea 11: 1-2, 'When Israel was a child I loved him and out of Egypt I called my son – yet it was I who taught Ephraim to walk, I took them up in my arms.' In our generation the image of God as mother and inclusive language about God is becoming increasingly prevalent. The challenge for male ministers, is to allow the Holy Spirit, to nurture the feminine qualities of God in their pastoral ministry. So that they may reflect the qualities of whole-hearted devotion, gentleness and affectionate relationships.

FIRM LIKE A FATHER

Anyone who has had the privilege of helping someone to respond to Christ, in effect becomes their spiritual father. So in 1 Thessalonians 1: 11, it comes as no surprise to read:

> For you know how like a father with his children, we
> exhorted each one of you and encouraged you and charged
> you, to lead a life worthy of God, who calls you into his
> own kingdom and glory.

While women have enjoyed considerable emancipation after
centuries of male domination, we might well reflect that in our
generation, it is men who are now often undervalued. In seeking a
contemporary understanding of our role as father, we may well find
that the ideal model is still God the father. Equally, understanding
Paul's fatherly role towards the Thessalonian Christians, can help
us to grow in our pastoral ministry. D. Tidball informs us, 'the
Roman father was a person with legal and financial authority over
his children. Moreover fathers not only had rights, they had very
significant responsibilities towards their children. These included
guarding, providing, nurturing and teaching them.'[13] In Paul's day
and in Greek culture, parents would receive respect from their
children, even when they were adults. Coming from a Greek
patriarchal society myself, I am aware that this description is not
too wide off the mark, even in the 21st Century.

Paul's use of the pastoral image of father, indicates that they
nurtured a close relationship with the Thessalonian Christians.
They made it their responsibility to initiate this close parental bond
with them all. Just as children demand their parents' time, love and
attention, so too these young Christians would have needed the
same things, in order to grow spiritually. Left to their own devices
they may well have faltered and not made much progress in
their faith. As a spiritual father figure Paul's role is one of
encouragement and exhortation. This would also have involved
giving guidance and teaching to these young Christians, and
building up their faith, so that they might lead a Christ-like life. A
life that is pleasing to the Lord – 1 Thess: 2: 12.

Another aspect of Paul as a father figure comes in 2: 10. 'You
are our witnesses and God also, how holy and righteous and
blameless was our behaviour to you as believers.' Paul and his
associates were setting these young Christians, a role model as an
example to follow. Just as parents nowadays expect their children

to behave in a certain way, so as not to embarrass them, so too Paul had no hesitation in setting an example for the Christians to follow. Setting an example as a father figure, whether as a minister or a lay person, reflects God's fatherly love.

PAUL THE THEOLOGIAN
JUSTIFICATION BY FAITH
A RIGHT RELATIONSHIP WITH GOD

It would be fascinating to have a conversation with Paul and enquire how his Christology, Ecclesiology and Soteriology evolved, and to discuss with him for example, his letter to the Romans written around 55 AD. Romans gives us a majestic exposition of salvation through faith in Christ, that embraces God's gifts of justification and righteousness. This gives us an insight into Paul's relationship with God, that was possible through Christ's atoning death.

Paul, like any religious Jew believed in righteousness through the Law, by obedience to it, as a response to God's grace that resulted in a right relationship with God – although a person could succumb to the temptation to think they merited this. After his conversion, it was revealed to him, that through his relationship with Christ he received the gifts of justification and righteousness – a right relationship with God. They were completely gratuitous and flowed from God's lavish grace, appropriated by faith through Christ's atoning death. 'Paul makes what most would agree to be an important statement, "we know that a person is justified not by works of the Law, but through faith in Jesus Christ" – Gal 2: 16-17, 3: 11, 24, 5: 4.'[14] The importance of this is evident, because 'justification by faith' led to a renaissance of faith for Martin Luther, and to the Reformation. Justification by faith has been a central theme in Pauline studies, and tends to dominate the Protestant perspective on salvation. Paul's perspective on justification, may be seen as the lens through which we have a panoramic view, of the benefits of our salvation. That justification is a central part of the scene is evident from Romans chapter 5 onwards.

THE OLD PERSPECTIVE

Before looking at 'the new perspective' (NP) on Paul, it is helpful to define what 'the old perspective' is. Here M. Thompson provides us with a concise assessment. 'Essentially, the NP represents a "reformation" of a few notions Christians have inherited primarily from the protestant Reformation. Scholars holding NP views, do not see themselves as a particular religious movement. They disagree among themselves about a number of interpretive details, and they do not reflect any one particular theological persuasion.

Influenced by Martin Luther's spiritual experience, a traditional Protestant interpretation, sees Paul reacting to a Judaism that was a religion of works instead of faith: of doing instead of trusting. Luther's own struggle to gain peace with God, was resolved when he began to interpret Paul as teaching a fundamentally different way of relating to God, in contrast to the way of Judaism. His understanding of justification by faith alone, apart from works, then became for him and his followers the decisive truth revealed in Christ, and crucial in Paul's theology. Acceptance by God was therefore seen as a gift, not as something to be earned. (This succinctly summarises the Old Perspective on justification).

A primary concern of evangelical critics of the NP is that the doctrine of justification by faith will be lost, or at least fudged. But no proponent of an NP reading denies that Paul taught justification by grace through faith in Christ. Also they do not deny that he would have rejected any notion that a person can earn salvation. The question Sanders and others rightly raise, is whether Paul's particular opponents, ever did think that membership in God's people was something to be earned. In practical terms, the NP helps us to better appreciate our Jewish heritage, and what we continue to share in common with Judaism. This can affect how we read the Old Testament, as well as how we relate to Jewish people. The NP also sheds light on a number of texts, for example, the Jewish boasting Paul opposes in Romans 2: 17, 23, 3: 27-29 and 11: 18, might not be the boast of an individual in his own meritorious deeds, but rather the nationalistic pride of Jews in the fact they were the chosen, covenant people of God who have been given the Law. And that by implication one had to become a Jew and keep the Law, to join and stay in the family of God. The NP does not deny the Bible's power to speak to individuals, but it reminds us that authentic Christianity is fundamentally corporate.'[15]

THE NEW PERSPECTIVE

Dunn points out, 'that towards the end of the 1970s, Pauline studies regained a new vitality, principally due to "the new perspective" provided by E. P. Sanders. He exposed the element of caricature (and worse) in much Protestant portrayal of Second Temple Judaism, more effectively than any previous protests. He demonstrated that Judaism has always been first and foremost a religion of grace, with human obedience understood as a response to that grace (obedience to the law). For Sanders a key descriptive phrase for Judaism's "pattern of religion," was a "covenantal nomism." He defined this as:

> Covenantal nomism is the view that one's place in God's plan, is established on the basis of the covenant, and that the covenant requires as the proper response of man, his obedience to its commandments while providing means of atonement for transgression…Obedience maintains one's position in the covenant, but it does not earn God's grace as such.

The Protestant Paul had always been a puzzle to Jewish scholars, because the Judaism which NT scholars posed as the foil to Paul's theology, was not one they recognised. The best solution they could think of was that he must have been reacting against a form of Judaism, of which no real trace now remains, except in his letters – a diaspora Judaism different from Palestinian Judaism.'[16] This may well be linked to the Judaizers who infiltrated Paul's churches, and insisted on keeping the Law and imposing circumcision on the Gentiles, as an integral part of belonging to God's people – rather than emanating from justification by faith in Christ. A strategy they adopted to counter their perception, that the significance of the Law was being diminished and eroded by Paul.

THE RIGHTEOUSNESS OF GOD

M. Hooker points out, 'the Hebrew word in the Old Testament for "righteousness" *is s-d-q*, which means "right-ness." Since God himself is righteous he can be relied upon to act rightly, and because he is the judge of all the earth, he will reward the righteous and punish the wicked. For the wicked, however, this revelation of righteousness will mean wrath – Rom: 1: 18. The idea that God might "justify" the ungodly – Rom: 4: 5 is clearly preposterous. And yet this is precisely what Paul claimed had happened. Moreover, he claims this righteousness has been revealed apart from the Law, and not on the basis if one has kept the Law: and it is therefore effective for all who have faith in Christ's atoning death. Paul's fellow Jews would have been shocked by the notion of righteousness apart from the Law. God's righteousness is offered to all who believe, but the basis on which this is done, is the grace of God. Paul thinks of righteousness as being imparted to men and women not just imputed – there is some truth in both these views. If Paul thinks of Christians as being declared righteous, it is because Christ himself has been declared righteous, and because those who are "in Christ" share his status – we note that being "righted," clearly involves also the idea, that men and women are restored to a right relationship with God.'[17]

Abraham must be introduced to the topic of justification by faith, because Paul traces his argument about this to him. In Romans 4, he argues that Abraham believed in God, and it was reckoned to him as righteousness. In other words he was not justified by his obedience to the Law, or through works of the Law. He says in 4: 13, 'For the promise to Abraham and his offspring, that he would be the father of many nations did not come through the Law, but through the righteousness of faith.' Here M. Hooker says, 'The Covenant between God and Abraham, had been made on the basis of God's grace and Abraham's faith – not his "works." His true descendents are in fact all who have faith, and not simply his physical descendents.'[18]

RIGHTEOUSNESS AND SALVATION

The concept of righteousness is a complex one that has various interpretations. J. Stott clarifies three variations and in effect says, 'Some emphasise the righteousness of God is a divine attribute or quality. This describes his character together with his actions. In Romans, God's personal righteousness is supremely seen in the cross of Christ, as his was a sacrifice of atonement that demonstrated God's justice. Others stress that the righteousness of God is a divine activity, his saving intervention on behalf of his people. These are frequently coupled in the parallelism of Hebrew poetry, especially in the Psalms and Isaiah 40-66. God's righteousness denotes his loyalty to his covenant promises, to come to the salvation of his people. Some stress that the righteousness of God, revealed in the gospel, is a divine achievement. It is a righteous status that God requires, if we are ever to stand before him. He achieves this through the atoning sacrifice of the cross of Christ, that he reveals in the gospel, and which he bestows freely on all who trust in Jesus Christ. God's righteousness is a gift that is offered to faith. It is at one and the same time a quality, an activity and a gift. All three views are true and have been held by different scholars, sometimes in relation to each other.'[19]

R. Hays points to the issue of righteousness in Romans 3, 'to mean as Kasemann advocated, "God's own righteousness" which encounters humanity as a "salvation-creating power." And that this could be best understood within the context of apocalyptic thought. However, Sanders pointed out that God's righteousness occurs primarily in hymns and prayers, not in apocalyptic narratives. Hays believes that the issue at stake, is God's own integrity, which in effect embraces his covenant faithfulness to Israel, alongside the inclusion of the Gentiles being justified.

Hays presents his argument about God's integrity, by summarising Romans 3 in this way.

3: 2-8   Has God abandoned his promises to Israel? Is he inconsistent or unjust?

3: 9-20   All such objections are invalid: humanity, not God, is guilty of injustice.

3: 21-26   God has not abandoned his people. He has now revealed his justice/righteousness in a new way, overcoming human unfaithfulness by his own power and proving himself faithful/just.

(Here Hays introduces psalm 143 which has several references to God's righteousness). The psalmist prays for and anticipates a salvation, that will be effected by God's faithfulness and righteousness. Terms that are strikingly reminiscent to Romans 3: 3-7. This righteousness according to Paul's proclamation, has now been made manifest in Christ Jesus. Psalm 143 illuminates the logic that underlies Rom 3, because the Psalm already contains both an affirmation of the unconditional inadequacy of human beings to stand before God – Rom 3: 9-20, and an appeal to God to exercise his own righteousness to rescue the psalmist – Rom 3: 21-26. There is no possibility of construing the righteousness of the Psalm, to mean some kind of imputed righteousness: it unambiguously means God's own righteousness, and this appears in this as a power of deliverance. Because Paul actually quotes from it precisely at this point in his argument, Rom 3: 11 provides much stronger support, for a righteousness that brings salvation. Consequently God's justice persistently overcomes human unfaithfulness.'[20]

BELONGING TO GOD'S PEOPLE

D. Horrell adds further to the debate when he points out, 'Further angles of the meaning of justification/righteousness in Paul, have recently been proposed by Tom Wright (Bishop of Durham). He argues against Sanders and others, that "justification" is not a matter of how someone enters the community of the true people of God, but of how you tell who belongs to that community. (Here, I think an important point of clarification is necessary. In Paul's day, the Jews would have understood this as a covenantal issue of belonging, not entry. However, in Paul's day if you were a Gentile, you would naturally interpret this as a sign of entry, and subsequently one of belonging. Alternatively, for someone coming to faith in Christ today, they are likely to feel they belong, precisely because they have entered the Christian community, by faith in Christ.)

T. Wright suggests that there are three aspects to the meaning of justification to Paul. 'Firstly, it is covenant language. In other words it is about the people who are in a covenant relationship with God, the traditional self-understanding of Israel. Secondly, it is law-court language: it is about the verdict that will be pronounced by God the judge, on the day of judgement. Thirdly, justification is inextricably tied up with eschatology: it concerns the declaration of who is included in the people of God, who will be vindicated and declared "righteous" by God, on the final judgement day…Now in Christ, by faith, people can belong to the covenant people of God, the people who will be declared righteous on the last day. Justification is essentially about membership of the covenant people of God.'[21] In fact Wright goes on to say, 'Justification' in the first century was not about how someone might establish a relationship with God. It was about God's eschatological definition, both future and present, of who was, in fact, a member of his people. In standard Christian theological language, it wasn't so much about soteriology, as about ecclesiology: not so much about salvation, as about the church.'[22]

While T. Holland agrees with T. Wright, that the language of justification is from the law court, 'in his view the setting was not the law court but the covenant. The law that has to be answered to is covenantal law – and what he has missed, is the fact that justification is used in the context of God, accepting Israel into the covenant. Wright acknowledges a New Exodus link, but does not develop it beyond noting the promise of return from exile, is fundamental to the covenant made with Abraham in Genesis 15. The fact is that there is far more than this promise in Genesis 15 for Paul to draw on. Israel was justified when she was released from her bondage and restored to her inheritance. Justification is foundational for New Exodus language as proclaimed by the prophets. This closely parallels the New Testament perspective, that links justification with entering the kingdom of God – Rom. 4: 25, 5: 1, 18: 8, 30. It is a corporate picture of the saving activity of

God towards his covenant people. Dunn has also missed this dimension, as a result of his faulty analysis of Paul's pre-conversion mind-set.

It surprising that Wright should miss the significance of what the prophets say, concerning this vitally important new Exodus setting for justification. Indeed, he has made much of Jesus' understanding of the new Exodus promises, and has used this model – although to my mind not to its full potential – to interpret Paul. Wright uses the wrong paradigms for unravelling his teaching. He uses covenantal nomism and martyrdom, as his hermeneutical keys. But justification in the Old Testament, spoke of Israel being released from exile, and being brought to her inheritance. In this redemptive historical setting, there is certainly a legal dimension to justification, in that it is Israel's sin that has caused her original exile, and this has to be dealt with. If justification is not considered within the context of this redemptive model, then it is bound to distort what Paul is saying, and we will be left with a deviation from his thought rather than with its essence. I have no doubt that Wright wholeheartedly agrees with the importance of the covenant, but he has inadvertently deflected the argument, by inserting it uncritically into Sander's covenantal nomism.'[23]

E. P Sanders perceptively raises an important issue about justification, that commentators tend to overlook. He says, 'we note that the judicial category is terminologically defective. We do not find the word "guilt" at all, which is the legal counterpart on the human side of God's condemnation, and the words "repent(ance) and forgive-(ness)" are virtually absent. These terms central to any scheme of judicial decision about guilt and innocence, play virtually no role in Paul's discussion of "being righteoused by faith." What is striking is that these categories, well known to any good Jew, play no role in the argument about "being righteoused" since that has to do with the question, "Who are in the people of God?" Another way of putting all this, is to say that, "righteoused by faith" means, being transferred from the group which will be destroyed, to that which will be saved.'[24] A view that T. Wright concurs with. This also highlights Paul's crucial theological thesis, that the Gentiles are now able to be in a right relationship with God, through faith in Christ and to be God's people.

One of the things that God's righteousness deals with is his wrath, as we see in Romans 5: 9. T. R. Schreiner refers to this when he says, 'It should be noted that righteousness is a forensic term, stemming from the law court. Believers are declared to be righteous before God as the divine judge, because Jesus, as the sinless one, bore their sins. God's righteousness, therefore, consists both of his judgement and salvation. He saves those who put their faith in Jesus, and he judges his Son at the cross. In other words, both the saving righteousness of God (by which he declares sinners to be right in his sight) and the judging work of God (by which he pours out his wrath on Christ) meet in the cross of Christ. It should be added that God himself sent his son to satisfy his wrath, and so righteousness is rooted in God's love.'[25]

A LENS WITH A PANORAMIC VIEW

In his relationship with Paul, the Lord revealed to him the outcome of being righteous and justified in God's sight, which he describes in Romans 5: 1, 'Therefore justified by faith we have peace with God.' This is not only to be understood in terms of a forgiven conscience and being at peace with God, but also as being at peace with himself. This was invaluable to Paul after his violent persecution of the church. Here J. Fitzmyer says, 'When human beings are in a correct relationship with God, their condition may be one of inner calm and quiet composure, of undisturbed conscience, but the essential thing is the experience of God-given salvation – those who are now at peace are no longer objects of God's wrath: for them Christ has removed all wrath.'[26]

As you read through Romans, it is unambiguously clear from the early chapters, that Paul's central theme in his theology, is the gospel of Christ and the person of Christ. Closely connected to this, is the inclusion of the Gentiles, as part of God's people. It is a main thrust of Romans that through faith in Christ, the Gentiles now belong to God's people, and Paul traces justification by faith back to Abraham, as God considered him righteous because of his faith. This is truly radical and revolutionary theology.

In Romans justification sits alongside Christ who dominates the scene, as Paul spells out the comprehensive nature of salvation. Romans 1: 5, speaks about receiving grace to bring about the obedience of faith, for the sake of his name among the Gentiles. In 1: 16-17, we read 'the gospel (of Jesus Christ) is the power of God for salvation, to those who believe, to the Jew first and also to the Greek. For in it the righteousness of God is revealed from faith to faith, as it is written the righteous shall live by faith.' L. Morris has this to say about the righteousness of God. 'In this passage, it is not completely certain whether we should understand the expression in the sense of a quality or attribute of God, or of a right standing which God gives. It makes good sense to say, "In the gospel it is revealed that God is a righteous God." But it also makes sense to say, "In the gospel it is revealed that people get a right standing, a status of being right from God." Cranfield sees as decisive, "the further point that the argument of the Epistle as a whole supports this view." Up to 4: 25, Paul is concerned with the man who by faith is just (it is only after this that he emphasises that the just "will live"). Here Paul is saying, that in the gospel God has acted decisively for our salvation, and in a way that is right. The "rightness" of the way of salvation will be further brought out in this Epistle, as Paul develops the concept of justification. We should further note, that the righteousness of God is here said to be "revealed" in the gospel. That is to say, it is something new, not simply a repetition of Old Testament truth (important as that is).'[27]

In Romans 3: 22, Paul speaks about the righteousness of God, that has been manifested apart from the Law, although the Law and the Prophets bear witness to it – the righteousness of God through faith in Jesus Christ. In chapter 4: 3, we learn that Abraham believed God and it was counted to him as righteousness, and Paul through Christ entered into a relationship with God and had access by faith into His grace – Romans 5: 3. As a result, God's love was poured into his heart through the Holy Spirit – 5: 5. A love God demonstrated through Christ's death and his shed blood – 5: 8-9, that leads Paul to say in 5: 11, 'More than that we also rejoice in God through the Lord Jesus Christ, through whom we have now received reconciliation.' In this context, the righteousness of God through faith in Christ, results in our justification and also in our reconciliation. On this theme L. Morris says, 'reconciliation is a vivid concept Paul uses to bring out the significance of the cross. It leads to a salvation that never ends. And Christ has done the great work of putting away our sin, and bringing about our reconciliation to God.'[28]

In Romans chapter 7, Paul makes a contrast between life under the Law and life under the Spirit, which is an expression of his life in Christ. At the beginning of Romans 8, he focuses on what may arguably be one of the pinnacles of his theology of being 'in Christ' – the subject of 'freedom.' This is an exhilarating theme for Paul as he compares this to being under the Law and captive to sin and death, and being justified by having faith in Christ. He emphatically states that Christ has liberated him from these things. He has been united to Christ – Romans 6 and enjoys the benefits of his liberty, so he says in 8: 1-2:

> There is therefore now condemnation for those who are in Christ Jesus. For the law of the Spirit of life in Christ Jesus has set me free from the law of sin and death.

The subject of freedom and liberty is something Paul also lays great stress on, in Galatians 5: 1-2 when he says, 'For freedom Christ has set us free: stand firm therefore and do not submit to a yoke of slavery. Now, I, Paul, say to you that if you receive circumcision, Christ will be of no advantage to you.' Dunn refers to Gal. 5: 1-2 as, 'The explosive conclusion to the main sequence of his argument' in Galatians 3-4.'[29]

The Galatians Christians were in danger of rejecting their freedom in Christ, and substituting this for being captive under the Law once again. Dunn picks up on this theme of liberty when he says:

> One other factor should be mentioned, since it is expressed with such intensity of feelings in Galatians. It is that justification by faith means liberty, and, most important of

all, liberty from the law. The antithesis of Paul's gospel of justification, as equally open to the Gentiles, was a divine righteousness restricted in it scope by the law, and in effect to those who practiced the works of the law.

Hence Paul's fear that the Gentile Galatians' freedom might be lost, if the demand for circumcision was accepted. Hence his revision of the theme in 4: 22-31, those born of promise and Spirit are the children of the free.

> Here again it simply needs to be underlined that Paul experienced his coming to faith in Christ as one of liberation. Paul's delight in justification by faith was that it had liberated him from what he recognised to have been a spirit of slavery, whose motivation was fundamentally one of fear – Rom. 8: 15. It was not least that liberating openness to the amazing riches of God's grace, which for him was one of the chief blessing of justification by faith, and one not to lightly let go.'[30]

Justification has been a central theme in Pauline studies, and tends to dominate the Protestant perspective on salvation. Arguably, too much of an emphasis on this can overshadow the benefits of being in a right relationship with God and Christ. For Paul the gospel and the person of Christ are his central themes. Justification explains to both Jews and Greeks, the inclusive nature of the Gentiles in God's universal plan of salvation, that also embraces them as the people of God. One perspective on justification, is that this is the lens through which we have a panoramic view, of the benefits of being in a right relationship with God and being his people. Too much of a focus on justification by faith, runs the risk that these benefits may not be given their due importance. Perhaps this has occurred because of the focus on the necessity of having 'faith' in the equation of justification. This could mean a false anthropological emphasis on this doctrine, thinking it depends on 'our having faith' to make it efficacious. Whereas, in reality, faith is a gift God gives us, to trust him for our justification, that he has provided through Christ's atoning death.

Justification has become a complex theological concept and truth, for scholars to debate. T. Wright quotes R. Hooker the great Anglican Divine, who makes an incisive contribution. 'One is not justified by faith, by believing in justification by faith.' Wright also adds, 'that one is justified by believing in Jesus. It follows that a great many people are justified by faith, who don't know they are justified by faith…They are constituted as members of the family. They must be treated as such.'[31]

GOD'S HOLINESS & JUSTICE

Ultimately, what may be crucial in the drama of Christ's salvation, is not necessarily a theological formula where everything has been worked out to perfection. Although it is important to get our theology right, what may be missed is the perspective from which God views this matter. Namely, that a person is acceptable in his sight and justified, when he/she has faith in Christ and trusts in his atoning death – without necessarily understanding the theological complexities, and the subtle nuances of justification by faith. Equally, from God's perspective, what we have to clearly grasp is that he has to maintain integrity with his character, which encompasses his holiness and his justice. It is important from His stance, that people being saved, understand that He has to reconcile his holiness and his righteous character, with his justice and his wrath: and that 'justification by faith' is his way of achieving this. Therefore, the resolution of this issue, may well be found in the double emphasis of justification by faith – that focuses on God's holiness and justice. Clearly, in the 21st century, the concept of God's holiness is important to grasp, as without this how can people understand the doctrine of sin and salvation? How the Church communicates these truths to those outside its boundaries, is another matter altogether.

Perhaps this is similar to what T. Wright is hinting at when he says, 'The discussions of justification in much of the history of the church, certainly since Augustine, got off on the wrong foot – at least in terms of understanding Paul – and they have stayed there ever since. Interestingly enough Alister McGrath in his monumental history of the doctrine, allows right from the start for exactly this possibility. The doctrine of justification he writes:

> Has come to develop a meaning quite independent of its biblical origins, and concerns the means by which man's relationship to God is established. The church has chosen to subsume its discussion of the reconciliation of man to God under the aegis of justification, thereby giving the concept an emphasis quite absent from the New Testament. The "doctrine of justification" has come to bear a meaning within dogmatic theology which is quite independent of its Pauline origins. Even if it could be shown that (justification) plays a minimal role in Pauline Soteriology, or that its origins lie in an anti-Judaism polemic quite inappropriate to the theological circumstances of today, its application would not be diminished as a result.[32]

A NEWER INTERPRETATION

This may well lead us to conclude, that justification by faith exists mainly in the rarefied atmosphere inhabited by scholars and theologians, and by Protestants who tenaciously cling to their traditional perspective of salvation. As an Evangelical these past forty years, in my experience it is rare to hear salvation spoken of in terms of 'righteousness and justification' – perhaps this is what A. McGrath was hinting at.

Having summarised the different views and perspectives on justification by faith, my perception is that the focus and relevance of this important doctrine has shifted. It may well be appropriate to now think of this in terms of an even – 'newer perspective.' The irony and paradox about justification by faith, that embraces the inclusion of the Gentiles as God's people alongside Israel, has now been superseded by its relevance to the Jewish people once again.

Because the Gentiles have been God's people since Paul's day, they and the Church no longer have to think in terms of belonging. They are most definitely in. The most contemporary and poignant perspective of justification by faith, is that this will once again have an apocalyptic relevance. Justification by faith through Christ's atoning death, will become the new way through which the Jews are once again numbered amongst God's people: when by faith they embrace the righteousness of God in Christ. But, this is likely to be in an 'apocalyptic setting.'

APPENDIX

CHRONOLOGY OF PAUL'S MINISTRY

It is hard to see how a Christian can work out the chronology of Paul's life without any help. So it seemed sensible to enlist the help of someone who has already done this, to give us an idea of the timescale of Paul's life. R. Mayhue's time-line on Paul's ministry that is essentially derived from F. F. Bruce, enables us to see when his missionary journeys occurred and when he wrote his letters.[1]

PAULINE HISTORY		ROMAN HISTORY	
c.33	Paul's conversion	14-37	Tiberius emperor
c.35	Paul's first post-salvation Jerusalem visit		
c.35-46	Paul in Cilicia and Syria		
46	Paul's 2nd Jerusalem visit	37-41	Gaius emperor
47-48	Paul & Barnabas on 1st missionary journey	41-54	Claudius emperor
48?	**Galatians**		
49	Council of Jerusalem & Paul's 3rd Jerusalem visit	49	Jews expelled from Rome
49-52	Paul's 2nd missionary journey		
49-50	Paul & Silas travel from Syrian Antioch through Asia Minor to Macedonia & Achaia		
50	**Thessalonian Epistles**		
50-52	Paul in Corinth	51-52	Galio proconsul Acahai
Summer 52	Paul's 4th Jerusalem visit		
52-56	Paul's 3rd missionary journey	52-58	Felix procurator of Judea
52-55	Paul in Ephesus		
55-56	**Corinthian Epistles**	54-68	Nero emperor
	Paul in Macedonia, Illycrium, & Achaia		
56	**Romans**		
Spring 56	Paul's last Jerusalem visit	58	Festus succeeds Felix as procurator of Judea

56-58   Paul's Caesarean imprisonment
Fall 58   Paul's voyage to Rome commences
Winter 59 Paul's arrival in Rome
c.59-61   Paul under house arrest in Rome
          Ephesians, Philippians, Colossians & Philemon
c.61-64   Paul's final travels   62   Death of Festus
                                                       Albinus procurator of
                                                       Judea
c.62-63   **1Timothy & Titus**
c.64-66   Roman imprisonment   64   Rome burns
          2 Timothy, & Paul's death

PAUL'S LAST YEARS

J. Stott says, 'Paul was imprisoned in Rome on two occasions. The first was under house arrest when he enjoyed comparative freedom, and the use of his own hired house. Luke records this at the end of Acts when he takes leave of Paul – Acts 28: 30-31, 'And Paul lived there two years at his own expense and welcomed all who came to him, preaching the kingdom of God, and teaching about the Lord Jesus Christ quite openly and unhindered.'

After being released Paul resumed his travels and went to Crete, where he left Titus behind –Titus 1: 3, and then onto Ephesus where he left Timothy behind – 1Tim. 1: 3-4. He may well have gone on to Colosse to see Philemon as he had planned – Philemon 22, and he certainly reached Macedonia –1Tim. 1: 3. Of the Macedonian cities he visited one will have been Philippi – Phil. 2: 24, from where he wrote his first letter to Timothy in Ephesus and his letter to Titus in Crete. He told Titus his intention to spend the winter at Nicopolis – Titus 3: 12 on the west coast of Greece, presumably he did so and presumably as he requested Titus joined him there. If the apostle was to fulfil his ambition of preaching to evangelise Spain – Rom. 15: 24, 28, it must have been in the following Spring that he set sail.

It is safe to assume that he later kept his promise to revisit Timothy in Ephesus – 1Tim. 3: 14-15. From there his itinerary seems to have taken him to the nearby port of Miletus, where he had to leave Trophimus behind ill – 2 Tim. 4: 20, and then on to Troas where he stayed with Carpus, and left behind his cloak and some books –2 Tim. 4: 13. Then on to Corinth where Erastus left the party – 2 Tim. 4: 20 & Rom. 16: 23 and from there to Rome. Somewhere along his journey he was arrested once again.'²

His arrest was probably unexpected as he had no time to collect his belongings, his books and his parchments which he asks Timothy to fetch to him when he visits him – 2 Tim. 4: 9-13. In 2: 14 he mentions that Alexander the coppersmith did him great harm, and the implication is that he was an informer who was responsible for his arrest. In this passage it is sad to learn, that on the occasion of Paul's first defence, no one supported him. Presumably they feared for their own lives. Reading about the circumstances of Paul's imprisonment is very moving, as this time around he is not under house arrest. Instead, 'he was shackled and placed in rigorous confinement in Rome, chained like a common criminal. He was incarcerated in some "dismal underground dungeon, with a hole in the ceiling for light and air." Perhaps it was the Mamertine prison as tradition says. But wherever he was, Onesiphorus succeeded in finding him only after a painstaking search – 1Tim. 1: 17. He was also suffering acutely from loneliness, the boredom and the cold of prison life.'³

J. Pollock adds, 'Paul was among the felons in Mamertine, or an equally obnoxious dungeon, reached only by a rope or a ladder let through a hole in the floor above. His weary body must lie on rough stones. The air was foul, sanitation almost non-existent. Of his trial, nothing is known, beyond a tradition that he was condemned by resolution of the Senate, on the charge of treason against the divine emperor. How long Simon Peter and Paul were in prison together before being executed the same day, as an early belief asserts, cannot be fixed: possibly as much as nine months. The date honoured in the city of their martyrdom is June 29, 67 AD, Peter nailed to a cross as a public spectacle at Nero's circus on the Vatican, head downward at his own request, and Paul, as a Roman citizen beheaded in a less public place.'⁴

WHO WROTE PAUL'S LETTERS?

In the New Testament there are thirteen letters that have Paul's name as the author. Those that are genuinely thought to be Paul's are Romans, 1 and 2 Corinthians, Galatians, Philippians, 1 Thessalonians and Philemon. 1 and 2 Timothy and Titus generally referred to as the Pastoral Epistles are widely, although not universally, rejected as coming from Paul's hand. Of those not considered to be Paul's, C. K. Barrett informs us, 'Their Greek style differs from Paul's, their theology is more developed but less profound, and they reflect a church order different from that which appears in the other letters. They (especially 2 Timothy), contain a few passages of historical reference, and it has often been maintained that these, or some of them, come from Paul's hand and were incorporated by the author as his own work. The Epistle to the Ephesians presents a more difficult problem. The style is closer to Paul's but not identical with it, and the same may be said of his theology. Here, however, there is a distinction. If it may be said that Paul writes of Christ and the church, one might say Ephesians writes of the church and Christ. This is not to allege a contradiction, but the reader is aware of a change of emphasis...There is a further problem in that the writer of Ephesians seems to presuppose that his readers do not know him personally – Eph. 3: 2-4, whereas Paul had ministered long in Ephesus. This argument however loses weight, in view of the fact that there is doubt whether the words "in Ephesus," were an original part of the manuscript.

Ephesians stands close to Colossians – indeed, its dependence on Colossians (and to a smaller degree on the Pauline letters), has been used as a further argument against its authenticity. The authenticity of Colossians itself is a difficult problem. In style, manner, pattern and thought it is closer to the other letters than Ephesians is. There are however differences and it is wise not to use it as a direct source for Paul's own thought. The same is true of 2 Thessalonians. The Epistle to the Colossians has all the appearances of a Pauline letter: indeed, if any one of his letters are considered genuine it is this one. A strong case can be made out for it. It is an attractive hypothesis, that the Epistle to the Ephesians, was written to introduce the collection of Paul's letters. Paul's letters were collected in the second century, and copies were made when he was not a well known figure. We know that in some of the genuine letters, Paul made use of a secretary – Rom. 16: 22, did this person take notes and elaborate on them? This may account for differences in vocabulary and style, which otherwise might indicate a different author. Or did Paul's theology evolve as he grew older? Whoever wrote them, they still testify to the importance of the name and of the man who bore it.'[5]

O'Brien gives an overview of what other scholars say about the author of Ephesians. 'The affirmation of the Pauline authorship of Ephesians, was universally accepted in the early church and was not challenged until the late 18th and 19th centuries. That there is a literary relationship between Ephesians and Colossians is clearly evident. Most scholars who regard Ephesians as pseudonymous, contend that it depends heavily on Colossians as its primary literary source. A. Lincoln for example, believes that this is the main reason for rejecting Paul as the author. Lincoln notes that in the first parts of the letters, the prologue, the thanksgiving period with its intercessory prayer report, the reminder of the readers' previous experience of alienation and their present reconciliation in Christ, along with the discussion of Paul's suffering as an apostle in his ministry of the mystery, are all parallel. He recognises that each letter treats these forms and subjects in a slightly different fashion, but even in those sections which appear to be distinctive, there are counterparts found elsewhere in the other Epistle…He draws attention to the distinctive ways in which each letter treats similar material. He claims it is inadequate to hold that the two letters simply reproduce common traditions…Lincoln concludes his overview by declaring Ephesians is dependent on a prior Colossians, in terms of its overall structure and sequence, its themes, and its wording." The author of Ephesians has, however, shown a "free and creative independence, not a slavish imitation or copying." As one who has immersed himself in his source material, to such an extent that it has become a part of his way of thinking, he frequently modifies the material of Colossians, through change of word order, omissions, additions and conflations.'[6]

What is striking is, that these very same arguments, could be used as a basis for Paul being the author of Ephesians. Instead of an anonymous author immersing himself in Colossians and writing Ephesians as a creative thinker, it could be argued that the latter, portrays the progressive development of Paul's theology.

O'Brien also points out that, 'Paul is certainly the 'implied' author of Ephesians. But what picture of the apostle is painted by the 'implied' author, and is it the same as that derived from his genuine letters? A range of scholars believe that the point of view presented by the 'implied' author, is later than that of the apostle. Ephesians 3: 1-13, is thought to look more like the estimate of Paul's authorship by someone looking back rather than Paul referring to himself and his ministry. Advocating his own insights in 3: 4, looks like the device of a person who wishes to "boost claims for the authority of the apostle's teachings for a later time." Missing from Ephesians is Paul's "personal presence – with its passion, urgency, joy and anger" – along with the tensions and struggles of his ministry.

The letter to the Ephesians is distinctive among the Epistles attributed to Paul. The early and consistent attestation to its apostolic authorship is highly significant, not only because Christians of the first centuries were closer than we are to the situation when it was written, but also because they were careful in weighing and evaluating their founding documents. This uniform testimony to its apostolic authority should not be easily dismissed. C. E. Arnold says, 'It is not unreasonable to think of Paul re-expressing, developing and modifying his own thoughts, for a different readership facing a different set of circumstances. D. A. Carson, D. J. C. Moon and L. Morris also say: 'The onus of proof is upon those who must establish, that Paul was incapable of this versatility. We agree – "that the best explanation seems to be, that the same man wrote Colossians and Ephesians a little later, with many of the same thoughts running through his head, and with a more general application of the ideas he had recently expressed.'[7]

J. Muddiman has this to say about Ephesians. 'There are several ways of answering the objection to Pauline authorship, on the grounds of differences in vocabulary and style. Paul may have given a co-worker, such as Timothy (F. F. Bruce), or Luke (R. Martin), a rough idea of what he wanted to say and allowed him to express it in his own way. Similarly, a secretary, could have been given more than normal freedom in this case.

The weakness in these counter-arguments is that while they may explain the differences, at the same time they make the similarities more problematic. The co-worker or secretary has been very free in certain places, but in others amazingly intuitive about what Paul himself would have said. A more plausible explanation of the variations in style within Ephesians, is to appeal to different types of source used by a pseudonymous writer. Alongside dependence on the Pauline Epistles, the author has incorporated elements of liturgy, like the blessing – 1: 3-10, or a hymn about Christ – 2: 14-16, 18, a creed – 4: 4-6, or a chorus – 5: 14. But this does not constitute a complete solution, since the elevated style of the opening blessing is maintained in the following material, right up to the end of chapter 3: it begins to fade in chapter 3 and more or less disappears thereafter. It is necessary to posit in addition to the use of liturgy-type sources, an author who himself prefers, and can reproduce when required, that style of writing.

The writer of Ephesians displays too much independence to be a mere imitator, and yet there is such a high degree of similarity with Paul that to imply that, unless it is by Paul, he must be a subtle and observant imitator. One solution to this dilemma, might be to say that there are whole sections of Ephesians that are genuinely Pauline, but there are also additional comments, expansion and other whole sections that are not.'[8]

Concerning Colossians J. D. G. Dunn highlights the fact that, 'probably the most contentious introductory issue is who wrote it. He believes there is a strong likelihood that the letter comes from a hand other than Paul's. Point after point in the letter, we are confronted with features characteristic of flow of thought, and rhetorical technique, that are consistently and markedly different, from those of the undisputed Paulines. Of course it is possible that Paul's style changed over the years. But it is more probable that the hand is different.

It is also difficult to deny that the theological and parenetic content is significantly different, from what we are accustomed to in all the other undisputed Paulines. The Christology expressed in 1: 15-20 and 2: 9-10 & 15, looks to be further along the trajectory, than that of the undisputed Paulines. Here again one could speak of the development of Paul's own thought, but again that would simply indicate that there is a later "Paulinism," that can be attributed to the late Paul, or to a close Pauline disciple, without altering the character of the "Paulinism" or the authentic character as "Pauline." In addition, we cannot ignore the degree to which Colossians and Ephesians overlap, sufficiently often with very similar phraseology and content. This feature is best explained by Ephesians being written, using Colossians as a kind of template. The fact this happened suggests that Colossians itself may have provided something of a "model" for Ephesians – that is, as an expression of "late Paulinism" or as written by a Pauline disciple close to Paul.

On the other hand, it is difficult to envisage a scenario where the autobiographical details of 4: 7-17, can be easily explained on a full-blown post-Pauline hypothesis. It is not simply because the passage contains a sequence of personal references. It is more the fact that these references are so closely related to the Colossian church: "to a concrete community." Here there is a close overlap with Philemon. The two letters name precisely the same authors (Paul and Timothy – Col. 1: 1, Phm. 1), and more or less the same list of greeters (Epaphras, Aristarchus and Mark, Demas and Luke – Col. 4: 10-14, Phm. 23-24). Such overlap can only be the result of deliberate contrivance (a later writer of Colossians simply copying Philemon, though with variations difficult to explain), or of closeness of historical origin (both letters being written at about the same time).

Although it is not absolutely clear, the most plausible solution is probably that the letter was written about the same time as Philemon, but actually composed by someone other than Paul. We may, for example, envisage Paul outlining his main concerns to a secretary (Timothy), who was familiar with the broad pattern of his letter writing, and being content to leave it to him to formulate the letter with a fair degree of license, perhaps under the conditions of his imprisonment, at that point able only to add the briefest of personal conclusions. The theology of Colossians could then be attributed to Timothy, or more accurately still, seen as the theology of Paul as interpreted by Timothy. If Timothy did write for Paul with his approval, then we have to call the letter Pauline in its fullest sense of the word, and the distinction between "Pauline" and "post-Pauline" – as applied to Colossians, becomes relatively unimportant.

At all events, whatever the precise circumstances of its composition, Colossians strongly suggests that the distinctions between a Paul who himself changed in style and developed in theology, a Paul who allowed someone else to interpret his thought and concerns, and a Pauline disciple writing shortly after his death, but seeking to be faithful to what he perceived would be the master's thought and concerns in the situation envisaged in the letter – become of uncertain and diminishing significance. And it is still in a proper sense Pauline.'[9]

While this sounds plausible, other characteristic features of Paul's Epistles make it unlikely, that he did not write Colossians and Ephesians. Bearing in mind the similarities between Ephesians and Colossians, it is just as natural, if not more natural, to assume Paul is the author. The development and progression of his style and theology, make this a natural explanation. Also he is in chains under house arrest in Rome when they were written, and he has time on his hands to compose them. So Paul has no logical reason or mitigating circumstance, to delegate their composition to anyone else. This may be one reason that accounts for the circular letter to the churches in Ephesus, it was an opportunity to capture in writing some important doctrinal truths, without the burden of addressing specific problems in the churches, such as happened at Corinth. Also what persuasively points to Paul's authorship, is that he is a very able theologian and a meticulous and precise writer.

When we look at 2 Corinthians, and the complex rhetorical arguments interwoven into the construction and flow of this letter, clearly Paul has taken care to organise his manuscript. The same can be said of Romans, another long complex letter of consummate precision. 1 Corinthians also shows the apostle's ability at organising his material in a logical sequence. Galatians too is carefully constructed to convey his theological thesis. Philippians is a gem of a friendship letter, that displays all of Paul's literary and theological expertise. And 1 Thessalonians portrays his intensely pastoral heart and apostolic concern.

These uncontested Pauline Epistles, do not give the impression of a man who would readily abdicate his pastoral concern and responsibility, to allow someone else to write the brief contested Epistles. And as they were written when he was under house arrest in Rome, when he had ample time on his hands, why should Paul delegate parts of Colossians and Ephesians to others to write? Even if he had asked Timothy to write parts of these, would he have had the literary skill to produce the apostle's level of theological competence? Bearing in mind his timid temperament, he probably would have felt somewhat intimated by this possibility. When considering whether Paul chose to delegate the responsibility of writing a letter or part of it, again it is difficult to imagine him giving a bare outline, and leaving it to someone else to compose this on his behalf. This is simply not representative of his temperament and way of doing things.

L. Morris believes that as in the case of the first Epistle, 'there are good reasons for thinking 2 Thessalonians is authentic. In the history of the church it has early attestation, for Polycarp, Ignatius and Justin all seem to have known it, possibly also the writer of the Didache. It is also quoted by Irenaeus and later writers. As with 1 Thessalonians, the mention of Silvanus and Timothy as associates of the author, and the obvious early date of the writing favour Pauline authorship...It is difficult to think of a forger entering so fully the mind of the apostle, as to produce a writing so redolent of the apostle as this one. There is also the point that had we not 1 Thessalonians, we would hardly call in question the authenticity of

2 Thessalonians. It is rather strange to call in question an Epistle which has all the hallmarks of a genuine Pauline writing, on the grounds it is similar to another Pauline writing.

Although there are similarities between the two letters, it is hard to imagine a forger who could imitate Paul's language so closely. Pauline words and phrases and constructions are everywhere. So too are Pauline ideas. If Paul wrote 2 Thessalonians not so long after the first letter, it would not be surprising if sometimes words and phrases were repeated, especially if as Neil thinks possible, he read through "the customary draft copy of his first letter before writing the second." This would be more likely, in that he had to bear in mind what was written in the first letter, because some of it had been misunderstood.

Concerning the suggested parallels between the two Epistles, these do not cover more than one third of the content, which is strange in a deliberate imitation. Identical language is also used in different ways. For example, there are marked resemblances, between the ways in which Paul describes his hard manual labour. In the first he does this to show his love for them, while in the second it is to bring out the force of his example. The differences are more compelling. So Paul's comment on the Man of Lawlessness in the second, is different from anything in the first. But the difference does not amount to incompatibility. The combination of likeness and difference is interesting – but the point is that it does not prove difference of authorship. Such a man as Paul was quite capable of both.'[10] Concerning the difference in tone between the two letters, the first is warm and friendly while the second appears cold and formal. The occasion of the first letter was a great relief to Paul, that the Thessalonians were standing firm in their faith. While the second letter appears cooler, this probably reflects the fact he was in a somewhat difficult situation 2 Thess. 3: 2.

W. Hendriksen adds the following arguments for those who reject Pauline authorship for 2 Thessalonians. '2 Thess. 2: 1-12, is an apocalyptic. This is in sharp contrast with Paul's emphasis on growth in faith, hope and love here and now. However, to reject it because it is apocalyptic, is arbitrary. If Paul wrote 1 Thess. 4: 13-

18 & 5: 1-1, he cannot have written 2 Thess. 3: 1-12. For while the first views Christ's coming as imminent, the second regards it as non-imminent. However, these two ideas are not mutually exclusive.'[11] Moreover, '2 Thess. 2: 1ff clarifies the reason for the apocalyptic content in this letter.' This is to counter any false teaching by a letter claiming to be from Paul, about the coming day of the Lord he alluded to in the first letter.' Hendriksen also points out the argument, 'that to a very large extent, 2 Thessalonians is a repetition of the first letter. However this argument can also be used to argue for Paul being the author.'[12]

J. Stott informs us that, 'ever since F. C. Baur of Tubingen rejected the Pauline authorship of all three Pastoral letters in 1835, the voice of critical orthodoxy have confidently followed this tradition. The letters are declared to be pseudonymous or deutero-Pauline, that is to say, composed by a disciple of Paul who attributed them to the pen of his master. In effect, he says, that the case for Pauline authorship has always rested on two foundations. The internal claim that they were written by the apostle, and the external claim of their acceptance as genuine from the earliest days until the last century. The internal evidence is so obviously comprehensive, that the theory of pseudonymity, credits Paul's imitator with historical and literary genius. All three letters begin by declaring Paul is the author. Both letters to Timothy affirm his authority as an apostle. The letters also claim to be addressed to Timothy and Titus, who are stationed in Ephesus by Paul, to silence false teachers – 1 Tim. 1: 3ff, and to appoint true teachers in their place.'[13]

Paul also alludes to their affectionate relationship, by addressing them as his 'dear son' or his 'true son.' Accompanying his instructions to Timothy are a number of personal references by the apostle, that indicate a first hand knowledge of him. He also concludes his letter with a moving appeal to him, to live a godly life and guard the truth entrusted to him. This is undoubtedly an authentic Pauline characteristic concern. 2 Timothy is the most personal of the Pastoral Epistles, and includes the apostle's farewell message to him, shortly before his anticipated execution. He also mentions Timothy's tears, the faith and ministry of his mother and grandmother, and his personal knowledge of his teaching and sufferings. Paul begs him to come and visit him and mentions a host of friends by name. Presumably, Timothy would have recognised these intimate details, that clearly indicate Paul was the author. To claim these letters were forgeries, is something Paul would probably have anticipated. If they were it is unlikely the person would have stressed the same concern for the truth they contain. After all the point of a forgery would be to change the content Paul might have included. Alternatively, why write a forgery and say exactly what Paul would say?! Equally, to enable Timothy to ascertain they were genuinely from Paul, all the intimate personal references he alludes to in such a touching manner, would have erased any concern of Timothy, as to whether they were genuinely from him.

There is nothing to be gained, by claiming these Epistles are the work of a forger, because the motive for writing them presumably was to change the content of what Paul might have said. After all why forge a letter and make it so transparently Pauline in content and tone? The apostolic heart and spirit of Paul, breathes through these atmospherically Pauline Epistles to Timothy – that I am sure would have been treasured by him as authentic. The very intimate and personal touches of these two letters, along with their doctrinal emphasis, convincingly testify to their being genuinely Pauline.

One last thought concerning Paul's Epistles. Perhaps it is time we read the briefer letters out aloud in church in one go, and read the longer ones during consecutive morning services: because that is how they were intended to be read.

FOOTNOTES

INTRODUCTION

[1] C. K. Barrett Saint Paul Continuum 2001 2

[2] K. Haacker Paul's Life In The Cambridge Companion To St. Paul Editor J. D. G. Dunn Cambridge University Press 2004 19

[3] Who's Who In The New Testament Brownrigg: Holt: Rinehart & Winston 1971 322

[4] J. M-O'Connor Paul His Story Oxford University Press 2004 199

[5] D. Wenham Jesus And Paul SPCK 2002 49

[6] Ibid 51

[7] F. F. Bruce Paul Apostle Of The Free Spirit Paternoster 1992 461

[8] E. Stourton In The footsteps Of St. Paul Hodder 2004 31

[9] F. F. Bruce ibid 457

[10] J. D. G. Dunn The Theology Of Paul The Apostle Eerdmans 1998 2-3, 11

[11] D. G. Horrell An Introduction To The Study Of St. Paul T & T Clark 2004 1-3

[12] Ibid 107-108

[13] J. D. G. Dunn in The Cambridge Companion To St. Paul ibid 2

[14] D. Horrell Ibid 126

[15] M. Hooker Paul A Short Introduction Oneworld 2004 2

[16] N. T. Wright Paul: Fresh Perspectives SPCK 2005 X

CHAPTER ONE

[1] D. Coggan ibid 17

[2] D. Wenham ibid 3

[3] J. M-O'connor ibid 3-4

[4] D. Coggan ibid 22-23

[5] J. M-O'connor ibid 4

[6] F. F. Bruce ibid 34-35

7. J. M-O'Connor ibid 36-37

8. D. Coggan ibid 25

9. J. M-O'Connor ibid 12-13

10. T. Wright What St. Paul Really Said Lion 1997 27-28

11. Ibid 29

12. C. K. Barrett ibid 5

13. E. Stourton ibid 23

14. J. M-O'Connor Paul A Critical Life Oxford University Press Eerdmans 1996 49-50

15. Ibid 56

16. Ibid 57

17. E. Stourton ibid 68-69

18. H. Montefiore Paul The Apostle Collins 1981 14-15 quoted by D. Coggan ibid 243

19. C. K. Barrett ibid 169

20. W. Trilling A Conversation With Paul SCM Press 1986 18

21. B. Witherington 111 The Paul Quest IVP 1998 15, 21, 24-26, 31

CHAPTER TWO

1. J. B. Lightfoot – This study was originally written in 1995. Although I have Lightfoot as the source I cannot trace this now.

2. J. D. G. Dunn The Theology Of Paul The Apostle ibid 350-352

3. T. Wright ibid 36

4. J. Calvin The Acts Of The Apostles Vol 1 Eerdmans 1987 257-258

5. J. Stott The Spirit, The Church & The World: The Message Of Acts IVP 1990 185

6. C. Swindoll Paul – A Man Of Grit & Grace Word 2002 2-4

7. Ibid 27

8. J. Calvin ibid 259

9. S. Christou The Priest & The People Of God Phoenix Books 2003 51

10. D. Wenham ibid 10

[11] F. B. Meyer Paul – Servant Of Jesus Christ Marshall Morgan & Scott 1953 38, 40

[12] J. Calvin ibid 258

[13] F. F. Bruce ibid 75

[14] F. F. Bruce Acts NICOT Eerdmans 1986 196

[15] U. Schnelle Apostle – Paul His Life & Theology Baker 2003 101

[16] E. Bock Saint Paul Floris Books 2005 17

[17] T. Wright ibid 37

[18] S. Christou Evangelism & Collaborative Ministry Phoenix Books 2004 43-44

[19] J. Stott Galatians IVP 1991 34

[20] J. D. G. Dunn Galatians A & C Black 1993 69-70

[21] C. Swindoll ibid 52

[22] J. B. Lightfoot Galatians 1865 Oliphants 1957 87, 90

[23] A. N. Wilson Paul –The Mind Of The Apostle Pimlico 1997 81

[24] J. M-O'Connor ibid 81-85

[25] L. Morris Galatians IVP 1996 57

[26] J.D. G. Dunn ibid 69

[27] D. Wenham ibid 28-29

[28] J. Stott ibid 23-24

[29] D. Wenham ibid 182-183

CHAPTER THREE

[1] T. Chester The Message Of Prayer IVP 2003 27
A quote from K. Barth Prayer & Preaching SCM 1964 19

[2] G. Hawthorne: R. Martin: D: Reid Dictionary Of Paul & His Letters IVP 1993 730-731

[3] W. W. Wiersbe The Bible Exposition Commentary 1989 31

[4] D. Carson A Call To Spiritual Reformation – Priorities From Paul & His Prayers. IVP 1992 85

[5] M. Bockmuehl Philippians A & C Black 1997 1

[6] P. O'Brien Philippians Eerdmans 1991 4-6

7. Ibid 1991 72-73

8. D. Carson ibid 83

9. P. O'Brien ibid 75

10. Ibid 127

11. A. Motyer Philippians IVP 1988 56-57

12. G. Fee Philippians Eerdmans 1995 83, 100

13. P. O'Brien ibid 76

14. M. Bockmuehl ibid 68

15. P. O'Brien ibid 74-75

16. R. P. Martin Ephesians, Colossians, Philemon John Knox 1992 3

17. P. O'Brien Ephesians Eerdmans 1999 1

18. H. C. G. Moule Ephesian Studies Pickering & Inglis (no date given) 52

19. J. Stott Ephesians IVP 1989 32

20. F. F. Bruce Ephesians Eerdmans 1984 58-60, 69

21. M. Stibbe Drawing Near To God –The Temple Model Of Prayer   DLT 2005 31

22. M. L. Jones God's Ultimate Purpose – Ephesians 1 Banner Of Truth 1978 343-344

23. M. L. Jones The Unsearchable Riches Of Christ – Ephesians 3 Banner Of Truth 1979 119

24. D. Carson ibid 131

25. M. L. Jones ibid 114

26. P. O'Brien ibid 255

27. F. F. Bruce ibid 132

28. F. F. Foulkes Ephesians IVP 1983 103

29. P. O'Brien ibid 257-258

30. H. C. G. Moule ibid 130, 137-138

31. H. W. Hoehner Ephesians Baker 2003 481

32. A. Lincoln Ephesians Nelson 1990 56

33. P. O'Brien ibid 257

34. Ibid 259

35. Ibid 260

36. J. Stott ibid 136

37. P. O'Brien ibid 261

38. J. D. G. Dunn Colossians Paternoster 1996 19, 36

39. Ibid 21

40. Ibid 26

41. B. J. Walsh & S. C. Keemaat Colossians re:mixed Paternoster 2005 7

42. J. D. G. Dunn ibid 55

43. H. C. G. Moule Colossian Studies Pickering & Inglis (no date given) 53, 56

44. R. C. Lucas Colossians IVP 1980 22-24

45. F. F. Bruce ibid 21

46. J. D. G. Dunn ibid 33-34

47. R. P. Martin ibid 82, 96

48. P. O'Brien Colossians Word 1982 20

49. Ibid 20

50. R. J. Martin ibid 94

51. S. Christou Evangelism & Collaborative Ministry ibid 3

52. P. O'Brien ibid 21

53. R. C. Lucas ibid 37

54. P. O'Brien ibid 74

55. J. D. G. Dunn ibid 129

56. H. C. G. Moule ibid 119

57. R. J. Martin ibid 82

58. P. O'Brien ibid 95

59. R. C. Lucas ibid 282-283

60. J. D. G. Dunn ibid 130

CHAPTER FOUR

1. B. Witherington 111 ibid 156

2. H. Ridderbos Paul An Outline Of His Theology SPCK 1977 448-449

3. Hawthorne: Martin: Reid ibid 45

4. P. O'Brien Ephesians ibid 84

5. J. M-O'Connor Paul A Critical Life ibid 80

6. D. G. Horrell ibid 27

7. B. Witherington 111 ibid 170

8. M. Bockmuehl ibid 51

9. G. Fee Philippians ibid 63-64

10. M Bockmuehl ibid 59

11. P. O'Brien Philippians ibid 486

12. G. Fee ibid 404-405

13. M. Bockmuehl ibid 162-163

14. J. D. G. Dunn Galatians ibid 147

15. P. O'Brien Ephesians ibid 165-166

16. Ibid 102-103

17. J. D. G. Dunn ibid 234

18. J. Stott Galatians ibid 193-194

19. G. Fee 1 Corinthians Eerdmans 1987 7

20. J. M. O'Connor ibid 252

21. P. Hughes 2 Corinthians Eerdmans 1986 462-463

22. C. M. Martini In The Thick Of His Ministry St. Pauls 1989 14-15

23. M. Hooker ibid 123

24. G. Fee 1 Corinthians ibid 627-629

25. T. Schreiner Paul Apollos 2001 313

26. M. Bockmeuhl Philippians ibid 260-262

27. G. Fee Philippians ibid 434-435

28. A. Motyer Philippians ibid 220

29. P. O'Brien Philippians ibid 533-537

30. R. Clements The Strength Of Weakness Christian Focus 1988 231-232

31. P. Barnett 2 Corinthians IVP 1995 177

32. D. Carson From Triumphalism To Maturity IVP 1986 144

33. P. Hughes 2 Corinthians ibid 443

34. Ibid 447-448

35. P. O'Brien Philippians ibid 388-389

36. Hawthorn: Martin: Reid ibid 562

37. M. Hooker ibid 50-51

38. J. D. G. Dunn The Theology Of Paul The Apostle ibid 251-254

39. P. O'Brien ibid 232-234

40. G. Fee ibid 222-223

41. Ibid 224

42. P. O'Brien ibid 238, 241

CHAPTER FIVE

1. W. Brueggemann 1 & 2 Samuel WJKnox 1990 123-124

2. Ibid 128-129

3. P. Hughes ibid 443

4. B. Witherington 111 A Socio-Rhetorical Commentary on 1 & 2 Corinthians 1995 463

5. Ibid 463-464

6. P. Hughes ibid 445

7. J. M-O'Connor ibid 302-303

8. F. B. Meyer ibid 81-82

9. Ibid 85

10. E. Best 2 Corinthians WJKnox 1987 119

11. R. Clements ibid 13-14

12. R. T. Kendall The Thorn In The Flesh Hodder 1999 10

13. John Newton Hymn – I asked The Lord That I Might Grow

CHAPTER SIX

1. M. Bockmuehl Philippians ibid 204, 206

2. A. Motyer Philippians ibid 160-161

3. P. O'Brien Philippians ibid 388

4. G. Fee Philippians ibid 315

5. M. Bockmuehl ibid 206

6. G. Fee ibid 127

7. P. O'Brien ibid 135

8. M. Bockuehl ibid 87-88

9. Ibid 91-93

10. G. Fee ibid 138-139

11. Ibid 113-114

12. P. O'Brien ibid 94

13. M. Bockmuehl ibid 76

14. P. O'Brien ibid 95

15. G. Fee ibid 100-101

16. M. Bockmuehl ibid 75

17. P. Hughes 2 Corinthians ibid 13-14

18. E. Best 2 Corinthians ibid 11

19. D. Dales Living Through Dying Lutterworth Press 1994 7-8

20. R. J. Martin Colossians & Ephesians ibid 111-112

21. F. F. Bruce Colossians ibid 81-82

22. J. D. G. Dunn Colossians ibid 114-117

23. P. O'Brien ibid 158, 162

24. M. Bockuehl ibid 102

25. P. O'Brien ibid 161

26. G. Fee ibid 1, 10-11

27. B. Witherington 111 ibid 12-13, 18, 20- 22, 24

28. G. Fee 1 Corinthians ibid 10-11

29. C. K. Barrett 1 Corinthians Hendrickson 1987 49

30. D. Dales ibid 7

31. C. K. Barrett ibid 54-56

32. D. Prior 1 Corinthians IVP 1985 41

33. C. K. Barrett ibid 62-63

34. Ibid 64

35. D. Prior ibid 49

36. A. Thiselton 1 Corinthians Eerdmans 2000 204-205, 209

[37.] G. Fee ibid 156

[38.] D. Dales ibid 7

[39.] G. Fee ibid 171

[40.] Ibid 157

[41.] Ibid 175

[42.] R. Martin 2 Corinthians WJKnox 1987 1-2

[43.] P. Barnett 2 Corinthians IVP 30

[44.] D. Dales ibid 9-10

[45.] R. Martin ibid 26

[46.] D. Dales ibid 11

[47.] R. Kent Hughes 2 Corinthians Crossway 2006 91

[48.] M. Harris 2 Corinthians Eerdmans 2005 343

[49.] P. Hughes 2 Corinthians ibid 136-137

[50.] M. Harris ibid 340-341

[51.] Ibid 345

[52.] D. Dales ibid 16.

[53.] P. Hughes ibid 142

[54.] Ibid 347

[55.] D. Dales ibid 19

[56.] M. Hooker ibid 113-114

[57.] J. M-O'Connor Paul A Critical Life ibid 314

[58.] M. Harris ibid 413

[59.] P. Hughes ibid 186

[60.] M. Harris ibid 419

[61.] Ibid 422

[62.] Ibid 430

[63.] P. Barnett ibid 118

[64.] E. Best ibid 52, 59

[65.] S. Christou The Priest & The People Of God ibid 126

[66.] Ibid 126

[67.] Ibid 128

68. B. Witherington 111 ibid 431-437

69. Ibid 441-442

70. D. A. Carson From Triumphalism To Maturity ibid 91-92

71. P Barnett 2 Corinthians Eerdmans 1997 534

72. P. Barnett 2 Corinthians IVP ibid 177

73. E. Best ibid 120-121

74. P. Hughes ibid 432

75. M. Harris ibid 864

76. R. Kent Hughes ibid 214

77. P. Barnett 2 Corinthians Eerdmans ibid 534, 567, 570, 574

CHAPTER SEVEN

1. J. Stott The Message of 1 & 2 Thessalonians IVP 1991 17

2. L. Morris 1 & 2 Thessalonians Eerdmans 1984 20

3. D. Wenham ibid 91

4. J. Stott ibid 9

5. W. Hendriksen 1 & 2 Thessalonians Banner Of Truth 1976 52

6. R. Mayhue 1 & 2 Thessalonians Christian Focus 1999 52

7. C. Cocksworth & R. Brown Being A Priest Today Canterbury Press 2002 33

8. Ibid 33-34

9. J. Stott ibid 52

10. C. Cocksworth & R. Brown Ibid 34

11. D. Tidball Builders & Fools IVP 1999 94

12. Ibid 88

13. Ibid 97

14. D. G. Horrell ibid 69

15. M. B. Thompson The New Perspective On Paul Grove Booklets 2005 4, 18, 22-23

16. J. D. G. Dunn The Theology Of Paul The Apostle ibid 336-339

17. M. D. Hooker ibid 73-75, 79

18. Ibid 73

19. J. Stott Romans ibid 61-63

20. R. B. Hays The Conversation Of The Imagination – Paul As Interpreter Of Israel's Scripture Eerdmans 2005 125

21. D. Horrell ibid 72

22. T. Wright What St. Paul Really Said ibid 117

23. T. Holland Contours Of Pauline Theology Mentor 2004 204-205

24. E. P. Sanders Paul Oxford University Press 1996 76

25. T. R. Schreiner ibid 201-202

26. J. A. Fitzmeyer Romans Anchor Bible 1993 395

27. L. Morris Romans IVP 1988 70-71

28. Ibid 225-226

29. J. D. G. Dunn ibid 388

30. Ibid 388-389

31. T. Wright ibid 159

32. Ibid 115

APPENDIX

1. R. Mayhue ibid 11

2. J. Stott 2 Timothy IVP 1973 17

3. Ibid 16

4. J. Pollock Paul The Apostle Kingsway 1999 304, 307

5. C. K. Barrett Saint Paul ibid 3-4, 144-154

6. P. O'Brien Ephesians ibid 4, 8, 11, 13

7. Ibid 33-34, 45-46

8. J. Muddiman Ephesians Continuum 2001 5-6

9. J. D. G. Dunn Colossians & Ephesians ibid 35-39

10. L. Morris 1 & 2 Thessalonians ibid 29-31

11. W. Hendriksen 1 & 2 Thessalonians ibid 25-26

12. Ibid 26

13. J. Stott 1 Timothy & Titus IVP 1996 21-22

BIBLIOGRAPHY

P. Barnett 2 Corinthians IVP 1995

P. Barnett 2 Corinthians Eerdmans 1997

C. K. Barrett 1 Corinthians Hendrickson 1987

C. K. Barrett Saint Paul Continuum 2001

E. Best 2 Corinthians WJKnox 1987

E. Bock Saint Paul Floris Books 2005

P. O'Brien Colossians Word 1982

P. O'Brien Ephesians Eerdmans 1999

P. O'Brien Philippians Eerdmans 1991

F. F. Bruce Acts NICOT Eerdmans 1986

F. F. Bruce Paul Apostle Of The Free Spirit Paternoster 1992

F. F. Bruce Colossians & Ephesians Eerdmans 1984

W. Brueggemann 1 & 2 Samuel WJKnox 1990

J. Calvin The Acts Of The Apostles Vol 1 Eerdmans 1989

D. A. Carson Spiritual Reformation – Priorities From Paul & His Prayers IVP 1993

D. A. Carson From Triumphalism To Maturity IVP 1986

S. Christou Evangelism & Collaborative Ministry Phoenix Books 2004

S. Christou The Priest & The People Of God Phoenix Books 2003

R. Clements The Strength Of Weakness Christian Focus 1998

C. Cocksworth & R. Brown Being A Priest Today Canterbury Press 2002

D. Coggan Paul Portrait Of A Revolutionary Hodder 1986

D. Dales Living Through Dying Lutterworth Press 1994

J. D. G. Dunn Colossians Paternoster 1996

J. D. G. Dunn Galatians A & C Black 1993

J. D. G. Dunn The Theology Of Paul The Apostle Eerdmans 1998

G. Fee 1 Corinthians Eerdmans 1987

G. Fee Philippians Eerdmans 1995

J. A. Fitzmeyer Romans Anchor Bible 1993

F. Foulkes Ephesians IVP 1983

G Hawthorne: R. Martin: D. Reid Dictionary Of Paul & His Letters IVP 1993

R. B. Hays The Conversion Of The Imagination – Paul As Interpreter Of Israel's Scripture Eerdmans 2005

W. Hendriksen 1 & 2 Thessalonians Banner of Truth 1976

H. W. Hoehner Ephesians Baker 2003

T. Holland Contours In Pauline Theology Christian Focus 2004

M. Hooker Paul A Short Introduction Oneworld Oxford 2004

D. G. Horrell An Introduction To The Study Of St. Paul 2000

P. Hughes 2 Corinthians T & T Clark 2000

R. Kent Hughes 2 Corinthians Power In Weakness Crossway 2006

M. L. Jones Ephesians Ch 1 – God's Ultimate Purpose Banner Of Truth 1978

M. L. Jones Ephesians Ch 3 – The Unsearchable Riches Of Christ Banner Of Truth 1979

R. T. Kendall The Thorn In The Flesh Hodder 1999

J. B. Lightfoot Galatians 1865 Oliphants 1957

A. Lincoln Ephesians Nelson 1990

R. J. Lucas Colossians IVP 1980

R. J. Martin Colossians WJKnox 1991

C. M. Martini In The Thick Of His Ministry St. Paul's 1989

R. Mayhue 1 & 2 Thessalonians Christian Focus 1999

F. B. Meyer Paul Marshall Morgan & Scott 1953

L. Morris Galatians IVP 1996

L Morris 1 & 2 Thessalonians Eerdmans 1984

A. Motyer Philippians IVP 1988

H. C. G. Moule Colossian Studies Pickering & Inglis (no date given)

H. C. G. Moule Ephesian Studies Pickering & Inglis (no date given)

J. Muddiman Ephesians Continuum 2001

J. Newton Hymn – I Asked The Lord That I Might Grow

J. M. O'Connor Paul A Critical Life Oxford U. Press 1996

J. M. O'Connor Paul His Story Oxford University Press 1997

J. Pollock Paul The Apostle Kingsway 1999

D. Prior 1 Corinthians IVP 1985

H. Ridderbos Paul An Outline Of His Theology SPCK 1977

E. P. Sanders Paul Oxford University Press 1996

U. Schnelle Apostle Paul – His Life & Theology Baker 2003

T. R. Schreiner Paul Apostle Of God's Glory In Christ Appollos 2001

M. Stibbe Drawing Near To God – The Temple Model Of Prayer DLT 2005

J. Stott The Spirit, The Church & The World: The Message Of Acts IVP 1990

J. Stott Ephesians IVP 1989

J. Stott Galatians IVP 1991

J. Stott 1 & 2 Thessalonians IVP 1991

J. Stott 1 Timothy & Titus IVP 1996

J. Stott 2 Timothy IVP 1973

M. B. Thompson The New Perspective On Paul Grove Booklet 2006

D. Tidball Builders & Fools IVP 1999

C. Swindoll Paul – A Man Of Grit & Grace Word 2002

A. Thiselton 1 Corinthians Eerdmans 2000

W. Trilling A Conversation With Paul SCM 1986

M. Volf Exclusion And Embrace Abingdon Press 1996

B. J. Walsh & S. C. Keesmaat Colossians re:mixed Paternoster 2005

D. Wenham Paul & Jesus SPCK 2002

W. W. Wiersbe The Bible Exposition Commentary 1989

A. N. Wilson Paul – The Mind Of The Apostle Pimilco 1997

B. Witherington 111 Conflict & Community In Corinth – A Socio-Rhetorical Commentary On 1 & 2 Corinthians Eerdmans 1995

N. T. Wright What St. Paul Really Said Lion 1997

N. T. Wright Paul Fresh Perspectives SPCK 2005